PUMA

PUBLIC MANAGEMENT

PRIVATE PAY FOR PUBLIC WORK

PERFORMANCE-RELATED PAY FOR PUBLIC SECTOR MANAGERS

ORGANISATION FOR ECONOMIC CO-OPERATION AND DEVELOPMENT

ORGANISATION FOR ECONOMIC CO-OPERATION AND DEVELOPMENT

Pursuant to Article 1 of the Convention signed in Paris on 14th December 1960, and which came into force on 30th September 1961, the Organisation for Economic Co-operation and Development (OECD) shall promote policies designed:

- to achieve the highest sustainable economic growth and employment and a rising standard of living in Member countries, while maintaining financial stability, and thus to contribute to the development of the world economy;
- to contribute to sound economic expansion in Member as well as non-member countries in the process of economic development; and
- to contribute to the expansion of world trade on a multilateral, non-discriminatory basis in accordance with international obligations.

The original Member countries of the OECD are Austria, Belgium, Canada, Denmark, France, Germany, Greece, Iceland, Ireland, Italy, Luxembourg, the Netherlands, Norway, Portugal, Spain, Sweden, Switzerland, Turkey, the United Kingdom and the United States. The following countries became Members subsequently through accession at the dates indicated hereafter: Japan (28th April 1964), Finland (28th January 1969), Australia (7th June 1971) and New Zealand (29th May 1973). The Commission of the European Communities takes part in the work of the OECD (Article 13 of the OECD Convention).

Publié en français sous le titre :
LES TRAITEMENTS DU PRIVÉ POUR LE PUBLIC :
rémunération liée à la performance pour les cadres de la fonction publique

FOREWORD

This report was prepared on behalf of the OECD's Public Management Committee by Robert Wood, Head of the Department of Management, University of Western Australia, and Maria Maguire of the OECD Public Management Service. It is based on information supplied by a panel of national experts and additional research undertaken by the authors. The case studies presented in Annex 2 were prepared by national experts or, where indicated, by consultants to the Secretariat. The report benefited from comments by and discussions with Panel members and consultants, and was reviewed in draft by the Public Management Committee. However, the views expressed here do not necessarily correspond to those of the national authorities concerned. The report is published on the responsibility of the Secretary General.

ALSO AVAILABLE

Administration as Service: The Public as Client (1987)				
(42 87 01 1) ISBN 92-64-12946-4	FF90	£9.00	US$18.00	DM40
Public Management Developments : Survey 1990 (1990)				
(42 90 03 1) ISBN 92-64-13437-9	FF130	£16.00	US$28.00	DM50
Public Management Developments: Update 1991 (1991)				
(42 91 01 1) ISBN 92-64-13546-4	FF90	£11.00	US$21.00	DM35
Public Management Developments: Update 1992 (1992)				
(42 92 01 1) ISBN 92-64-13729-7	FF95	£13.50	US$22.00	DM39
Public Management Studies : Flexible Personnel Management in the Public Service (1990)				
(42 90 01 1) ISBN 92-64-13353-4	FF90	£11.00	US$19.00	DM35

Prices charged at the OECD Bookshop.

THE OECD CATALOGUE OF PUBLICATIONS and supplements will be sent free of charge on request addressed either to OECD Publications Service, or to the OECD Distributor in your country.

CONTENTS

LIST OF TABLES

LIST OF FIGURES

INTRODUCTION

Schemes to link pay to performance are becoming widespread in the public sector in OECD countries, especially at managerial levels. Performance-related pay is one of a range of reforms that have been introduced since the early 1980s in an attempt to develop a performance oriented culture in public sector organisations, in the expectation that this would increase their productivity and effectiveness. What advantages does performance-related pay offer for the public sector and what problems does it pose?

The adoption of performance-related pay in the public sector reflects the influence of the private sector culture of incentives and individual accountability championed by the rationalist economic policies that were in the ascendancy throughout the 1980s. The main rationale for establishing these schemes is to improve performance. Yet there has been very little evaluation of whether improvements have actually occurred and whether benefits justify costs. Many public sector schemes have not been in operation long enough for a thorough assessment, and even in the case of longer running schemes, there has been very little systematic analysis of their impact on organisations. Studies reveal a similar lack of evaluation of many private sector schemes.

Despite this lack of evaluation, and notwithstanding evidence that some schemes have experienced serious problems, there appears to be widespread support both among elected officials and public sector managers themselves for the principle of linking pay to performance. Support for performance-related pay among public sector managers may in fact be a key indicator of the acceptance of a performance oriented culture within the public sector. Surveys in several countries have shown that a large majority of public sector managers believe that some proportion of their pay should be linked to assessments of their performance, so that those who perform well are paid more than those who perform poorly. These attitudes are more widely held by managers who have had some direct experience of performance-related pay schemes, even when those schemes have been judged to have been failures. Such attitudes appear to be motivated by beliefs that performance-related pay will enhance the performance of public sector organisations and that it is more equitable to allocate rewards on the basis of managerial contributions to organisational outputs and outcomes.

The OECD's Public Management Committee requested this study because of the growing interest in applying performance-related pay to public sector employees in OECD countries. The brief was to review performance pay schemes covering middle management and senior management levels in departments and agencies of central government and to look also, on a selective basis, at schemes for managers in other parts of the public sector. The objectives of the study were to investigate why performance-related pay schemes are being introduced at management levels in the public sector, to examine how these schemes operate, to assess whether the schemes are meeting their stated objectives, and to see whether and under what conditions performance pay can operate successfully in public sector settings.

This report presents the findings from the first phase of the study. A second and final phase, to be concluded in 1993, will attempt a more rigorous evaluation of the impact of performance-related pay schemes in the public sector in terms of variables such as motivation, pay costs, performance, equity and staff turnover. The report is intended as a contribution to the partial but growing body of information on the experience with performance-related pay in the public sector. Although an attempt is made to cover all of the relevant issues, variations in the data available for analysis have meant that some topics could only be discussed in a relatively cursory way. Differences in the data available have inevitably meant that longer running schemes, particularly those in Canada, the United Kingdom and the United States, have been given greater emphasis in the discussions of some issues. The main body of the report presents the analysis of schemes in central government departments and agencies. Annex 1 presents summary descriptions of these schemes. Some case studies of schemes in other parts of the public sector and some comments on these schemes are presented in Annex 2.

Throughout the study, the terms *performance-related pay* and *performance pay* are used to refer to a variety of systems for linking pay to performance. Two main types of system can be identified: merit increments and bonuses. In many cases the two are combined in a single scheme. Under merit increment schemes, all or part of the annual pay increase is linked to the employee's performance in the job. The merit increment takes the form of either a fixed or variable increase which is added to and becomes a permanent part of basic pay. Pay progression is thereby linked, wholly or in part, to individual performance rather than seniority.

Bonuses are once-off payments which are not consolidated into basic pay. They may be expressed in either cash terms or as a percentage of basic pay. In most of the schemes examined in this study bonuses are allocated on the basis of individual performance, but a few examples of group bonus schemes are included. Under these latter schemes, bonuses are awarded on the basis of some measure of the performance of a work unit or an organisation. Group schemes are relatively rare in the public sector at managerial levels.

Another feature of public sector schemes is that they rarely take the form of pure incentive schemes in which individual rewards are determined solely by individual performance against agreed standards. Limited budgets, and in some cases quotas on the number of recipients for performance awards, mean that public sector managers are often forced to compete with their peers for merit increments and bonuses, based on an annual rating of performance.

There are numerous variations in how performance is assessed and how the assessment is linked to the allocation of performance pay awards. In some schemes performance appraisal is a detailed and formalised process, with performance pay linked in a mechanistic fashion to performance ratings. In others, the performance rating is informal, no written appraisal may be required, and there is a large element of managerial discretion in the allocation of performance pay awards. Systems of performance appraisal based on management-by-objectives are becoming more widespread, although other approaches are also to be found in the schemes examined here.

An important contrast in the performance pay systems to be found in central government concerns the degree of centralisation and standardisation. Some longer running schemes, particularly those in Canada, the United Kingdom and the United States, have been centrally imposed on line departments and agencies and, with the exception of certain aspects of the United Kingdom schemes considered, have adopted fairly standardised approaches to performance appraisal and to the allocation of bonuses and merit increments. Another common feature of schemes in these three countries has been their evolutionary nature. As problems have arisen, various components of schemes have been adjusted to deal with them.

More recently implemented schemes in countries such as Denmark, the Netherlands, New Zealand and Sweden present some interesting contrasts in their approaches. Most importantly, schemes in these countries are less standardised and allow individual departments and agencies greater latitude in the design and implementation of schemes. In these countries, central frameworks outline general principles governing performance pay, conditions for giving awards and, in most cases, budgets and maximum awards payable. Within these general frameworks, individual departments have considerable flexibility in areas such as the approach to performance appraisal, the distribution of awards amongst eligible staff, the size of individual awards and the form of payments. Future evaluations will be needed to determine whether these schemes will prove more effective than more standardised, centrally imposed schemes. Revisions to some of the longer-established schemes have shown a more decentralised approach, which suggests that there may be advantages in flexibility.

The report is organised as follows. In Chapter 1 we provide an overview of the context in which performance-related pay schemes have been introduced into the public sector. The theory and evidence supporting the use of performance-related pay are reviewed in Chapter 2. Issues relating to performance measurement, performance appraisal and how the linkage between assessed performance and pay is made are analysed in Chapters 3 and 4. Chapter 5 describes and analyses the characteristics of performance pay schemes, including coverage, pay allocation processes, forms and size of performance payments, budgets and methods of controlling the distribution of awards. Chapter 6 reviews evidence on the impact of performance pay schemes. In the final chapter the findings and conclusions of the study are presented.

Chapter 1

THE CONTEXT FOR INTRODUCING PERFORMANCE-RELATED PAY

The new managerialism

Performance pay schemes are part of a wider set of reforms to the structures and managerial processes of public sector organisations that were implemented in many OECD countries during the 1980s. These reforms have been described as the "new managerialism" because of their frequent adoption of techniques from the private sector and the elevation of managerial skills, relative to policy and advisory skills (Flynn, 1990). The new managerialism has involved a comprehensive process of change to public sector organisations, with an emphasis on decentralised managerial and financial control and the fostering of what is described as a "performance culture" that places greater emphasis on accountability and value for money.

Across a range of OECD countries, the reforms have marked a shift away from a focus on input measures of performance, such as the allocation of cash resources and staff. Under this previous regime the traditional measure for which public sector managers were held accountable was performance against budget. This remains an important measure; public sector organisations cannot continually overspend. However, much greater emphasis is now being placed on output measures that focus on the goods and services produced and outcome measures that assess contributions to the aims of government. Senior managers are now being held accountable for the delivery of outputs at an agreed cost and level of performance as specified in departmental corporate plans and programme budgets. In several countries annual departmental reports to government must account for the effective use of resources against objectives established in corporate plans.

Performance-related pay is a logical component of reforms aimed at more efficient and more effective delivery of public services and is consistent with the rationalist economic philosophy that began to influence policy makers in OECD countries in the 1980s. The rationale for the shift toward economic policies of smaller government, privatisation and low inflation was outlined in an OECD report dealing with structural adjustment and economic performance (1987). These policies were, in a general sense, a response to the economic malaise that struck many OECD countries in the 1970s and early 1980s, the symptoms of which were low growth, low productivity and weak investment in conjunction with high unemployment and inflation.

Flynn (1990) has identified several themes in the policies and reform agendas of the economic rationalists. Some of these themes, but not all of them, are consistent with the measurement and rewarding of performance in the public sector. The themes identified by Flynn include the use of market mechanisms to allocate resources wherever possible. These have been implemented through a range of policies, including privatisation, corporatisation and user-charges. In government commercial enterprises, where these policies have been taken much further than in central government agencies, managers are now being appraised and rewarded against financial and market performance indicators similar to those used in private industry. In central government agencies there are no effective market-based measures of managerial performance and assessments of outputs and outcomes must rely instead on performance appraisal systems.

A second policy theme has been the introduction of competition between providers of goods and services, including those which have been traditional government monopolies. This highlights the comparative performance of managers in the public and private sectors and puts pressure on managers in the public sector to strive for higher standards of service and greater efficiency. Competition is both a process of comparison and a source of performance standards. Through the introduction of performance pay, public sector managers have been placed in competition with one another for monetary rewards.

A third theme, according to Flynn, has been the emphasis on individualism and individual choice in the selection of goods and services, such as schools and health insurance. The logic of individualism applies equally to both accountability and responsibility, and in the public sector there has been a move toward managerial systems which delegate responsibility to individual managers and then hold them accountable for their contributions. Performance-related pay schemes typically attempt to hold managers accountable for their individual contributions. Performance pay can, of course, be based on collective outputs, but that has not been very common.

A fourth theme has been the reduction of state provision of goods and services, resulting in the reduction of government bureaucracies. In many countries, reforms of the public sector have included reductions in the work force and cuts in programme budgets. It is, perhaps, the policies related to this theme that are most inconsistent with performance pay strategies. Compensation theorists generally argue for a de-emphasis of performance-related pay during periods of divestment or reductions in organisational size (*e.g.* Milkovich and Newman, 1990; Ellig, 1982).

It is within the context of these policy themes and the performance-oriented culture that they engendered in public sectors and communities at large that reforms to management of the public sector have occurred throughout the 1980s. In many instances, governments, and public sector managers themselves, have turned to the private sector for examples of managerial models and systems that would produce a greater responsiveness to clients, more flexible, goal-oriented allocations of resources, and higher levels of accountability. Corporate planning, accrual accounting, programme budgeting, performance measurement and appraisal, and flatter, more decentralised organisational structures are among the many changes that have been introduced to public sector organisations in recent times as part of this process. The adoption of performance-related pay schemes and other reforms to compensation systems, such as the simplification of salary structures and the decentralisation of salary negotiations, were part of this general milieu of reform to public sector management structures and systems.

The public-private compensation gap

The review and reform of public sector compensation systems during the 1980s was also influenced by a widening gap between public and private sector levels of management compensation. Data collected by the OECD show that across a range of OECD countries, salary levels of public sector managers lagged behind those of private sector managers by as much as 30 per cent to 50 per cent during the 1980s, and the disparities were greatest at the most senior levels of management. As a result of the disparities in salaries, public sectors in several countries have experienced difficulties in recruiting and retaining managers and those with specialist qualifications. The adoption of performance pay schemes was, in part, an attempt to improve the flexibility of public sector organisations in rewarding managers and to improve the competitiveness of the public sector in labour markets.

Adoption of performance pay schemes

Beginning with schemes introduced in the United States in 1979 for the Senior Executive Service and in 1981 for middle-level managers, there has been a significant growth in the adoption of performance pay schemes by public sector organisations in recent times. Denmark, Ireland, the Netherlands, New Zealand, Spain, Sweden, and the United Kingdom, have all adopted some form of performance-related pay in central government agencies during the 1980s. Experimental schemes have been tried in selected government agencies in Finland and Italy, a scheme has been introduced in the German postal service and a proposal to introduce a scheme for the Senior Executive Service in the Australian Commonwealth public service is currently under consideration. Performance pay schemes have also spread in other parts of the public sectors in many of the above countries, in regional and local government, state enterprises and trading organisations, and service areas such as health authorities.

However, the experience with such schemes in OECD countries goes much further back than the reforms introduced in the 1980s. In Canada, for example, a formal system of merit increments for senior civil servants was first introduced in 1964. In France, the earliest version of the General Regulations for civil servants, enacted in 1946, specified that individual or collective bonuses could be granted periodically to civil servants in the recognition of exceptional performance achievements. Since those initial regulations, a series of inter-ministerial decrees have specified the amounts and types of awards for the different categories of staff, and bonuses are now a major component of salaries for some groups of French civil servants. In Japan, there has been provision for a "diligence allowance" for national public employees since the early 1950s.

Interest in performance-related pay is now so widespread among OECD countries and experimentation with various schemes so common that it appears unlikely to fade quickly. In several countries schemes have now been running for a decade or more and, despite many problems, appear to have become part of the public sector management framework. Further, support for performance-related pay on the part of politicians in many countries means that it is a reality for public management. Across many countries and different political parties, performance pay is seen as an exemplar of reforms modelled on practice in the private sector that are expected to lead to improved efficiency and effectiveness in the public sector.

Further support for performance-related pay comes from those public sector managers who are covered by schemes. Claims that pay is not a significant motivator for public sector managers, particularly those at senior levels, are not supported by the available evidence. Implementation processes in most countries with performance pay schemes have included extensive consultation with the managers affected and their support has been a necessary condition for introduction of the schemes. Public sector managers appear equally as likely as their private sector counterparts to believe that pay can be motivating and that some portion of pay should be based on performance achievements.

Support for the principle of performance-related pay among public sector managers is not diminished by experience and even remains high among managers who are dissatisfied with schemes currently in use. In the United Kingdom civil service, for example, most staff in the management grades concerned remained in favour of pay being linked to performance following the termination of the experimental bonus scheme for managers in 1988. This was despite the fact that there had been widespread dissatisfaction with the scheme among managers and that it had failed to establish a clear relationship between pay and performance. There were similar negative evaluations by senior managers of a merit scheme in the state of Victoria in Australia, but an overwhelming majority of them (83 per cent) continued to support the principle of performance-related pay (Public Service Board of Victoria, 1987). In the United States, annual surveys show that a similar proportion (86 per cent in 1989) of the middle managers in the Federal civil service who are covered by merit and bonus schemes support the idea of some portion of their pay being based on performance (U.S. Office of Personnel Management, 1990*a*).

The widespread support by public sector managers for performance pay may in itself be indicative of a shift toward a performance culture. Performance-related pay schemes represent a major shift away from traditional seniority-based reward systems for public sector managers. In several countries the introduction of performance-related pay has also been part of a plan to move managerial compensation in public sector organisations away from incremental pay structures within national wage systems in which progression was automatic, irrespective of performance. Under the new pay schemes, increments are no longer automatic and can be withheld from managers who are not performing satisfactorily. In some schemes in Canada, the United Kingdom and the United States, even annual cost-of-living adjustments to the pay schedule are withheld from managers whose performance is judged to be unsatisfactory.

Policy objectives

Different countries have identified different policy objectives for the introduction of performance-related pay. However, there are several common themes in the objectives identified. These include:

a) To create greater accountability for individual performance and strengthen the belief that rewards are linked to performance;

b) To strengthen the relationship between individual job goals and organisational goals;

c) To provide agencies and individual managers with greater flexibility to recognise and reward individual performance contributions, thus allowing them greater discretion in their management role;

d) To contain salary costs by reducing the incidence of automatic progression through salary levels;
e) To enhance job satisfaction and the belief that rewards are fairly distributed;
f) To reduce the turnover among high quality public sector managers who are being recruited to higher paying jobs in private sector organisations.

In a later chapter, following a discussion of the characteristics of schemes in different countries, data relating to the impact of performance pay schemes on several of these objectives will be discussed.

Chapter 2

THEORY AND EVIDENCE FOR PERFORMANCE-RELATED PAY

The theory

The idea that pay should be related to performance is a dominant theme in both economic and psychological writings on rewards and compensation. Baker, Jensen and Murphy note that "... (e)conomic models of compensation generally assume that higher performance requires greater effort ... In order to provide incentives, these models predict the existence of reward systems that structure compensation so that a worker's expected ability increases with increased productivity" (1988, p. 594). Matching compensation to the productivity of individual workers, particularly managers, is considered necessary as an incentive for effort and to attract and retain more competent managers. In the human resource management literature arguments for the adoption of performance pay schemes are usually based on expectancy (Vroom, 1964), and equity (Adams, 1963) theories of motivation. The incentive effects of performance-related pay, it is argued, lead to higher levels of effort that, in turn, lead to higher levels of performance.

According to the theory, the major requirements for effective performance-related pay schemes include:

a) rewards of sufficient size so that, in economic and expectancy theory terms, bonuses or merit increments are of sufficient value to recipients to be motivating;

b) the distribution of rewards so that there is a significant positive relationship between performance and pay awards, and that this relationship is understood by potential recipients of awards;

c) equal rewards for staff who perform at the same level, so that rewards are perceived as equitable.

This simple and compelling logic for linking pay to performance as a means of motivation and enhancing performance is based on several assumptions, as follows:

a) that organisations can accurately measure individual outputs;

b) that individual outputs contribute to organisational performance;

c) that individual outputs and the resulting organisational performance are a product of individual effort;

d) that rewards, including pay, can be administered in a way that captures their expected incentive value for the potential recipients.

In fact, these assumptions are difficult to satisfy in many types of organisations, particularly in relation to managers. First, it is very difficult to measure the marginal product of a manager. The value created by an individual manager's efforts and decisions is often inseparable from the value created by others; or from external factors such as changes in budgets, political decisions or industrial unrest. Furthermore, the efforts of individual managers may contribute to organisational performance in complex and uncertain ways (Kotter, 1982). Much of a manager's activity at work is spent in seemingly unproductive communication with other managers, subordinates and clients (Mintzberg, 1975, Kotter, 1982). As a result, the assessment of managerial performance often depends upon subjective performance appraisals against job performance criteria with ambiguous links to organisational performance. The resulting ambiguity about the link between performance and pay weakens the effect of pay on subsequent performance (Konrad and Pfeffer, 1990). Ambiguous performance criteria are also associated with lower levels of perceived pay equity and lower pay satisfaction (Lawler, 1990; Wallace and Fay, 1988).

Despite the difficulty of doing so, the importance of attempting to satisfy the above mentioned conditions has been recognised as a necessary part of the design and ongoing modification of performance-related pay schemes in the public sector in several countries. In Ireland, for example, the Review Body on Higher Remuneration in the Public Sector, in its 1987 report, identified the following as preconditions for the successful introduction of performance pay schemes:

- it must be possible to identify clear objectives for an individual on an annual basis;
- an organisation must already have a system of performance management, a result-oriented system of management, in operation;
- it must be possible to have informed, consistent and objective performance appraisal;
- a job holder must be capable of exerting control over the achievement of set objectives.

Many of the previously mentioned reforms in performance planning and appraisal systems have taken public sector organisations a considerable way towards satisfying the conditions for building a stronger relationship between performance and pay. However, there is a broader set of issues to be considered when deciding whether to introduce performance pay and, if so, in what form. These issues concern the relationship between performance pay and the strategic orientations of an organisation. Several authors have questioned the widespread adoption of performance-related pay schemes in private sector organisations and have argued that for such schemes to be effective over the long-term they must:

a) support corporate values and beliefs;
b) be derived from business strategies and goals;
c) fit the management style and culture of the organisation;
d) support and reinforce the desired behaviour;
e) be linked to outputs and outcomes which contribute to organisational performance. (Lawler, 1990; Wallace and Fay, 1988; Milkovich and Newman, 1990).

Differences in the size and functions of government departments, to mention but two possible bases for comparison, would suggest that they must pursue radically different human resource management strategies. This, of course, would include different compensation strategies. The New Zealand Public Service, for example, is made up of 39 departments employing approximately 47 000 staff. The departments range in size from Social Welfare with 7 650 staff to Pacific Island Affairs with six staff. Most other countries have much larger public services and much larger departments, but display a similar range in the size of departments.

The ability of government departments to tailor performance-related pay schemes to their own corporate strategies and cultures will depend upon the degree of standardisation imposed on them in the implementation of schemes. Standardised schemes imposed from the centre offer the promise of more equitable and more consistent allocation of performance pay, but this may be at the cost of a poor fit with the strategies and cultures in some departments. Allowing departments to develop and manage their own performance pay schemes may enhance their strategic orientation within departments.

The evidence

The research evidence on the effects of performance pay schemes is based mainly on private sector experience and focuses primarily on the impact of schemes on performance. Studies of the effects of schemes in the public sector are very limited, but some evidence is beginning to appear, mainly from research conducted in the United States. This will be discussed in a later section on the impacts of performance pay schemes in the public sector. Research on the performance effects of schemes has focused mainly on individual incentive plans, such as piece rates, bonuses and commissions, and group incentive plans, such as gain sharing and profit sharing. There have also been some studies of executive compensation. A related body of research has developed in the study of goal setting and feedback (Locke and Latham, 1990). Much of the available evidence is reviewed by Milkovich and Wigdor (1991) and need only be summarised briefly here.

Studies of individual incentive plans in private sector settings have shown that such plans can improve individual performance by an average of almost 30 per cent over pay plans that are not based on performance (Locke *et al.*, 1980). But there is also evidence that individual incentive plans can have unintended, negative consequences, such as neglect of job aspects not covered in performance goals, reporting of invalid data on performance, and negative social sanctions for high performers (Lawler, 1973). Research suggests that such plans work best when the employees covered have relatively simple, structured jobs, when performance goals are quantitative and relatively unambiguous and are under the control of the employees, and when frequent, relatively large payments are offered for performance achievements (Milkovich and Wigdor, 1991, pp. 82-3).

Research on gain sharing, profit sharing and other types of group incentive plans indicates that such plans are associated with improved productivity at the level of the group or organisation (Locke *et al.*, 1980; Milkovich and Wigdor, 1991). But, as noted by Milkovich and Wigdor (1991), the research evidence does not enable the performance effects of group plans to be disentangled from the effects of other, contextual factors relating to tasks, organisations and environmental conditions. The evidence on gain sharing comes almost exclusively from plans in manufacturing firms, covering non-managerial employees. Profit-sharing plans are used mainly as a component of pay for managers and there is evidence in the executive compensation literature that such schemes lead to higher stock values and better financial performance of organisations.

Figure 1. **The performance, appraisal and pay allocation process**

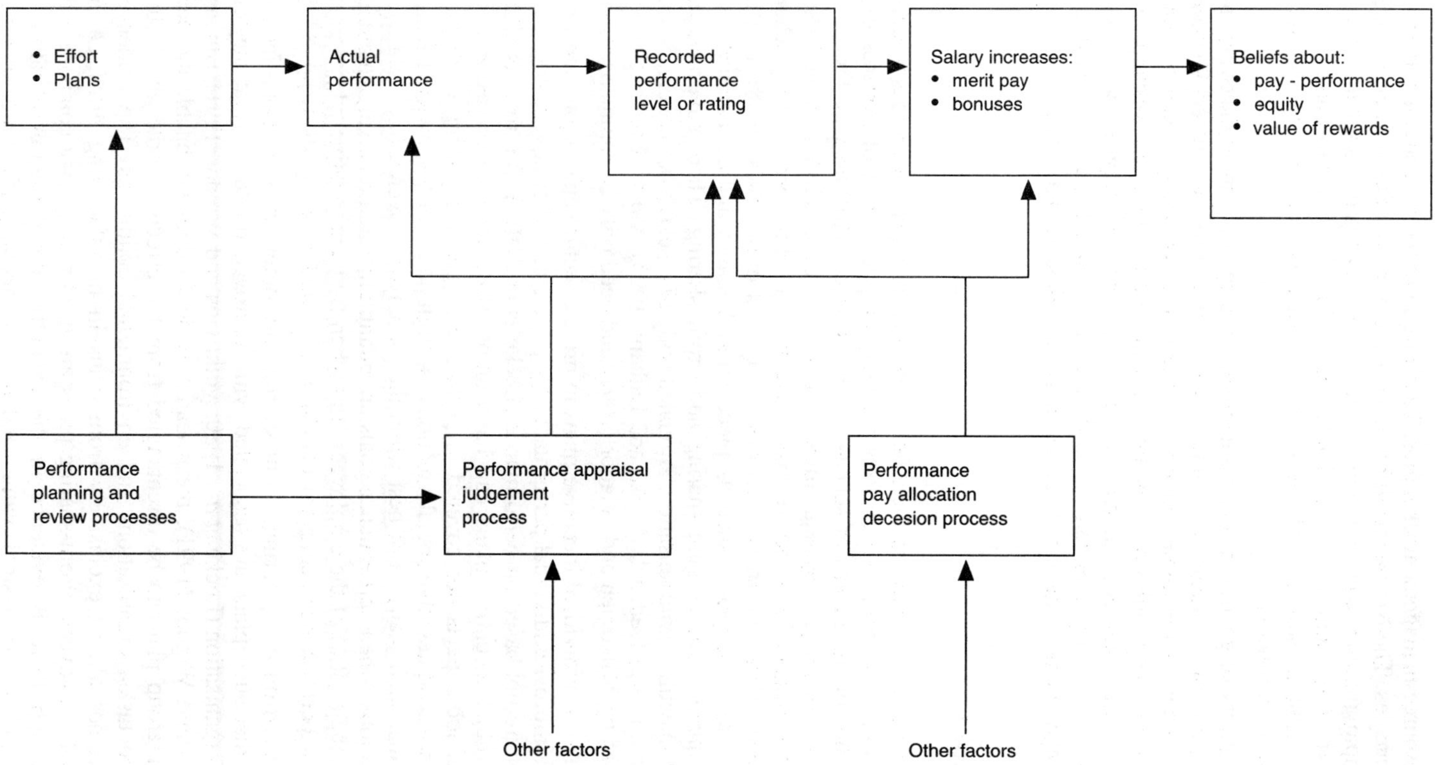

Two recent large-scale, longitudinal research programmes have investigated the relationship between managerial pay strategies and financial performance of organisations in the United States (Gerhart and Milkovich, 1990; Jensen and Murphy, 1990). In both studies, performance pay strategies have been shown to have a positive relationship with financial measures of organisational performance.

Other performance management programmes, particularly goal-setting and feedback programmes, have been found to have less pronounced but very significant impacts on individual and group performance. Based on the evidence for individual performance effects, a performance management system which combines goal setting and feedback with performance-related incentives appears to offer the greatest potential for productivity improvements (Locke and Latham, 1990).

Most studies of the relationship between performance-related pay and performance have examined schemes that include objective measures of performance with clearly defined relationships to levels of performance pay. By design, these schemes closely represent the incentive conditions prescribed by motivational theories that were mentioned above. There are, however, at least two limitations in the application of these results to public sector organisations. The first is the problem of performance measures being based on subjective performance appraisals. A second problem arises because of the inability to link pay mechanically to performance in a way that clearly establishes the incentive values for different levels of performance in advance of the task.

A model

Figure 1 presents a simplified model of activities and outcomes in the relationship between individual motivation (*i.e.* effort and work plans) and the pay allocation process. The design of performance-related pay schemes must attempt to maximise the validity of the two judgement and decision processes shown in the model, the performance appraisal judgement process and the pay allocation decision process. The relationship between these two processes must be such that the appraisal judgement process provides useful inputs for the pay allocation decisions. This will typically require a ranking of employees, with levels of discrimination that are at least as detailed as the discriminations required in the allocation of pay awards.

The logic of performance-related pay often assumes a model that includes only the steps in the main horizontal flow of Figure 1. That model applies to pure incentive schemes such as piece-rate incentive schemes, sales commissions and executive compensation that is based on financial measures of performance. From a pure incentive perspective, the performance appraisal judgements and pay allocation decisions shown as in Figure 1 weaken the relationship between pay and performance by introducing subjectivity and uncertainty into the performance measurement and pay allocation processes. In later sections we will organise our discussion of performance-related pay schemes around the performance appraisal judgement and pay allocation decision processes and discuss how these affect the outcomes shown in Figure 1.

Chapter 3

PERFORMANCE MEASUREMENT

The proper assessment of performance is generally considered to be a necessary condition for the establishment of effective performance-related pay schemes (e.g. Wallace & Fay, 1988; Milkovich and Wigdor, 1991). Compensation decisions are the most frequently mentioned use of performance appraisal data in surveys in Australia, the United Kingdom and the United States. The assessment of managerial performance, however, is one of the more problematic areas in human resource management, primarily because of the elusive nature of the concept of performance when referring to managerial work (Wood and Mitchell, 1990). Control of inputs, work behaviours, outputs and outcomes are all potential criteria for assessment of a manager's job. During the 1980s, reforms to public sector management practices in a range of OECD countries have radically altered the definition of managerial performance and related performance measures, placing greater emphasis on output and outcome criteria and, relatively, less on the traditional criteria of inputs such as expenditures and staff levels.

The importance of the choice of criteria was reflected in the performance appraisal research agenda for several decades, until the beginning of the 1980s. Until that time, research on performance appraisal was dominated by the measurement tradition and was concerned with identifying the dimensions of job performance that could be used as criteria for assessing performance, and developing rating scales for recording human judgements of performance against criteria that were free from bias, valid and reliable.

In the 1980s, paralleling the reform of management practices in the public sector, performance appraisal systems for managers were redefined as performance management systems. Researchers felt that the study of measurement precision in performance appraisal had reached its limits (Ilgen et al., 1992; Murphy and Cleveland, 1991). Studies are now beginning to address questions of how performance appraisal affects employee motivation and how the appraisal process is related to the organisational context. At the same time, performance management systems represent an integration of planning and appraisal systems that attempts to capitalise on the well documented motivational effects of goal-setting and feedback (Locke and Latham, 1990). The process of performance management is typically an annual cycle that starts with a performance agreement between a manager and subordinate that sets out the job goals and developmental needs of the employee. Monitoring, assessment and review occur at agreed periods throughout the year and, if circumstances change, may lead to modifications of the performance agreement. The annual review includes an appraisal, typically a rating of the employee's performance throughout the year. This appraisal then becomes an input to decisions regarding performance-related pay.

Although research on the development of performance criteria and rating scales has begun to wane, the choice of criteria and methods of recording performance remain as central problems for public sector performance appraisal systems. Identifying performance indicators and standards that are seen as being objective, job-related and fair in comparisons across managerial jobs is often difficult because of the nature of managerial work in the public sector. The choice of criteria will determine the performance that gets rewarded and, therefore, will have a major influence on the contributions of performance pay schemes to the efficiency and effectiveness of public sector organisations. We begin our discussion of the criteria used with a consideration of the conditions that appraisal criteria are supposed to satisfy before performance-related pay can be expected to have positive effects on the attitudes and performance of managers (e.g. Wallace and Fay, 1988; Milkovich and Newman, 1990). The difficulties in satisfying these conditions in the jobs of many managers in the public sector are highlighted.

Choosing performance criteria

First, it is argued, managers must have some control over the performance to be assessed and must be able personally to perform better or worse against the chosen performance criteria. Choosing criteria which are responsive to individual efforts will help enhance the impact of pay which is related to performance against those criteria. In many public sector jobs, however, managers are dependent upon the action of others and may have little direct control over the outputs and outcomes that their efforts are directed towards achieving (Wood, 1989).

Second, it is argued that performance must be verifiable. However, performance criteria and their related performance indicators vary quite markedly in their ease of measurement and in the degree of objectivity with which they can be observed and recorded. Criteria that can be measured quantitatively through impersonal recording systems are generally considered to be more objective than those which require more qualitative assessments based on personal evaluations of performance. In general, the less easily verifiable the actual performance attainments the more human judgement involved in the observation, recording and evaluation of performance and the greater the potential for uncertainty and conflicts about them. In the public sector, much of a manager's time is spent giving advice, counselling employees, making decisions and presenting recommendations. The outcomes of these service activities are often intangible and highly transient in nature. This makes them difficult to observe and record in ways that allow comparisons amongst staff or against established standards. Commonly cited examples of areas of work in which these problems are most pronounced are ministerial advising and staff relations. The appraisal of work activities in these areas requires the use of behavioural criteria and more subjective forms of recording and evaluation.

Third, performance criteria must have a positive relationship with organisational performance. That is, the appraisal process must capture the value added by a manager and not just measure job activities and outputs that do not contribute to the attainment of organisational goals. The reforms of the 1980s have meant that public sector organisations now better satisfy this condition for performance-related pay schemes. The integration of performance appraisal with other planning systems such as programme budgets, corporate plans and business plans helps ensure that individual managers contribute to organisational performance.

In the public sector performance-related pay schemes examined in this study, the two most common types of performance criteria used are those which define the critical elements of jobs and those which are based on setting job objectives. Objective-setting approaches are used in schemes in Australia, Canada, Ireland, the United Kingdom and the United States. In the United States, critical elements criteria that are developed through a proper job analysis may be used in place of job objectives. Many schemes combine both approaches and some also use supplementary criteria such as personal skills and job worth in the pay allocation decisions. A few schemes still use job inputs, such as hours worked, in their allocations of individual bonuses. In Spain, for example, bonuses are based on the amount of work done. The development of criteria to represent the critical elements of managerial jobs typically involves the analysis of work activities for a range jobs. The results of the job analyses are then used in the development of standardised criteria for a managerial job family within a department or across the whole of government. Examples from the United States scheme for the Senior Executive Service, shown in Figures 4 and 5, are discussed later. In Denmark and the Netherlands, critical elements criteria have been developed without any systematic job analyses or deliberate attempt to standardise them for different jobs. In those countries, departments have considerable discretion in their choice of performance criteria and their level of definition.

Appraisal based on job objectives

In the objective-setting approach, managers and their supervisors normally collaborate in developing job objectives for the appraisal period. This is often done within the context of corporate plans and programme budgets and some of the manager's job objectives may come directly from those documents. Guidelines for developing individual job objectives frequently stress the need for them to contribute to the achievement of goals defined for the work unit and the organisation. The agreed job objectives then become the criteria against which a manager's performance is appraised at the end of the period.

The use of individual job objectives for the purposes of appraisal and pay allocation decisions requires the identification or development of performance indicators and performance standards, as well as a method of recording achievements against objectives that can be used to compare managers from a range of different jobs. The requirements of verifiability and organisational contributions have led to an emphasis on indicators that are results-oriented and quantifiable. At the same time, it is recognised that the choice of specific indicators may result in an over-emphasis on those aspects of a manager's job that are most easily quantifiable, at the expense of more important qualitative aspects. Also, it is recognised that managers remain responsible for inputs and work processes that may have indirect impacts on outputs and outcomes which are difficult to measure. Figure 2 shows the range of performance indicators that are used in establishing individual job goals for public sector managers.

The standards included in individual job objectives vary with the task. Standards may be established using historical performance data, comparisons with performance in similar jobs, formal estimates, (e.g. budgets), or projections (e.g. guesses or forecasts) about what might be feasible. On more routine or repetitive tasks, standards can be established using historical data or formal estimates. For the more complex, novel tasks

Figure 2. **Types of performance indicators**[1]

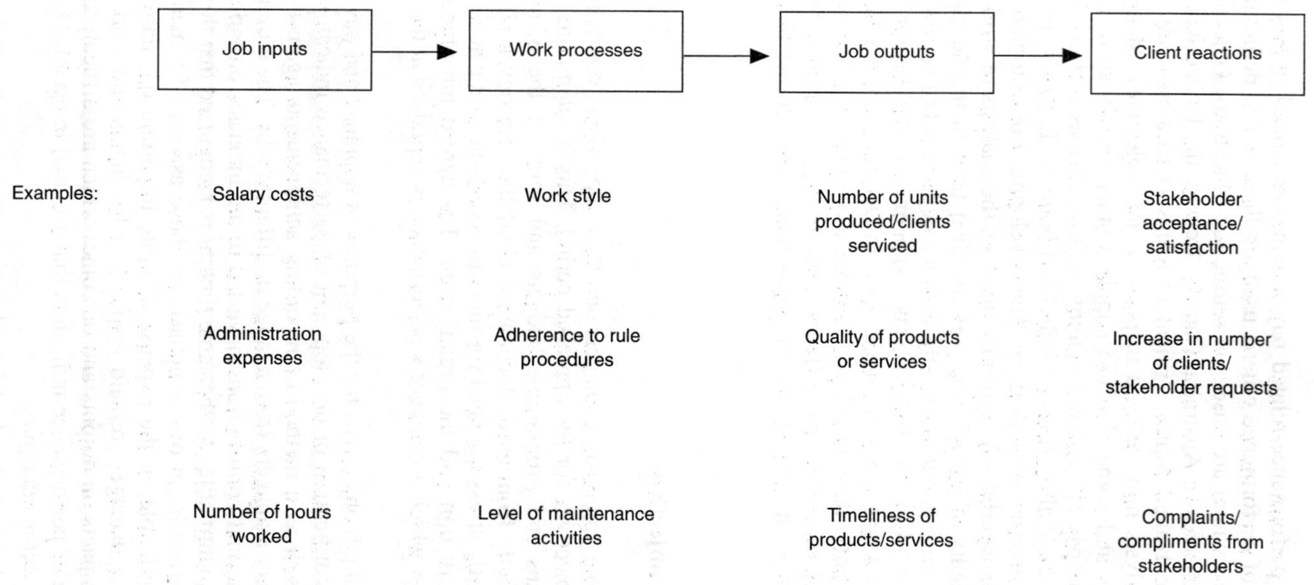

1. Based on framework used in Programme Budgeting by Commonwealth Department of Finance, Australia.

that are often part of a public sector manager's job, more subjective comparisons with other managers and guesses are more commonly used to establish standards. This leads to considerable variance in the standards chosen and in their accuracy as estimates of performance achievements. Because of this, most performance management systems require periodic reviews and revisions of job objectives during the appraisal period.

The diversity of job objectives and variations in the level of difficulty of performance standards are seen as major problems affecting comparisons of public sector managers during the pay allocation process. Criticisms of performance-related pay schemes from managers in a range of countries make frequent mention of inconsistency in standards as a major source of dissatisfaction with schemes.

From a practical standpoint, appraisal systems based on job objectives present several problems for pay decisions that require comparative judgements of performance. First is the problem of how to combine performance against several goals of differing importance and differing degrees of difficulty into a single evaluation of performance that can be equated to a pay award. A second problem is how to compare individuals in different jobs with different job goals and different levels of resources and support. The standard solution to these problems is to use a global graphic rating scale. A typical example of this type of rating scale is the one used in the appraisal scheme for managers in the Canadian public service, shown in Figure 3. Ratings on the scale may be based on objective work outcomes assessed against quantitative performance indicators that a manager has incorporated into his or her goal statements. Alternatively, they may be based on more subjective assessments of attainments against more qualitative goals, such as "delivers high quality advice to the minister in a timely manner".

Several different approaches are taken to the definition of anchors for global rating scales in the schemes examined. A common approach is to define performance levels relative to the achievement of the objectives set for a manager's job, as is done in the Canadian example in Figure 3. As a variation on this approach, the labels for performance rating levels may include statements such as "fell far short of meeting objectives set", "substantially met objectives set" and "far exceeded objectives set". This approach, taken from a scheme used in the New Zealand State Services Commission, limits the judgements of a manager's performance to comparisons against expectations for his or her job. Other schemes employ anchor statements that attempt to force a comparison of a manager's performance with the standards normally expected of a competent manager at his or her level. For example, the midpoint on the rating scale used for managers in the United Kingdom civil service is labelled "performance fully meets **normal** requirements of the grade". Performance ratings above and below that point are also labelled relative to normal requirements for competent performance at the manager's level.

Research suggests that global ratings on graphic scales are very susceptible to bias and, as a result, often lead to inconsistencies in appraisals of performance (Carroll and Schneier, 1982). Such ratings are often used to rationalise decisions (e.g. "Monique deserves a 10 per cent raise so I will give her an 'outstanding' rating"), as a result of uncertainty about the relationship between the observed performance and appropriate rating level. More detailed definition of the labels used, as shown in Figures 3 and 5, may help to improve the validity of ratings if they are widely understood and can be related to particular job performances. The same effect may be true of labels that require judgements against established norms, if there is common agreement on performance norms for different managerial jobs.

Figure 3. **Example of five-point graphic rating scale rating scale used to assess overall performance**

Performance Rating	Anchor points	Definition
5	Outstanding	Achievement consistently and substantially beyond what is expected.
4	Superior	Performance generally beyond the requirements of the position and established criteria.
3	Fully satisfactory	Criteria and established expectations, without significant exception, met and sometimes exceeded.
2	Satisfactory	Many expectations met and fundamental requirements adequately discharged, but recognisable need for further development of skills and knowledge.
1	Unsatisfactory	One or more fundamental requirements not met.

Source: Canadian public service appraisal scheme for managers.

Standardised critical elements criteria

In several countries (*e.g.* Australia, Canada, the United Kingdom, and the United States) standardised criteria have been developed to cover the more important areas of work that are common to a range of managerial jobs. These generic or core criteria are often known as job accountabilities or job responsibilities. In the United States they are referred to as critical job elements. The definition of criteria may describe a range of inputs, work processes, outputs and even outcomes for an identified set of tasks, such as ministerial advising, personnel management, resources management, and so on. Examples of these criteria from the United States civil service are provided in Figure 4. The proper development of criteria such as those shown in Figure 4 requires extensive job analyses for the family of jobs to be covered by the criteria.

Standardised criteria lack the specificity of job goals but do provide a common framework for a family of jobs that include similar but not identical tasks. The common framework allows comparisons of performance across jobs and at the same time permits some flexibility in the monitoring and evaluation of performance for individual jobs. The manager and the appraiser may choose the aspects of performance that they wish to emphasise in an appraisal. When properly developed and validated, standardised criteria can be used to appraise performance in areas where specific job goals may not adequately represent the complexity of the task or the difficulty of specifying expected standards in advance (Wood, 1991).

In the United States, the development of critical elements criteria includes the definition of standards. Figure 5 contains an example of these standards for the programme monitoring and evaluation criteria in Figure 4. Standards are stated as a set of behaviours that a manager would be expected to perform for the different levels of performance ratings. The definition of standards further clarifies the meaning of performance ratings for the appraiser and appraisee and can help to reduce bias and inconsistency in appraisal judgements.

One approach which combines standardised critical elements criteria with objective setting is to require managers to develop job objectives for each of the critical elements criteria. At the end of the appraisal period performances against the job goals for each critical element are then used to rate the manager's performance.

Non-standardised criteria

Not all performance pay schemes are based on job goals or highly defined standard criteria. While there has been a move away from the use of traits and loosely defined criteria in public sector appraisal systems, this approach has some appeal in countries where there has been limited development and use of performance appraisal schemes. The use of non-standardised criteria also fits with the highly decentralised nature of the public services in some countries. In countries such as Denmark, France, the Netherlands and Sweden, it is felt that any attempts by a central department to impose standardised criteria or methods of appraisal on other departments would be rejected. Sweden, for example, has no requirement for a formal appraisal system in departments, and relies on informal dialogues between managers for the assessment of performance. In Denmark, where performance payments are based on a mixture of job demands and individual

Figure 4. **Critical job elements criteria and definitions for senior executive jobs**

Critical elements	Definitions
Organisational planning	Determines goals and objectives. Develops policies and procedures. Assigns priorities. Develops specific programme plans and milestones. Establishes budget and resource allocations.
Programme direction and communication	Articulates and communicates agency goals in terms of specific programme outcomes. Maintains internal and external communications. Directs a management system, including a performance appraisal system, for meeting organisational goals. Makes decisions to facilitate programme accomplishment. Carries out work responsibilities.
Human resources management	Delegates work and monitors work progress. Motivates employees. Appraises employees. Acts as liaison between staff and higher management. Gives technical advice. Selects, places, develops employees. Manages performance through appropriate rewards and corrective action.
Programme monitoring and evaluation	Develops procedures and guidelines to review programme quality and progress. Revises programmes as needed, based on review results. Revises monitoring procedures as required.

Source: U.S. Office of Personnel Management , *Appraising Managerial Performance: Suggested Elements and Standards for Executives, Managers and Supervisors,* Washington D.C. april 1984.

Figure 5. **Behaviourally defined standards for general job criteria**

Criteria	Unsatisfactory	Standards Fully successful	Exceeds fully successful
Programme and evaluation	Does not develop procedures for monitoring and review. If such procedures exist does not use them to identify problems.	Determines that review/ monitoring procedures and guidelines are clearly and concisely stated.	Actively involves staff and/or users in developing review plans.
	Projects are frequently late without acceptable reasons.	Uses monitoring and evaluation procedures which ensure that outputs are of good quality and on time.	Anticipates situations where assistance or changes in direction will be necessary.
	Reports and projects have frequent inaccuracies due to careless review.	Recognises when current review is inadequate and makes appropriate changes.	Uses reviews to identify new approaches that will accomplish work more quickly or effectively.
			Frequently suggests creative improvements to review plans.

Source: U.S. Office of Personnel Management , *Appraising Managerial Performance: Suggested Elements and Standards for Executives, Managers and Supervisors,* Washington D.C. april 1984.

performance, central guidelines recommend, but do not require, that the following criteria be used in pay allocation decisions:

- willingness and ability to establish a motivated, result-minded team;
- good co-operative relations with external associates;
- working efficiency;
- resource conscious leadership;
- willingness and ability to delegate tasks;
- willingness concerning mobility;
- active participation in management development;
- service-minded leadership;
- development-oriented leadership.

Although not defined in detail, these criteria present a vision of an effective manager in the Danish public service. They are in marked contrast to the criteria developed in the United States civil service where, under laws relating to the use of appraisal data, criteria are typically developed in much greater detail in order to demonstrate job relevance and validity. In Denmark, the level of detail in defining criteria and the specific criteria used to assess performance are left to the discretion of individual departments. A review of the Danish scheme showed that there were very large differences in the weightings given to different criteria across departments.

In most countries, concerns about equity within and across agencies have led to efforts to standardise appraisal criteria. In schemes that use non-standardised criteria, individual managers have considerable discretion in deciding what aspects of performance to recognise and record. In France and in the Netherlands, departments may develop their own appraisal schemes, including standardised criteria and objective setting, to assist them in their pay allocation decisions. However, there is no formal requirement for them to do so. This decentralised approach lacks the consistency and control of centrally imposed schemes, but it allows departments greater opportunity to develop schemes that fit with their culture and departmental strategies.

Supplementary criteria

In several countries, the criteria used in performance pay decisions go beyond performance to include elements that are more closely related to the comparative weight of the job or the manager's personal market worth. Evaluations of performance are frequently supplemented by a consideration of criteria such as skills and experience of the manager. The introduction of supplementary criteria may confound performance pay with other components of salary, such as market loadings or base salary for the position. However, this is sometimes done quite deliberately when it is felt that judgements regarding job demands, individual merit and market worth are inseparable. In the United Kingdom, for example, decisions about performance-related pay awards for senior civil servants include consideration of job weight and the demands of the job. In New Zealand, one departmental scheme requires that a number of factors be taken into account when determining an employee's salary progression. These are:

- achievements against position objectives;
- contributions to the wider goals of the organisation;
- particular skills and experience;

– ease or difficulty in recruiting or retaining people.

While an employee's pay progression would normally be based on achievements against job objectives, there is flexibility under this scheme to increase an individual's salary in response to labour market conditions or specific needs of the agency.

Ratings distribution

In most countries with formal performance appraisal schemes, five-point scales similar to the one shown in Figure 3 are used to rate annual performance. The distributions of ratings on these scales have tended to be both highly skewed toward the top of the scale and highly compressed. Less than 1 per cent of the mid-level managers covered by the Performance Management and Recognition System in the United States civil service are rated as less than fully satisfactory, the mid point on the five-point scale (U.S. Office of Personnel Management, 1990*a*). In the United States scheme for the Senior Executive Service (SES), only 0.2 per cent of the SES managers appraised in 1989 received ratings of less than fully satisfactory, more than half (53 per cent) were rated outstanding, the top rating, and over 90 per cent were rated in the two top categories on the five-point global scale (U.S. Office of Personnel Management, 1990*b*). The distributions of ratings for selected departments in the United States Federal Government are shown in Table 1. Although there are differences between departments, ratings are generally very high and often provide poor discriminations for pay allocation purposes. The highly skewed nature of the ratings distribution could be due to a range of factors, including leniency by raters, poorly defined standards for rating levels, insufficiently challenging goals being set by managers, or other sources of ambiguity about rating

Table 1. **Distribution of ratings in United States Federal Government performance appraisal schemes**

	Per cent of staff assigned Performance rating levels[1]					Average rating
	1	2	3	4	5	
SES-Total[2]	0.1	0.1	8.0	38.0	53.0	4.44
SES-Airforce[3]	–	–	–	3.0	97.0	4.97
SES-Agriculture[4]	–	–	30.0	60.0	4.0	3.73
PMRS-Total[5]	0.1	0.2	22.3	49.4	27.9	4.05

1. Rating levels: 1 = Unacceptable; 2 = Minimally successful; 3 = Fully successful; 4 = Exceeds fully successful; 5 = Outstanding. All data are for 1989.
2. SES = Senior Executive Service.
3. Airforce was the agency with the highest average rating for SES officers in 1989.
4. Agriculture was an agency with one of the lowest average ratings for SES officers in 1989.
5. PMRS = Performance Management and Recognition System.

Sources: U.S. Office of Personnel Management (1990), *The Status of the Senior Executive Service: Tenth Anniversary Edition,* Washington, D.C.
U.S. Office of Personnel Management (1990), *Performance Management and Recognition System, 1988 and 1989: A Report to the President and the Congress of the United States,* Washington, D.C.

standards. Research has shown a similar skew in ratings in private sector organisations in the United States (Bretz and Milkovich, 1989).

The data in Table 1 highlight several points about the use of global rating scales. First, the five-point scale is effectively modified to a three-point scale, with practically all managers being rated as fully satisfactory or better. This is true even for agencies such as the United States Department of Agriculture that have lower average ratings. Second, despite the restriction of the range to the top three points on the scale, there are considerable differences in the distributions and their potential usefulness for salary discrimination. The distribution of ratings for SES managers in the United States Air Force is almost totally non-discriminating, with 97 per cent of managers being rated as outstanding, the highest point on the scale. As a result, the ratings would be useless as information on which to base allocations of performance pay in a system that is constrained by budgets and quotas. The distribution in the Department of Agriculture is less skewed and provides sufficient discrimination for the allocation of bonuses to the top two rating categories.

Poor discrimination in performance ratings seems to be more of a problem at the upper levels than at the lower levels of government departments. Figure 6 shows how average ratings correspond with grade level in the United States civil service. Managers are on average rated more highly than staff at lower levels. One justification presented for this state of affairs is that managers, having gone through many more selection processes to get to the higher levels of the organisation will, on average, be a more capable and higher performing group than employees at lower levels in the organisation. This argument, however, assumes that employees at different levels are compared against similar standards. The performance appraisal process is meant to compare managers at roughly equivalent levels of responsibility with one another. The purpose is to identify variation in performance amongst individuals covered by performance-related pay within groups that are, at least partly, defined by levels of responsibility and difficulty of the work. The data in Table 1 and Figure 6 clearly indicate that existing ratings of performance are failing to do that adequately within most federal government departments in the United States.

The United States appraisal schemes are not the only ones to experience problems of ratings inflation. In Australia, a scheme for Senior Executive Service officers in the state of Victoria that operated from 1982 to 1990 showed a similar lack of discrimination between different levels of performance in annual appraisal ratings (Public Service Board of Victoria, 1989). Surveys showed that, as a result, there was a close to automatic movement through the pay levels in the merit pay scheme. In Canada, the Senior Merit Pay Plan, a forerunner to the present Management Category salary plan, revealed similar trends toward higher performance ratings. As early as 1976, for example, ten of the 14 Canadian government departments with more than 20 executives rated more than 60 per cent of their executives as superior or outstanding. The Advisory Group on Executive Compensation, clearly thinking about differences in performance within the management group, stated in its 1977 report that, "...It is difficult to accept that there could, in any service, be over 30 per cent of the people ranked superior or outstanding". This led to the "30 per cent rule", which states that no more than 30 per cent of executive employees can be rated superior or outstanding (*i.e.* points four and five on the five-point performance rating scale). The 30 per cent rule has applied to executive compensation in the Canadian public service since 1978.

Figure 6. **Average performance rating by grade in the United States civil service**

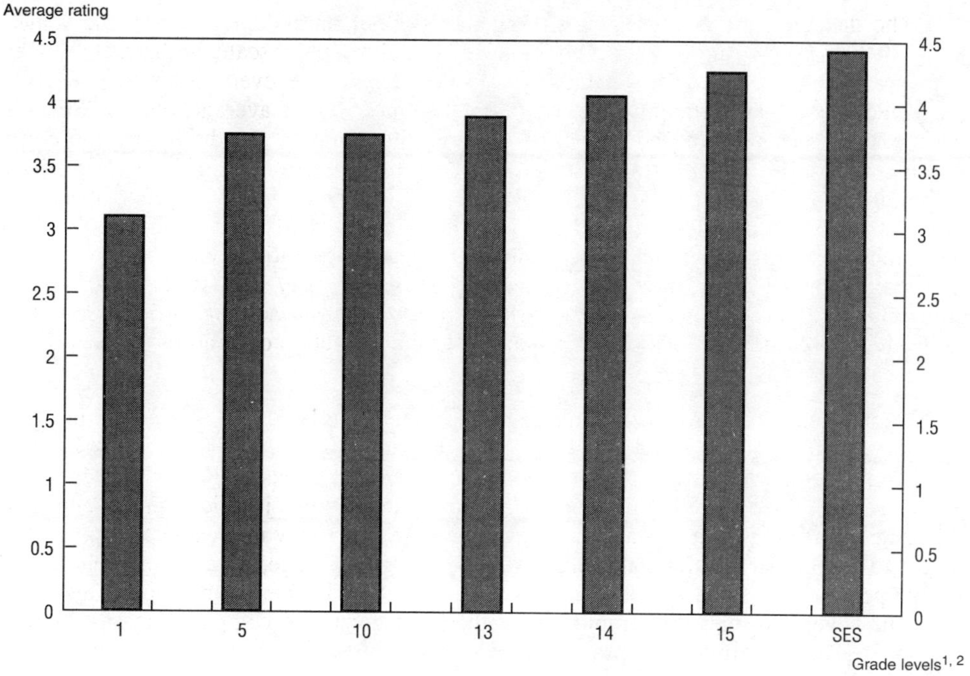

1. Grade levels 13 - 15 are management levels covered by the PMRS scheme.
2. The SES average is for all grades in the senior executive service.

Various steps can be taken to alleviate the problems created by highly skewed performance ratings. One option is to use a ranking of employees within a comparable group, such as those in a single work unit or those reporting to a single manager. Alternatively, the rankings may be done by a committee or some higher level manager, using the rating data as one input to that judgement. A second approach is to use a forced distribution of the ratings, in which a manager is required to place a certain percentage of employees at each rating level. In the United States civil service, the use of forced distributions is forbidden by law. Alternatively, a quota may be imposed on the proportion of employees placed in higher categories of the rating scale, particularly those which qualify for performance pay awards, such as the ''30 per cent rule'' in Canada.

Chapter 4

LINKAGES BETWEEN PERFORMANCE APPRAISAL AND PAY

Performance-related pay, to be effective, requires clear discrimination between those managers whose performance qualifies for an award and those managers whose performance does not. In the absence of standardised, objective measures of performance, the quality of discriminations in the allocation of rewards will be determined by the quality of performance ratings and their relationship with pay awards. Standardising the appraisal process and formally linking performance ratings to pay increases can help to produce a more consistent and equitable distribution of rewards across work units and departments. At the same time, however, it reduces the discretion of managers and departments to tailor the distributions of awards to suit their own strategies and local circumstances. Table 2 shows the differing levels of centrally imposed standards for both performance appraisals and the relationship between performance ratings and pay awards in different countries.

The relationship between the performance appraisal judgement process and performance pay allocation decisions is a reciprocal one. The reliability and validity of performance ratings will determine their usefulness as information on which to base pay allocation decisions. A lack of distribution in performance ratings will undermine attempts to make fair and valid discriminations in the allocation of pay awards. For those managers eligible to receive pay awards, any uncertainties or mistrust regarding the accuracy of

Table 2. **Linkages between pay and performance appraisal in central government performance pay schemes**

Country	Formal appraisal required	Appraisal-pay relationship specified
Australia	yes	no
Canada	yes	yes
Denmark	yes	no
France	no	no
Ireland	yes	yes
Netherlands	no	no
New Zealand	yes	yes
Sweden	no	no
United Kingdom	yes	no
United States	yes	yes

performance ratings will undermine their belief that awards are based on performance. This, in turn, can heighten dissatisfaction with pay and diminish the motivational effects that performance pay is intended to achieve. Clearly specifying the relationship between performance ratings and pay awards will not remove these problems, which are characteristics of the appraisal system and not the pay allocation decision process.

When pay awards are based directly on performance ratings, there is a reciprocal pressure on managers to use the appraisal process effectively and to be able to justify their ratings of their staff. Without this pressure managers often fail to spend adequate time or effort on appraisals, and related benefits of the process, such as work planning and staff development, are lost. Against this position is the argument that linking the performance appraisal process to pay awards induces behaviours directed at improving ratings without necessarily improving performance. The inflation in ratings across several countries, discussed earlier, may be a product of such behaviours.

There are two issues to be considered in relation to the link between performance appraisals and pay awards. First is the question of whether there should be any link at all? Second, if there is a link, how standardised should it be? In this chapter we will outline how standardising the relationship between performance ratings and pay awards can affect different policy objectives and then discuss the different approaches taken to link pay to observed levels of performance. In later chapters, evidence regarding the actual distribution of awards and the perceived link between pay and performance will be discussed.

There are those who object to any link between performance appraisal ratings and pay awards. Their objections are based on one of two concerns. First, that performance-related pay will lead to a preoccupation with the monetary awards during the performance planning and review process and will undermine the developmental purposes of appraisal, and that it may also create an added pressure for lower standards and inflated ratings in appraisal. One approach to dealing with this problem is to conduct the performance review at a different time from the pay review.

The second concern relates to the reliability and validity of performance appraisals as a basis for discrimination. In some countries there has been a reluctance to create a formal link between awards and performance appraisal schemes because of a general scepticism and concern about the subjectivity of performing ratings. For example, the lack of objective performance measures for managerial jobs in the public sector is one of the reasons given for not adopting performance-related pay schemes in the German civil service. In government business enterprises, where products and services are sold to the public, often in competition with private sector organisations, there is often greater opportunity to identify objective performance indicators for managerial jobs. These can range from unit production costs to sales revenues to financial indicators of corporate performance for the business enterprise. In central government agencies, the less tangible nature of job outputs and the lack of well defined markets for outputs makes the use of objective indicators less feasible.

In addition to the general problems of linking pay to performance appraisals there are several issues that relate to the level of standardisation in these linkages. The degree of standardisation reflects a choice between equity and consistency on the one hand and the degree of flexibility managers are allowed in managing their staff on the other. Although it could be argued that standardisation of the relationship between performance rating and pay also affects the resulting salary costs, these are more directly related to the use of quotas and budgets which will be discussed separately.

One potential benefit of a standardised relationship between performance ratings and pay awards is that it can strengthen the incentive value of the awards by providing a clearer link between performance and pay. There is likely to be greater ambiguity regarding the relationship between performance and pay in more discretionary schemes in which the award for a given level of performance is decided after the fact. This argument, of course, assumes that the performance appraisal system distinguishes effectively on a single scale between the different levels of performance. Against this must be weighed the evidence discussed earlier which indicates that the appraisal systems used in at least some schemes are not effectively discriminating between managers. Added to this is the fact that performance appraisals are used for purposes other than salary decisions, such as the motivation and development of staff. Performance ratings which serve these other purposes may not provide the level of discrimination required for pay allocation decisions. Judgements of an individual's contribution may also include a range of factors that are not included in specified performance criteria or appraisal plans. Non-standardised relationships between performance ratings and pay allow greater latitude for these supplementary factors to be taken into account in the decisions on pay awards. But they carry the risk that decisions will be based on factors that conflict with the criteria used in the appraisal process so that pay awards do not appear to be related systematically to performance ratings.

In the schemes considered here, the levels of standardisation in the relationships between performance ratings and pay awards range from no specific links to standardised, mechanistic linkages.

No specific links

In some public service schemes, such as in France, the Netherlands and Sweden, where there is no requirement to link performance pay awards to formal appraisal, managers are allowed considerable discretion in their choice of criteria and standards used to decide on pay awards for their staff. A manager, for example, may choose to give an award to a long-term employee who is a consistent but not outstanding contributor, as a form of encouragement or to maintain his or her morale. Another employee may be rewarded for efforts on a necessary but particularly difficult task with little in the way of achievements. The effects of these different awards on the productivity and morale of the work group will depend upon the quality of the manager's judgements and their acceptance by group members. The risks of arbitrariness, favouritism and other sources of bias will also be dependent upon the level of trust between the manager and the employees.

In the absence of formal appraisal systems, norms regarding levels of awards and the criteria and standards on which they are based will develop as part of the decision process for allocating performance pay awards. In the Swedish system, for example, all recommendations for personal salary adjustments are sent for approval to salary review boards that include union members. Local unions are quite involved in the establishment of local salary norms for different occupational categories. Although formal data are not available, it does appear that the review boards discriminate amongst individuals and that the range of salaries paid is increasing. Individual bonuses are reported to range from zero to over 30 per cent, although bonuses at the upper end of the range are rare. In this system, individual awards include market loadings and adjustments for job worth, making it difficult to establish how much of the bonuses paid is based on assessments of performance or whether there is any significant discrimination in awards that is due to differences in performance.

In France, a range of bonuses and allowances is given for performance and other factors and there is a long history of bonuses being paid without any required links between performance appraisals and bonus payments. Managers are allowed to use their discretion in allocating bonuses to subordinates, subject to the constraints of budgets and the specified bonuses for different occupational categories. The total amount of bonuses and allowances may not exceed 100 per cent of base salary. Attribution of bonuses is based on a global evaluation of work accomplished rather than on a formal link between pay and performance.

In summary, the methods of allocating pay awards in countries without a formal link between performance appraisal and performance pay indicate some factors which, potentially, could diminish the dependence on a performance appraisal system. These include the use of consensual decision processes, such as committees including union representatives, to allocate awards and a lack of general knowledge about the exact sizes of performance bonuses and how they are distributed.

Appraisal-based but links not standardised

In several schemes performance-related pay awards are based on a formal appraisal, but managers have considerable discretion about the number of staff to whom awards are given and the size of individual awards. The costs of the system are limited by the budget allocated for performance-related pay awards. In the United Kingdom civil service, for example, the revised performance pay scheme introduced in 1991 for the senior grades (Grades 2 and 3) has no requirement that levels of awards be tied to markings on the performance rating scale, though heads of departments do have the discretion to do so. The size and number of awards are only constrained by the budget. The only requirements relating to distribution of awards are that staff judged to be performing at the fully satisfactory level (rating level three on the five-point scale) or above should be awarded at least the annual standard pay increase for the grade, and that staff performing less than satisfactorily (rating levels four and five) should not be considered entitled to any salary increase, even if this means their pay falls below the newly adjusted minimum for the grade. However, heads of departments have the discretion to award increases up to the standard amount to staff rated below fully satisfactory if they believe this is justified by the circumstances. Discretionary pay increases over and above the standard increase for the grade may be awarded to staff performing at the fully satisfactory level or above, within the limits of a fund available to departments for this purpose. Therefore, heads of department who are willing to use their discretion have considerable flexibility to develop departmental rules for the allocation of awards.

A hypothetical example of how pay increases could be distributed within a department of eight staff in the United Kingdom civil service scheme for Grades 2 and 3 is shown in Table 3. In this example, the department head has decided to give the individual A, who is performing at the less than fully satisfactory level, half of the annual standard pay increase for these grades. All other staff receive the full standard increase. Table 3 also demonstrates two alternative distributions of increases given in addition to the

Table 3. **A hypothetical example of possible performance pay allocations in the United Kingdom civil service scheme for Grades 2 and 3**

Staff member	Current salary £	Performance rating [1]	Standard increase or less [2] %	Additional cash increase (£) Possible distributions [3]		New salaries (£)		Salary increases (%)	
				(X)	(Y)	(X)	(Y)	(X)	(Y)
A	47 300	4	2.5	–	–	48 480	48 480	2.5	2.5
B	45 000	3	5.0	–	700	47 250	47 950	5.0	6.6
C	50 900	3	5.0	–	700	53 450	54 150	5.0	6.4
D	47 500	3	5.0	–	700	49 880	50 580	5.0	6.5
E	48 600	3	5.0	400	700	51 430	51 730	5.8	6.4
F	45 000	2	5.0	1 400	900	48 650	48 150	8.1	7.0
G	52 100	2	5.0	1 000	900	55 705	55 605	6.9	6.7
H	52 100	1	5.0	2 800	1 000	57 505	55 705	10.4	6.9
Salary dispersion [4]	15.8%					21.7%	16.2%		

1. Performance ratings are: 1 = Outstanding; 2 = Well above standard requirements; 3 = Fully meets normal requirements; 4 = Not fully up to requirements; 5 = Unacceptable.
2. Standard increase is awarded each year (5% is illustrative). Full standard increase requires a performance rating of 3 or better.
3. Assumes departmental budget of £700 per staff member for additional performance-related increases (£700 x 8). This is the maximum sum available for distribution. Where awards made total less than the maximum, the remainder may be carried forward to the following year.
4. Salary dispersion (highest salary – lowest salary)/lowest salary.

standard increase, (X) and (Y) and the resulting impacts on salary dispersion within the department. A head of department could choose either of those distributions, or some other distribution, under the rules governing the scheme. In distribution (X), the head of department has exercised discretion and given additional increases to the staff he or she judges to be the top performers in the department. Distribution (X) also shows that the head of department used supplemental criteria when allocating increments. This is demonstrated by the fact that staff with the same performance rating received different awards. This approach increased the dispersion of salaries within the department from 15.8 per cent to 21.7 per cent.

Lack of discrimination in awards may be the result of group norms regarding equity or equality of treatment. It may also be due to the manager lacking the confidence or ability to discriminate effectively between employees or to gain acceptance by employees of performance pay awards that do discriminate. Distribution (X) in Table 3 demonstrates how a highly discriminatory allocation of awards may leave the large proportion of staff rated as fully satisfactory (rating level three) feeling inadequately rewarded. Four out of the eight staff were rated fully satisfactory, but only one of them received any additional pay award above the standard increase. Discriminating in favour of those whose performance is more than fully satisfactory or outstanding increases the risk of demotivating the majority of staff whose performance is rated as fully satisfactory. A second potential problem with schemes that allow managers the discretion to discriminate widely in their allocations of increments is that practices will diverge between work units or departments. This could lead to gross inequities as staff with similar histories of performance ratings come to have significantly different earnings.

By way of contrast, distribution (Y) in Table 3 is less discriminatory; all staff with the same performance rating received the same award and differences in the awards for different levels of performance were small. As a result, the salary of the highest performer in the department received an increment of 6.9 per cent and the lowest performer an increment of 2.5 per cent, as compared with relative increments of 10.4 per cent and 2.5 per cent under distribution (X). The resulting dispersion of salaries under distribution (Y) is much narrower than for distribution (X) and, therefore, less susceptible to the potential problems discussed above. But the resulting compression of increments and base salaries may weaken the perceived relationship between pay and performance, thus diminishing the motivational effects of the scheme.

The discretion allowed under this particular United Kingdom scheme and under similar systems in Australia and New Zealand, as well as in all those countries in which there are no specific links between performance appraisal and pay awards, allows individual managers or departments much greater flexibility in their use of a critical resource, monetary rewards. At the same time, however, it increases the risk of bias and inconsistencies in the allocation of awards. Another potential problem under discretionary systems is a lack of adequate discrimination between individuals whose performance clearly warrants different levels of awards.

Standardising the links between appraisals and pay awards is one response to the potential problems that arise when individual managers or departments are allowed full discretion in their allocation of merit increments and bonuses. There are, however, alternative control mechanisms for managing the potential risks associated with decentralised systems that allow greater discretion to individual managers. These include consensual decision processes in the allocation of awards, and regular monitoring and review of the operation of systems. In the United Kingdom, the operation of the system described above will be monitored by the Review Body on Top Salaries. In addition, pay awards for all Grade 2s, and for Grade 3s in departments where the head of the department is below a certain level, are subject to approval by the Head of the Home Civil Service. All awards that are higher or lower than the standard increase must be supported by a copy of the most recent performance appraisal.

In the Australian public service a proposed scheme of performance payments for senior executives requires that performance pay decisions be based on ratings achieved in the performance appraisal process. However, within the budget limits set, it is proposed that the allocation of bonuses be left to departments. The aim of this approach is to achieve a balance between the consistent service-wide application of principles outlined in guidelines on performance appraisal and performance pay and the flexibility within departments to manage performance-related pay according to their specific circumstances. The specific circumstances could include factors such as the staffing profile or the corporate strategy of the department. It is now widely recognised that compensation strategies for senior executives need to be matched to corporate strategies and that different strategies, such as cost minimisation versus growth in products or services, will require different performance pay strategies. In the public sector this may mean different distributions of awards in different departments.

Standardised relationships between performance ratings and pay

In several countries, schemes have been adopted in which the links between performance ratings and performance payments are stated as either requirements or guidelines. There are two different formulae used in determining the size of performance-related payments. The first is a simple scaling of awards based on performance rating levels. The second approach employs a matrix formula in which the size of a performance pay award is determined by both a manager's performance rating and his or her position in the salary range. Within each of these approaches, awards may be either stated as a fixed cash amount or calculated as a percentage of base salary. The approach used to determine individual awards can influence the effectiveness of a performance pay scheme through a range of intervening outcomes. These include the size of awards paid and their distribution among staff, rates of progression through the salary range, and the resulting distribution of base salaries.

Two examples of the simple scaling approach, as used in the scheme for Assistant Secretaries of departments in the Irish civil service and in the scheme for the Management Category in the Canadian public service are shown in Table 4. These two schemes can be used to illustrate several differences in the way standardised links between performance ratings and performance pay can be applied. The Irish scheme uses fixed increments of varying sizes to reward performance. These increments are equivalent to one-third, one-sixth and one-ninth of the span of the salary range for Assistant Secretaries. Departments have no discretion to vary these amounts. In Canada, an open pay range is used and the manager's position in the range will be determined by his or her history of performance awards. There are no fixed steps and it is possible for every manager in a department to have a different salary level. Departments are issued with the guidelines shown in Table 4 but are not obliged to follow them exactly. In both systems, the base pay of a manager cannot exceed the maximum of the pay range for the position. However, in the Canadian system a manager whose salary reaches the range maximum

Table 4. **Examples of standardised relationships between performance ratings and performance pay awards**

Performance rating level	Performance payments		
	Canada[1] (guidelines for awards)		Ireland[2] (fixed scale of awards)
	In-range increase %	Bonus %	£
1	7–10	up to 10	2 830
2	5–7	up to 7	1 415
3	3–5	up to 5	943
4	0	–	0
5	0	–	n.a.

n.a. = Not available.

1. Management Category Salary Plan. Merit increments or bonus payments, calculated as a percentage of base salary. The descriptive anchors used for the five rating levels in the scheme are: 1 = Outstanding; 2 = Superior; 3 = Fully Satisfactory; 4 = Satisfactory; 5 = Unsatisfactory.
2. Performance pay scheme for Assistant Secretaries of civil service departments. Fixed merit increments, 1991 rates. The descriptive anchors for the five rating levels used in the scheme are: 1 = Outstanding; 2 = More than satisfactory; 3 = Satisfactory; 4 = Less than satisfactory. The pay range for Assistant Secretaries in 1991 was £35 212 to £43 701.

can be paid the equivalent amount of the performance payment as a lump-sum bonus. Bonuses must be re-earned each year, but they are treated as part of salary for pension purposes.

Another difference between the Canadian and Irish systems is the manner in which adjustments in the salary range (*i.e.* general wage increases or cost of living adjustments) are handled. In the Irish system range adjustments are not linked to performance appraisal ratings and all managers receive the increases that result from those adjustments, even if their performance is rated as less than satisfactory. In the Canadian system, managers do not automatically receive the full amount of increases due to range adjustments. Managers whose performance is rated unsatisfactory receive no range adjustment. Managers whose performance is rated as satisfactory may be paid either the full amount of a range adjustment or some lesser amount at the discretion of the head of their department. This further increases the variation in individual salary levels.

The different methods of calculating the performance payments under the Canadian and Irish schemes will also affect the relative sizes of awards received by individuals and their progression through the salary range. In the Irish system the size of awards is expressed as a fixed cash amount and is not affected by the manager's existing salary level. In Canada, the award is calculated as a percentage of base salary so that managers higher up the salary range will receive a larger increment in cash terms than managers lower in the range who receive the same performance rating and the same percentage increase. An example of the impact that this approach can have on the size of awards for managers at different points in a salary range is shown in Table 5. In the example given, the cash value of bonuses paid to managers at the top of the salary range is over 50 per cent greater than the value of the payments received by managers at the bottom of the range. The differences in the salary levels of managers that are produced by this approach

Table 5. **An example of the differences in sizes of lump-sum bonuses paid as a percentage of position in salary range**[1]

Performance rating	Bonus %	Corresponding cash awards	
		Manager at bottom of salary range A$	Manager at top of salary range A$
Outstanding	15	10 102	15 465
Superior	10	6 735	10 310
Fully Effective	5	3 367	5 155
Marginal	0	–	–
Unsatisfactory	0	–	–

1. Based on the new bonus scheme for Senior Executives in the state of Victoria, Australia, which commenced in 1990.

reflect differences in base salary that are due to level of appointment in the salary range and past performance achievements.

An alternative to the simple scaling approach is a matrix approach, in which performance pay awards are based on both the manager's performance rating and his or her position in the salary range. An example of how a matrix can be used to determine merit increments as a percentage of base salary is shown in Table 6. It should be noted that the scheme from which this example is taken has since been altered substantially and no longer uses this matrix. It is included here purely because it provides a useful illustration of several features common to matrix approaches. By explicitly adjusting the size of the percentage increment received on the basis of the existing position in the salary range, the matrix approach shown in Table 6 reduces the variation in the cash value of awards. It also slows down the rate of salary progression as the individual

Table 6. **An example of a merit increment matrix based on position in the salary range and performance rating**[1]

Current position in salary range[2]	Performance rating[3]				
	1	2	3	4	5
Less than 80%	–	5	10	15	20
80% and over	–	2	5	10	15
Maximum salary[4]		90	100	115	130

1. Based on 1990 guidelines for scheme covering advisory and professional staff in New Zealand State Services Commission. The guidelines can be altered from one year to the next. In the 1991 guidelines for the same department, the recommended merit increments were set at lower levels due to financial restraints and were based solely on performance rating. The recommended merit increments for each performance rating level in 1991 were: 1% for rating 3; 2% for rating 4; and 3% for rating 5.
2. Current position in salary range is expressed as a percentage of the range mid-point.
3. Performance ratings are as follows: 1 = Fell far short of meeting objectives set; 2 = Fell short of meeting objectives set; 3 = Substantially met objectives set; 4 = Exceeded objectives set; 5 = Far exceeded objectives set.
4. Maximum salary levels are expressed as a percentage of the range mid-point.

approaches the top of the salary range and may avoid problems associated with employees reaching the top of the range too long before they are likely to be promoted. However, because of the relatively large increments paid under this particular matrix, progression through the range is quite rapid.

Several other features of the matrix approach shown in Table 6 are worthy of note. First is the fact that there is a negative adjustment for experience and a history of better performance. That is, individuals who are further up the salary range due to higher performance ratings in previous years, receive a lower award, as a percentage of base salary, than those at a lower point in the range who receive the same performance rating in the current period. Individuals who are close to the maximum salary point may be further penalised because they may not be able to take their full increment for a given period. For example, a more junior manager who receives a lower performance rating could receive a higher percentage increment than an outstanding senior manager who is near the top of the range. If managers compare increments in percentage terms, then this situation may lead to feelings of inequity and may undermine the perceived link between pay and performance among the more senior, high performing managers. The magnitude of this problem will depend upon the promotion rates for managers at the top of the range and rates of progression through the salary range.

Another feature of the matrix approach illustrated in Table 6 is that it sets maximum limits on the levels of pay that an individual can receive for different performance ratings. Over the longer term, this may have several effects. First, it will constrain the overall cost of salaries. Second, it will create some dispersion of salaries between individuals who perform at different levels over several years, assuming those differences are accurately reflected in the ratings. Therefore, if a manager consistently fails to achieve objectives his or her salary will not go above 90 per cent of the median. A manager who consistently meets all objectives will earn the median salary while a consistently outstanding performer would be paid 30 per cent more than the median. This, in turn, could create incentives for managers to improve their performance and to maintain high levels of performance once they are attained.

Table 7. **Merit increment matrix based on position in the salary range and performance rating**[1]

Performance rating	Position in salary range[2]			
	1st tercile	2nd tercile	3rd tercile	Step 10[3]
Outstanding	Full MI[4]	Full MI	Full MI	0
Exceeds fully successful	Full MI	1/2 MI	1/2 MI	0
Fully successful	Full MI	1/2 MI	1/3 MI	0
Minimally successful	0	0	0	0
Unacceptable	0	0	0	0

1. Formula used for Performance Management and Recognition System in United States civil service.
2. 1st Tercile = Step 1 up to $1 below Step 4. 2nd Tercile = Step 4 up to $1 below Step 7. 3rd Tercile = Step 7 up to $1 below Step 10.
3. Step 10 is top of the range.
4. MI = merit increment, equivalent to approximately 3% of base salary.

The merit increment formula of the Performance Management and Recognition System for mid-level managers in the United States, shown in Table 7, illustrates several features of a different matrix approach. First, movement up the salary scale is based on merit increments that are equivalent to a single step increase in a ten-step scale. The maximum salary is the top of the range, irrespective of the performance rating received. Therefore, in this system all managers progress through the same salary range, whereas in the example shown in Table 6, the width of the salary range varies as a function of the different maximum salaries payable for different levels of performance ratings.

Chapter 5

PERFORMANCE PAY

In earlier chapters we have discussed the performance measurement systems and their linkages with performance-based pay. In this chapter we turn our attention to the specifics of the performance-related payments themselves. In particular we will consider the decision process used to allocate pay awards, the nature of payments and factors that affect their size and distribution.

Staff covered by performance-related pay

Staff covered by performance pay schemes range from the highest positions in the public service to the lowest levels of clerical and manual staff. However, the majority of schemes concentrate on middle and senior managers. The number of staff covered by particular schemes in different countries varies dramatically. In Ireland, the scheme for Assistant Secretaries covers 95 staff at the second most senior level in civil service departments. The Performance Management and Recognition System in the United States covers over 140 000 middle-level managers in the federal government. Surprisingly, there appear to be no clear relationships between the number of employees covered by schemes and the characteristics of the schemes. For example, the degree of formalisation and the constraints applied to schemes seem to be more a product of experience and the public sector culture within different countries than a response to the control problems of large schemes. In France, for example, performance bonuses are paid to all managerial and technical staff without any formal appraisal requirements and few rules regarding the allocation of bonuses.

Performance-related pay schemes often, but not always, exclude the highest positions in the public service because of the difficulty of finding an appropriate appraiser for performance in these posts. As the nexus between the political system and the public administrative institutions, heads of departments must respond to a wide variety of political and institutional demands, making appraisal of their performance by a single person or a single group inappropriate. In both Ireland and the United Kingdom, Permanent Secretaries of departments are excluded from the schemes that cover managers in the two levels immediately below them in the hierarchy. In both countries, appraisals by ministers are considered inappropriate because they are outside the authority of the civil service system. In Canada, which is one of the few countries with a scheme that covers the heads of central government departments, four different appraisals are used to determine salary increases. This approach is described in some detail in the next section.

The pay allocation decision process

The allocation of performance pay amongst staff can place heavy demands on the individual responsible for this. Effective use of performance pay requires discrimination in the awards given to different staff who must work together and collaborate with their superior if he or she is to function effectively. Lack of confidence in the accuracy of appraisals and potential negative reactions by staff can make it difficult to discriminate amongst staff in the allocation of pay and to gain staff acceptance of decisions regarding pay. In pure incentive systems, where performance pay is determined by performance against agreed quantitative measures of individual job performance, these pressures are minimal. However, this is rarely the case for the work performed by public sector managers in central government agencies. Standardising the relationship between performance ratings and pay awards in the ways discussed earlier will shift the pressures associated with pay allocation decisions onto the performance appraisal judgements. However, formal links between performance appraisal and performance pay are widely believed to add to the inflation of performance ratings that has been evident in the appraisal systems for managers in many countries.

Added to this are the problems of inconsistencies in rating standards and pay allocations between supervisors, work units and departments. A supervisor may accurately rate the performance of his or her own staff and then allocate pay awards on the basis of those performance ratings. However, if his or her staff compare themselves to staff in units where lower standards are used to allocate performance awards they may still be dissatisfied with their own awards and believe that pay increases are not related to performance. Better design and development of performance appraisal systems will help to reduce inconsistencies and bias in the appraisal judgements used to allocate awards. However, experience in the United States has shown that there are clearly limits to the consistency and accuracy of performance judgements in even the most developed systems.

Different schemes have taken different approaches in their attempts to minimise the problems which insufficient discrimination in pay awards and inconsistencies in performance ratings cause in the allocation of performance pay. One approach has been to apply quotas to either the number of staff who can receive the top performance ratings or to the number of staff who can receive performance pay. However, as discussed later, quotas often lead to widespread dissatisfaction among the large majority of staff who are judged to be performing satisfactorily but are excluded by the quota requirements from receiving a performance pay award.

Another approach to the problem of inconsistency in performance ratings and inadequate distributions of performance pay awards is to create compensation committees to either decide or recommend what the final allocation of awards should be. Compensation committees reduce the power and discretion of the individual supervisor to decide which of his or her staff should receive particular awards. At the same time, however, they protect the supervisor from the pressures that go with the responsibility for that decision. Committees may also ensure greater consistency in ratings and awards by reviewing the performance ratings and other data for staff from a range of work units or departments. In this way they are better able to identify biases and the different standards of individual supervisors and to correct for them in pay decisions. There is, however, the risk that compensation committees in their deliberations may introduce data and criteria that are not part of the supervisor's appraisal of his or her staff. This may add to uncertainties about the relationship between performance and pay and undermine a supervisor's standing with staff. For this reason, compensation committees for mid-level managers are usually given monitoring and review roles rather than a direct responsibility for recommending or deciding on performance pay awards.

Heads of departments typically have the final authority to determine performance pay awards for managers in their departments, within the limits of any budget constraints, quotas or other requirements which may apply to performance appraisal and the allocation of pay awards. However, compensation committees with direct responsibility for recommending individual pay awards are more commonly used when managers at very senior levels, heads of departments, for example, are covered by performance pay plans. In Canada, for example, all pay increases for Deputy Ministers (heads of government departments), including performance bonuses, are decided by Cabinet on the recommendation of a broadly-based committee of peers, the Committee of Senior Officials on Executive Personnel (COSO). This is an example of how compensation committees can help overcome the problems of inconsistency and pressure on individual supervisors in the allocations of pay awards.

The COSO is comprised of four permanent members who are Deputy Ministers of central agencies with service-wide responsibilities in relation to various aspects of public service management: the Secretary of the Treasury Board, the Chairman of the Public Service Commission, and the Secretary and Deputy Secretary to the Cabinet. Four other Deputy Ministers serve on a rotating basis. The committee bases its recommendations on a range of assessments of each Deputy Minister's performance. These include:

- the Minister's assessment of his or her deputy's performance;
- an assessment by the Treasury Board Secretariat of the performance of the Deputy Minister's department against corporate goals and financial indicators;
- an assessment by the Public Service Commission of the performance of the Deputy Minister's department against corporate goals and staff management indicators;
- a voluntary self-assessment by the Deputy Minister.

Based on these assessments, each Deputy Minister's performance is evaluated relative to that of his or her peers in the same grade and recommendations are made to the Prime Minister regarding individual pay increases (both range adjustments and performance bonuses). When the pay awards have been approved by Cabinet, Deputy Ministers are informed of their evaluation grades and pay awards by letter.

There are several features of this committee review process that are likely to lead to more valid discriminations in the pay awards given to individuals and greater acceptance of the award distribution by Deputy Ministers. First, the broad-based membership of the committee and the range of data sources considered ensures a comprehensive view is taken of each Deputy Minister's performance. Second, the comparison across a range of departments will mean that some attempt is made to establish comparable standards and to reflect differences in departmental conditions in the final evaluation of performance. Finally, accountability for the Deputy Minister's pay award is shared by a group of peers. As a result, no single person is fully exposed to the pressures and demands of the performance pay decision.

In most cases where compensation committees are used to recommend or approve pay awards their membership is drawn from within a department. One interesting exception is the Salary Review Boards in Sweden, which include union representatives. All recommendations for performance payments go to the Review Boards for approval. In other countries where compensation committees are used, their composition varies with the level of managers under review. At the more senior levels, the head of a department and a selected group of his or her deputies will comprise the compensation committee. For middle-level managers, if committees are involved at all in the decision process, they will often include divisional managers and senior human resource managers.

For middle-level managers it is more common for recommendations of pay awards made by the immediate superior to go to a more senior manager in the same hierarchical line of authority for review and approval. This review process serves many of the same functions described earlier for the COSO compensation committee in Canada. However, individual managers, depending upon the number of staff reporting to them through their subordinates, will generally have a narrower range of comparisons than compensation committees.

Form of payment

A key issue in the design of performance-related pay schemes is whether or not payments are to be in the form of merit increments that are added to the base salary of the recipient, or lump-sum bonuses that have to be re-earned in each appraisal period. Merit increments link progression through a pay scale or pay range to employee job performance rather than seniority. If pay is effectively linked to productivity increases, then increases in payroll costs may be offset by performance improvements under a merit scheme. Under a seniority-based scheme, payroll costs increase as a function of the age and experience profile of the workforce. The workforce profile is, in turn, related to the turnover of staff and the recruitment policies of the organisation. The net costs of a seniority-based scheme will also depend upon the productivity effects of having an experienced, stable workforce.

Bonus payments do not affect base pay and the employee must re-earn the bonus each year. With less of the total compensation budget allocated for base pay, bonus schemes allow greater flexibility in the allocation of rewards and in the control of payroll costs. Also, because bonuses are typically not counted in the calculation of benefits that are related to base pay, such as pensions, the indirect payroll costs are usually less under a bonus scheme than a merit scheme. Several countries have performance pay schemes that combine merit increments and lump-sum bonuses. These combinations include schemes in which employees may be paid either a bonus or a merit increment (e.g. the Netherlands), schemes in which bonuses are paid instead of merit increments when a person has reached the top of the merit range (e.g. Canada, United Kingdom,) and schemes in which bonuses and merit increments can be earned simultaneously (e.g. United States).

Table 8 shows the different types of performance payments that are used in central government schemes in different countries. As can be seen, pure merit schemes are rare. The recently introduced scheme for Assistant Secretaries in Ireland is the only pure merit scheme. Countries with longer-running merit schemes, such as Canada and the United Kingdom, have introduced bonus payments for managers who have reached the top of the merit salary range. The United States runs both merit and bonus schemes concurrently for mid-level managers covered by the Performance Management and Rec-

Table 8. **Forms of performance payment in central government schemes in selected countries**

Country	Bonus	Merit Increments	Special Awards[1]	Comment
Australia	Yes	–	–	–
Canada	Yes	Yes	–	Bonuses are paid when managers reach top of merit range. For Deputy Ministers larger bonuses are paid.
Denmark	Yes	Yes	–	Includes temporary salary increases (*e.g.* 3 months).
France	Yes	–	–	Bonuses are paid for a range of purposes, including performance.
Germany	–	–	–	–
Ireland	–	Yes	–	Non-competitive scheme. No quotas or budget limits.
Netherlands	Yes	Yes	Yes	Includes temporary salary increases for periods of up to one year. Bonuses are paid for special achievements.
New Zealand	Yes	Yes	–	Performance pay schemes vary between departments.
Spain	Yes	–	–	Bonuses are paid quarterly. Mainly based on hours worked.
Sweden	Yes	Yes	–	Bonus scheme is self-financing. Merit payments based on national awards.
United Kingdom	Yes	Yes	–	Bonus paid at top of range.
United States	Yes	Yes	Yes	PMRS scheme includes all forms of awards. SES scheme includes different types of bonuses.

1. Special awards here refers to small tokens (*e.g.* bottles of wine, dinner vouchers) or small cash awards given as recognition for completion of a project, a special effort, etc.

ognition System, although payments under each scheme are made at different times of the year in many agencies. The schemes for senior executives in Australia and the United States are pure bonus schemes with no merit increments. In Denmark and the Netherlands, departments are given greater flexibility in their choice of the form of payment and individuals may be paid a bonus, a merit increment, or a temporary salary increase. In these countries, the allocations of awards between bonuses and merit increments must be managed within the available budgets. In the Netherlands, for example, managers who overspend the centrally allocated performance pay budget must find the additional funds from other budget sources. Therefore, temporary allowances and bonuses, which require no future commitments of funds, tend to be preferred to merit increments, which must be funded on a continuing basis.

Merit increments

Merit increment schemes require that there be a salary range for each position covered by the scheme so that differences in performance can be recognised. Movement through the range from the minimum to the maximum can be through fixed steps or through variable increments, as in the case of open range schemes in which the minimum and maximum are the only defined points in the range. In some countries, the introduction of merit increments required the introduction of a salary range in place of a single salary point for positions. In other countries, the merit pay range replaced existing fixed incremental salary scales. By way of contrast, bonus payments may be based on pay structures that include a single salary point for each position.

A critical issue in the design of merit increment schemes is the time it takes a manager to move through the full width of the pay range. If managers reach the top of the range too quickly, salaries can become clustered within a narrow range and supplemental payments (e.g. bonuses) that go outside the established salary range are needed. The rate of progression through a salary range is a function of both the size of merit increments and the width of the merit pay range. The impact of these two variables can be illustrated by a comparison of the United States merit scheme for mid-level managers, shown in Table 7, and the Irish scheme shown in Table 4.

Merit increments in the scheme shown in Table 7 represent around 3 per cent of base salary and the width of the salary range (differential between the minimum and the maximum of the range) is 27 per cent. As a result, movement through the range is relatively slow. An individual with a consistent performance rating of fully satisfactory would take 18 years to move from the bottom to the top of the range. A consistently outstanding manager would move through the range in nine years. In the Irish scheme shown in Table 4, by comparison, the increment for an outstanding performer is equivalent to 8 per cent of base salary, that for a more than satisfactory performer is 4 per cent, and that for a satisfactory performer is less than 3 per cent (1991 figures). The width of the salary range is 24 per cent. Under this scheme a consistently satisfactory manager would reach the top of the range in just nine years. For a consistently outstanding manager the larger increments would take him or her through the range in three years. Therefore, if supported by an appraisal scheme that effectively discriminates between outstanding and fully satisfactory performers, the matrix shown in Table 7 is less likely than the matrix in Table 4 to confront problems due to large numbers of staff who reach the maximum rate and are ineligible for further increments.

Several problems may arise in merit increment schemes. If new employees are normally brought in at the bottom of the pay range, then the whole range must rise with market rates. Failure to adjust for the market in this way will mean that new employees, particularly those in areas of high demand, will have to be brought in at salary levels above the bottom of the range. This may result in situations where a new manager with little experience in his or her job earns more than an outstanding manager with several years experience. The resulting feelings of inequity and perceived distortion of the link between pay and performance may affect morale and can lead to increased turnover among more experienced, high performing managers (Milkovich and Newman, 1990).

Year to year fluctuations in performance levels of individuals present another problem, particularly in schemes with relatively large merit increments where movement through the salary range is quite rapid. Someone who performs well for several years will progress quickly through the range. If their performance rating then drops in subsequent years, they will receive smaller increments or no merit increments, but because they retain the increments received in earlier years they may be paid more than their peers who are performing at the same (lower) level and may also, for a time, be paid at the same level as higher performing managers who have entered the pay scheme later. The relatively slow movement through the pay range in the United States scheme shown in Table 7 makes it less likely that this problem will occur. Lower rated managers who are paid at the same level as their higher performing peers will generally be much older than them.

Another problem that has affected the impact of merit payments in some countries has been the relatively high rates of inflation that occurred during the 1980s. As a result of inflation, merit increments are often smaller than annual cost of living adjustments in salary ranges. In the United States civil service, for example, the annual general increase in pay rates for mid-level managers has been around 4 per cent in the latter half of the 1980s, while the maximum merit increment in the scheme for these managers is 3 per cent. In Canada, recent cost of living increases of around 4 per cent to salary ranges for managers have been less than the 10 per cent maximum merit increment that can be earned. However, since only a small proportion of managers receive the maximum increment under the Canadian scheme, the cost of living adjustment is about the same size as the merit increment earned by the almost 70 per cent of managers who are rated as fully satisfactory. The expected lower inflation rates for the 1990s should mean that merit increments will be more significant relative to cost of living adjustments and therefore will have greater motivational value for public sector managers.

Bonus schemes

Bonus schemes in the public sector differ markedly from those in the private sector in one critical way; they are more likely to be based on performance appraisal ratings than on objective, quantitative measures of performance. In the public sector, quantitative targets for awarding bonuses are more common in government commercial enterprises. Quantitative targets may also be used in the assessment of heads of departments when this group is included in performance pay schemes. In Canada, for example, Deputy Ministers are paid bonuses following a review of the performance of their departments against financial targets.

A major advantage of bonuses paid as a lump sum is that they highlight the total size and the performance-related nature of the reward. Merit increments, although they represent a much larger contribution to the employee's lifetime stream of earnings, are less dramatic in their immediate impact. For example, a 10 per cent merit increment on a salary of $52 000 per annum would mean an extra $140 in a fortnightly pay packet, assuming a marginal tax rate of 30 per cent. A 10 per cent bonus at the same marginal tax rate would mean a lump-sum payment of $3 640. There is no research evidence regarding the effects of lump-sum payments versus merit increments, but some compensation experts believe lump-sum payments provide the individual with greater discretion in satisfying personal needs and that they enhance performance and satisfaction more than do merit increments.

Lump-sum bonuses also offer several advantages over merit increments in controlling payroll costs. Because they are not perpetuated as part of base salary, bonuses do not add to the fixed payroll costs. Also, because they are a variable cost, the government has greater flexibility to vary the budgets and number of awards available from year to year. However, experience in the United States, where Congress cut the Senior Executive Service bonuses budget in half during the first year of the scheme's operation, has shown that the budgets for performance payments can lead to widespread dissatisfaction with schemes (Ingraham and Colby, 1982). Lump-sum bonus payments also allow greater flexibility in adjusting pay to performance when an individual's performance level drops. Under most merit increment schemes, a manager whose performance declines after a few years of good performance will retain the merit increments earned in those years.

The maximum bonuses payable in the schemes examined here range from 10 per cent upwards, as shown in Table 9. Based on salary rates for 1991, the largest possible bonus that may be earned in a single year is in the United States, where a Senior Executive Service officer on a base salary of $87 000 who received the maximum 20 per cent performance bonus and a $20 000 Presidential Rank Award in the same year would receive bonuses equal to 43 per cent of his or her base salary (see Annex 1). A $10 000 Presidential Rank Award plus a full performance bonus would equal 31.5 per cent of salary. These levels of bonus payments are uncommon, however, due to the small percentage of staff who receive Presidential Rank Awards. No more than 1 per cent of SES officers may receive an award of $20 000 each year and no more than 5 per cent may receive an award of $10 000, and an individual may receive the same Rank Award only once in a five year period.

In several countries there are bonus schemes with no defined maximum payments. These include Denmark, the Netherlands, Sweden, and the United Kingdom. In Sweden, bonuses paid are believed to be as high as 35 per cent of salary, although awards at this level are extremely rare. In Denmark, limits imposed by departments have resulted in maximum bonuses of around 15 per cent of base salary. In the Netherlands, special achievement bonuses, when awarded, are believed to be typically around 20 to 25 per cent of monthly salary (equivalent to 1.5 to 2 per cent of annual salary), but may be higher in special cases. To this can be added any performance allowance paid as a temporary salary increment, which may be as much as 15 per cent of base salary for senior managers. In both the Netherlands and Denmark, performance pay budgets are relatively small (see Table 9), suggesting high levels of discrimination in the allocation of awards. In all of these countries, bonuses can be offered as alternatives to merit increments and, therefore, the size of awards given may be constrained by the generally lower levels of merit increments.

Table 9. **Budgets and maximum awards for selected performance pay schemes**

Country	Scheme type	Budget[1] %	Other funds	Maximum[2] awards %
Australia[3]	Bonus	11.0	Salary savings	24
Canada	Merit and Bonus	5.0	None	10+[4]
Denmark	Merit and Bonus	0.4[5]	Salary savings	15
Ireland	Merit	n.a.[6]	None	8
Netherlands	Merit and Bonus	0.75[7]	Salary savings, budget transfers	15[8]
Sweden	Merit and Bonus	7.5[9]	Cost savings[10]	n.a.
United Kingdom	Merit and Bonus	2.0	Funds carried forward	n.a.
United States (PMRS)	Merit and Bonus	1.5	None	0
United States (SES)	Bonus	3.0	None	20+[11]

n.a. = Not available.

1. Centrally allocated budget expressed as a percentage of payroll for eligible staff.
2. Maximum bonuses or merit increments based on recommended maximums (Australia, Canada, Ireland, Netherlands, United States) or estimates of actual payments where there are no limits on payments (Denmark). In Ireland and Australia awards are stated in cash amounts and the maximum percentage award for individuals varies with position in the pay range.
3. Estimated budget for proposed scheme for Senior Executive Service in the Australian Public Service based on recommended dollar awards.
4. 10% is for Management Category. Senior Deputy Ministers may earn up to 25% of salary and junior Deputy Ministers up to 15%.
5. The budget comprises 0.3% of the total salary budget for the performance pay scheme covering all staff and 0.1% for the special scheme for managers. Negotiations with unions have produced an agreement to raise the budget to 0.8%.
6. No specific budget; non-competitive scheme; increments are included in overall salary budget.
7. This comprises 0.5% for merit increments and 0.25% for other performance awards (see Annex 1).
8. 15% is the maximum temporary salary increase for managers in grades 16-18. Award of a merit increment (3%) and a special achievement bonus could be in addition to the 15%.
9. No separate budget; collectively bargained wage agreements include an amount specifically earmarked for individual salary setting, which is based on level of responsibility and skill as well as performance. In 1990 the total increase in the wages budget was 6%, of which 3.5% was earmarked for individual salary setting.
10. In some agencies there are local bonus systems which are financed through higher efficiency or cost savings.
11. 20% is for performance bonuses only. Top Presidential Rank Awards range from 24% (SES, level 6) to 28% (SES, level 1). These are limited to 1% of the SES.

In the United States, until recently, the minimum bonus payable to staff who receive outstanding ratings was specified, as well as the maximum. Although the minimal amount specified was very low (2 per cent), this approach was intended to ensure that high performers received significant awards and that there was some dispersion in awards paid for different levels of performance. However, in April 1991, this statutory requirement was removed in order to give agencies more flexibility in managing their bonus funds. Another approach is to fully specify all possible levels of awards that can be paid, as is done in Canada and Ireland (see Table 4). Information concerning the actual distribution of awards under these different approaches would be of great interest. Unfortunately, data are not available to show whether one system is better than another in producing a valid dispersion in the allocation of awards.

Specifying the levels of awards will not, by itself, ensure a dispersion of awards. The level of discrimination in the performance appraisals on which bonuses are based, the use of quotas, the size of budgets and the norms governing merit and equity will all influence the actual distribution of awards. In a later section we will discuss the available evidence on the actual distributions of awards and attempt to relate them to characteristics of the systems.

Special achievement bonuses

Another form of bonus is an award given for completion of a task or some other special achievement. These bonuses are usually given at the time of the achievement and may range from a special gift (e.g. a bottle of wine or dinner vouchers) to cash awards. There is little data or research evidence on the effects of these special awards. However, they have several features which suggest that they could have very high incentive value for recipients.

First, managers usually have greater discretion in their allocation of awards to staff. This, in turn, means they can be used to recognise a range of different contributions and to motivate staff in different ways. Another benefit is that they can be given in a timely manner, immediately following the completion of a task or the achievement being recognised. Finally, experience with these schemes in the United States and the Netherlands shows that people respond positively to the recognition by their peers even when the awards are of quite small monetary values.

Size of potential payments

The sizes of merit increments and bonuses vary widely across different schemes. Table 9 shows the maximum awards payable under a selected set of performance pay schemes in different countries. Potential merit increments range from 10 per cent in the scheme for the Management Category in Canada to 3 per cent in the scheme for mid-level managers in the United States. Maximum bonuses payable are generally higher than merit increments. Upper limits of 20 per cent or more are not uncommon for senior managers across a range of countries.

Several factors may influence the size of performance payments. First is the government's willingness and ability to pay. Pay awards to public sector managers may have flow-on effects to other sectors of the economy and create problems for a government's macroeconomic policy. A government's commitment to the rationalist economic principles discussed earlier may also influence its willingness to base greater proportions of public sector managers' pay on performance. Another factor that influences the potential size of performance payments is the substantial salary gap between managers in public and private sector organisations in many OECD countries. As previously discussed, performance-related pay was introduced in several countries as a means of reducing the disparities in salaries between public and private sector managers. According to the equity theory of pay, the level of satisfaction and the effects on performance of compensation for public sector managers will be influenced by comparisons with the compensation packages of managers at equivalent levels in private sector organisations (Adams, 1963; Mahoney, 1979). Therefore, one possible benchmark for establishing the size of bonuses or merit increments is the resulting total compensation for public sector managers compared to that of equivalent managers in the private sector.

In most schemes the potential cash value of awards available to more senior managers is greater than that available to managers at lower levels simply because awards are calculated as a percentage of base salary. In some schemes the bonuses available to more senior managers also represent a greater percentage of salary than awards for more junior managers. For example, in the United States, members of the Senior Executive Service may receive annual performance bonuses of up to 20 per cent of their base pay. Among mid-level managers covered by the Performance Management and Recognition System, bonus awards can be worth up to 10 per cent and merit increments around 3 per cent of salary. Higher bonuses are payable, but only in exceptional circumstances. In Canada a maximum award of 10 per cent, including both bonus and merit increments, is payable to senior managers up to, but not including, the Deputy Minister level. For Deputy Ministers the bonus maximums are set at 25 per cent of salary for the most senior Deputy Ministers and at 15 per cent of salary for the others.

Budgets

Budgets for performance pay schemes serve many different functions and, in combination with other design features such as quotas, may act as a major constraint on the success of a performance-related pay scheme. Inadequate funding and changes in budgets have hindered the operation of several schemes. The Canadian performance pay scheme for the Management Category was suspended for several years due to a lack of funding, and even when it did operate the rewards paid were often small due to budget constraints. From 1985 to 1991, funds were available for the scheme to operate as intended.

In the United States, the performance bonus scheme for the Senior Executive Service which was introduced under the provisions of the 1978 Civil Service Reform Act was originally budgeted for up to 50 per cent of staff in each agency to receive awards in any year. Soon after the first round of awards was announced, Congress effectively halved the budget for the scheme by reducing the quota of staff who could receive an award to 25 per cent. The Office of Personnel Management (the central personnel agency of Federal government) further reduced the quota to 20 per cent. This generated dissatisfaction and cynicism among executives whose salaries had been limited by a ''pay cap'' for several years and who viewed the performance awards as an opportunity to gain justified salary increases (Milkovich and Wigdor, 1991). The limitation on the percentage of SES members eligible for awards was removed in 1984, but the negative perceptions created by the earlier alterations in the scheme have proved difficult to eradicate. A number of performance pay schemes in state and city administrations in the United States have also suffered problems as a result of failure to fund, or only partial funding, in some years (Ingraham, 1991).

The experience in Canada and the United States provides some specific illustrations of the more general problem that funding for performance pay schemes in the public sector may be vulnerable to budgetary cutbacks in times of economic constraint. This is a critical issue because the level and stability of funding for schemes are likely to have a major impact on the success of schemes.

In private sector organisations and government business enterprises, the use of quantitative financial indicators and other performance measures that can be converted to monetary equivalents makes it possible to justify performance pay budgets in terms of expected financial gains and to establish more clearly the net benefits of the schemes. By contrast, the lack of productivity and financial performance measures for many public sector activities means that cost-benefit assessments for performance pay schemes are extremely difficult to make. As a result, attention is more likely to be focused on the direct cost of the schemes rather than on the overall cost-benefit equation. Curtailment of the funding available for performance pay, by limiting the rewards which the schemes can deliver, undermines the likelihood of achieving performance gains or other organisational benefits.

The size of a performance pay budget, as a percentage of payroll, reflects a government's support for the principle of performance-related pay. Evidence from research in the private sector indicates that the proportion of total compensation that is performance-related is a significant predictor of organisational performance (e.g. Jensen and Murphy, 1990). There is no obviously consistent logic to the establishment of budgets across schemes in different countries. As shown in Table 9, they vary quite markedly, ranging from 3 per cent of payroll in Denmark to a projected 11 per cent in Australia. It should be noted that in some merit pay schemes there is no budget specifically earmarked for performance pay. The merit increments are taken to be part of the normal cost of salaries for the groups concerned and are provided for in the overall allocation to departments for staff costs. This is the case with the Irish scheme for example. In the New Zealand system, performance pay must be funded from departmental budgets and no separate funding is provided.

The size of the budget will also affect the size and number of awards that can be given out and, therefore, will influence the competition for awards, the incentive value of awards, and the perceived links between pay and performance, as well as the cost of the programme. The smaller the budget, the fewer the significant awards that can be given out. This may result in the scheme being perceived as being elitist and unattainable for the vast majority of people. An alternative response may be to give small awards to the greatest number of people, thus undermining the principle that pay should vary as a function of performance. These two approaches to the distributions of awards and their impact on salary dispersion are illustrated by the (X) and (Y) distributions in Table 3, discussed earlier. The number of potential recipients, which is a function of both quotas and budgets, will influence the overall acceptance of a performance pay scheme. A problem with many existing schemes is how to provide awards to the large percentage of staff whose performance is fully satisfactory, while, at the same time, providing significant recognition to outstanding performers. The ability to do both is of course determined by the funds available.

The size of the budget should be related to the aims of the performance pay scheme. For example, if the intention is to recognise and reward outstanding performance and promote a general culture of striving for excellence, then a small budget may be appropriate. The Presidential Rank awards in the United States Senior Executive Service are examples of such awards. As noted earlier, no more than 1 per cent of the senior executives may receive the Distinguished Executive Award of $20 000 plus a gold pin and no more than 5 per cent may receive a Meritorious Executive Award of $10 000 plus a silver pin. These awards are for executives whose performance is judged to be exceptional over an extended period of at least three years and they are awarded by the President at a special ceremony. For the vast majority of senior executives, the recipients of the awards represent models of outstanding public sector managers and a demonstration of a commitment to excellence in public service. For the average senior executive, the prospects of receiving a Presidential Rank award would be remote and therefore not directly motivating in his or her own job. The aim of such highly competitive awards for outstanding performance may therefore be directly to enhance the performance of the most talented managers and to support a culture of excellence among the broader group covered by the awards. As we will discuss shortly, it is important to the success of such schemes that selections be viewed by staff as impartial, unbiased and valid.

Alternatively, if the aim is to raise the overall level of performance for the majority of managers, then this may be better achieved through a less competitive system that recognises a wider range of levels of performance and places a significant proportion of the salaries of all managers at risk each year. This is more like the systems of performance awards for managers used in private sector organisations (Merchant, 1989). Such schemes require larger budgets however, and these may be more difficult to justify. The risk is that such a large proportion of managers may receive increments under this type of scheme that it operates as a *de facto* seniority system. Tight budgets force some discrimination in the allocation of awards but this may also be achieved through the use of quotas.

In the Canadian Management Category salary plan, calculation of the 5 per cent performance pay budget is closely linked to the expected distribution of awards, in the manner shown in Table 10. By matching the budget calculations to the expected distribution of awards the central agency can indirectly influence the distribution of awards within departments. In some departments there may be insufficient staff to establish reasonable approximations of the forced distributions assumed in the calculation of budgets or allocation of quotas. In response to this problem small departments with fewer than 20 eligible managers are usually given a greater percentage of payroll as a performance pay budget. Budgets for smaller departments are allocated on a sliding scale that ranges from 10 per cent of payroll for departments with a single eligible manager down to 5.1 per cent for those with 19 eligible managers.

Another issue in the budgeting of funds for performance pay is whether programmes should be self-funding within agencies or automatically provided for in budget allocations to departments. The most common approach is the latter. Agencies are allocated a certain level of funds based on existing staffing levels and are then required to allocate that amongst managers according to whatever rules and guidelines may exist regarding quotas and relationships between performance appraisals and awards. In most countries the performance pay budget is calculated as a proportion of total salary costs and, therefore, will increase when there are standard increases or cost of living adjustments to the pay scale, as well as when there is an upward movement in the average wage levels of

Table 10. **Calculation of a performance pay budget based on an assumed distribution of performance ratings and related pay awards**[1]

Performance rating	% of eligible[2] managers	Recommended awards as % of base pay	Budget as % of payroll[3]
Outstanding	5	10	0.50
Superior	25	7	1.75
Fully satisfactory	68	4	2.72
Satisfactory Unsatisfactory	2	0	0.00
Budget total			4.97

1. Based on Canadian public service performance pay scheme for the Management Category.
2. Expected distribution of managers across different performance rating levels.
3. Per cent of eligible managers multiplied by recommended awards, for each performance rating level.

the staff. This latter development may be due to the hiring of more senior staff, to increases in average salaries due to the granting of merit increments, or to reduced turnover. Promotion and staff turnover at more senior levels will lead to a reduction in budgets. In this way, performance pay budgets are indexed to general salary trends and are upgraded every year without any renegotiation with central financial authorities being necessary.

Some responsibility for funding performance pay may be delegated to departments and agencies, who must find the funds from savings or productivity improvements. Examples of supplementary funding sources for performance pay budgets are shown in Table 9. In the Netherlands and Denmark, departments can supplement their relatively small performance budgets with funds from established positions that are not filled (*i.e.* salary savings). Therefore, a department head could reach an agreement with his or her staff not to fill a position and have them carry the additional workload. Allowing agencies to fund performance pay programmes from savings in other areas of the budget may help ensure that pay awards are linked to performance improvements. However, it also carries the risk of departments generating short-term cost savings to pay performance bonuses at the expense of providing quality services over the longer term.

Another approach to the budget allocations is to require departments to make regular bids for funds. Under this approach, performance pay is funded from centrally allocated budgets, but the allocation of funds is not automatic nor is it necessarily standardised across agencies or departments. In the Australian state of New South Wales, departments must make a bid to Treasury for performance pay funds, in the same way that they would bid for funds for any other programme. Before introducing a performance pay scheme, agencies must demonstrate that they have adequate corporate planning and performance appraisal systems operating. This decentralised approach gives agencies considerable discretion in designing their schemes, and requires them to justify the costs in terms of demonstrated outputs and outcomes, similar to other programmes included in the budgeting process. It also gives the Treasury or other central agencies involved in the budget allocations the power to reject schemes that they believe are inadequately developed or not justified in terms of outputs or outcomes.

Quotas and forced distributions

One of the major requirements for effective performance pay schemes is that the award differentials between high and low performers be sufficient to emphasise to employees that high performance is well rewarded and that low performance is not rewarded at all. There are two components to these differentials. First, there must be a dispersion of awards across individuals so as to reward a range of performance levels. Second, there must be significant variations in the size of awards given to staff whose performance is at different levels in a given period.

Quotas are one mechanism for ensuring dispersion in awards while at the same time keeping overall performance pay expenditure within the allocated budget. Quotas or forced distributions can be applied in either the performance appraisal judgement phase or in the reward allocation decisions. Their primary effect is to force supervisors to discriminate between staff in their performance ratings and in the award of performance pay. This is consistent with the underlying logic of performance-based pay but cuts across the idea of managerial discretion in the allocation of rewards. The experience in both Canada and the United Kingdom shows that this loss of discretion is a major problem for managers who must make these decisions. Compensation experts have also argued that forced distribution policies, particularly for merit increment schemes, are ineffective (Wallace and Fay, 1988).

On the surface it would appear that a system that applied quotas on pay allocation decisions but did not apply the same restrictions on performance appraisal ratings would run the risk of limiting the usefulness of performance ratings for pay allocation decisions. Off-setting this is the fact that performance appraisal ratings may serve several other purposes for the manager and the people he or she appraises and some of these purposes, such as maintaining commitment and morale of staff, could be adversely affected by forced distributions of ratings.

Most of the performance appraisal systems that provide formal ratings as inputs to the performance pay allocation decision do not require ratings to follow a predetermined distribution. In the United States, predetermined distributions of performance ratings are forbidden by law. An exception is the Canadian system for the Management Category, which requires that no more than 30 per cent of a department's managers should be rated as "outstanding" or "superior", the top two ratings on their five-point scale. The standardised link between performance appraisal ratings and salary allocation in this scheme means that the 30 per cent quota on the top two levels of ratings creates an equivalent limit on performance pay awards. Within this constraint, the actual distribution of merit increments and bonuses will be further determined by the budget.

In other countries, quotas have been applied to the pay allocation decisions, without any equivalent restrictions on the performance ratings distribution. In an experimental bonus scheme that ran in the United Kingdom civil service from 1985 to 1988 there was a quota of 20 per cent on the number of staff who could receive a bonus but there was no requirement that the bonus decision be based on a formal appraisal. In a review of that scheme, the 20 per cent quota was one of the factors that was criticised. However, the scheme was not formally linked to any performance appraisal system and there was a general lack of understanding about what kind of performance would lead to an award. The consultants who carried out the review of the scheme observed that staff viewed the scheme as a "a competition which only 20 per cent of people can win and where the rules are not clear'' (see Annex 1). Therefore, it is not clear if the scheme's lack of acceptance was due to general uncertainty about the appraisals used to allocate bonuses or dissatisfaction with the quota.

The merit pay scheme for senior grades 2 and 3 in the United Kingdom civil service also had a quota on the number of staff who could receive merit increments. When the scheme was introduced in 1987 the quota was set at 25 per cent of those in each of the two grades covered by the scheme. In response to criticism from both management and staff that the quota was unduly restrictive, it was raised to 35 per cent in 1989. The merit awards in this system were not mechanistically linked to performance appraisal ratings and the quota was seen as further limiting the establishment of mechanistic links. As a result of the quota, 65 per cent of staff in the grade received no benefit from the merit increment scheme. The vast majority of these were rated as ''fully satisfactory'' and yet did not move from the bottom of the pay range, creating dissatisfaction with the scheme. In response to these problems, a new scheme was introduced in 1991 with the quota removed.

In response to a range of problems experienced with the Canadian Management Category salary plan, the system was modified so that Deputy Ministers now have the discretion to make awards of up to 10 per cent of base salary (merit increments or bonuses) for staff rated at fully satisfactory. Previously, awards at this level were restricted to those who were rated as superior or outstanding. This revision to the level of discretion in performance pay decisions was made within the existing restrictions on performance appraisal ratings, *i.e.* that no more than 30 per cent of managers can be rated superior or outstanding, and the budget limit of 5 per cent of management payroll.

If the aim of the performance pay system and other motivational processes is to raise the performance of all managers then any assumptions regarding normal distributions of performance, and the resulting forced distributions of rewards, may be dysfunctional. Forced distributions and quotas create ''winners'' and ''losers'', with the latter suffering some loss of self-esteem and becoming demotivated (Kohn, 1986). These reactions may undermine the motivational and developmental function of performance appraisal and lead to distortions in appraisal information that undermine the effective solution of performance problems. Employees' expectations concerning reward distributions can have strong feedback effects on performance appraisal processes.

Distributions of awards

In previous sections we have argued that major requirements for effective performance-related pay include:

a) Significant awards so that, in expectancy theory terms (Vroom, 1964), the bonuses or merit increments have sufficient value to be motivating for recipients; and

b) A distribution of awards such that there are clear relationships between performance levels and awards and these relationships are perceived by the managers covered by the schemes. In expectancy theory terms, this is referred to as the instrumentality of performance and, in combination with the value of the rewards, will determine the motivational effects of performance-related pay (Vroom, 1964).

A major aim of performance-related pay is to produce some differences in the salary levels of managers that reflect their differing levels of performance. There are data available from some performance pay schemes which enable us to examine the size of awards and their distribution among managers covered by the various schemes.

In France, it has been noted that at a time when the notion of performance in terms of management criteria is becoming more widely accepted in the public service, there is a tendency among those responsible for granting bonuses to take less than full advantage of their authority to vary the amounts of awards.

The difficulties of establishing a clear link between performance and pay awards in merit schemes are highlighted by the experience in Canada where surveys of managerial attitudes in the public service in 1986 and 1988 found that only 21 per cent and 16 per cent respectively of respondents believed that job performance was reflected in salary increases (Zussman and Jabes, 1989). In the Australian state of Victoria, a 1989 survey found that only 40 per cent of senior managers covered by a merit pay scheme that had been running for seven years felt that pay was related to performance (Public Service Board of Victoria, 1989). In the three years leading up to the survey, all but the smallest minority (around 4 per cent) of the managers surveyed had received merit increments. However, because of budget constraints, higher performing managers at the top end of the salary range were paid at levels below the level recommended for their performance.

In Canada, a 1980 review of the Senior Merit pay plan, the forerunner to the current Management Category plan, found a reluctance on the part of managers to use the scheme to discriminate between their subordinates. They were very lenient in their ratings, with the majority of managers being rated as superior or outstanding. They did not regress the salaries of those whose performance dropped and no longer warranted a superior salary treatment. In 1979, 18 per cent of managers covered by the scheme were paid at a rate higher than their performance ratings justified. Also, there was a reluctance to treat the mid-rate of the salary range as the maximum for fully satisfactory performers, as was the intention of the scheme. These fully satisfactory performers were, therefore, able to advance into the upper portion of the salary range, which should have been reserved for the best performers. As with other merit schemes, there was strong pressure on managers to maintain a steady upward movement in the salaries for their subordinates.

In response to these problems the Canadians introduced a revised scheme where the maximum of the salary range for each level of the Management Category was defined as the pay rate attainable by a manager whose performance had been fully satisfactory over a period of time, and progression through the range was by merit increments. Once a manager reached the top of the range all performance payments were one-time bonuses that were not added to base salary. Under this new system of payments, the lack of variation in salaries persisted. In 1989, 94 per cent of the managers covered by the scheme were at or within 5 per cent of the range maximum. This meant that the vast majority of managers were receiving no performance pay because only the 30 per cent of the managers that could be rated as superior or outstanding received bonuses once their salary reached the range maximum. This had a demotivating effect on the managers rated fully satisfactory, the majority of whom were at the job maximum and, therefore, not eligible for a merit increment.

As noted earlier, in the context of the discussion on quotas, a similar set of circumstances arose in the United Kingdom performance pay scheme for Grades 2 and 3 where variations in pay levels were created by a 35 per cent quota on the number of staff in each grade who could receive merit increments. As a result, the majority of eligible managers could expect no benefit from the performance pay scheme. As in the Canadian scheme, this created a problem in that approximately two-thirds of managers, whose performance was rated fully satisfactory, did not receive any increase. Revisions to both the Canadian and United Kingdom schemes have changed the rules so that the large majority of managers rated fully satisfactory can receive a greater amount of performance pay. The changes in the two schemes reflect different tradeoffs in their attempts to broaden the distribution of awards.

In the United Kingdom, the quota on merit increments has been replaced by a salary range in which all increases, including the annual standard increase, are based on performance ratings. Previously all managers received the annual standard increase as an adjustment to the salary range. At the same time, the budget available for merit increments and bonuses has been set at 2 per cent of the pay bill. Under this new scheme all managers rated at fully satisfactory or above will receive the standard increase and will be eligible for an increment or bonus. Those rated at one of the two levels below fully satisfactory will receive less than the standard increase and may receive no increase at all, thereby experiencing a drop in real income in times of inflation. These two changes will have the effect of creating greater differences between the salaries of low performers and the rest. The variation in salaries between the fully satisfactory and better performers however, will depend upon how departments choose to distribute merit increments and bonuses among the approximately 95 per cent of managers rated fully satisfactory or better. Under the new scheme heads of departments can elect to allocate smaller awards to a larger number of staff or larger awards to a more limited number of staff. Examples of these alternative distribution patterns, illustrated in Table 3, were discussed above.

In Canada, managers at the top of the pay range who receive a fully satisfactory rating will now be eligible for the bonus of up to 10 per cent of base pay that had previously been restricted to the 30 per cent of managers who received a superior or outstanding rating. This will mean that approximately an additional 40 per cent of managers covered by the scheme will be eligible for bonuses, based on 1989 figures. Without an increase in the performance pay budget, any resulting wider dispersion of bonuses will mean lower average bonuses and, potentially, less variation in the bonuses awarded.

Experience in the United States has shown that bonus schemes also have a tendency toward a wider dispersion amongst eligible staff with a resulting reduction in the average monetary value of rewards. In 1989, 63 per cent of all eligible staff covered by the Performance Management and Recognition System received bonuses, with an average award of 2.04 per cent of base pay, down from 2.15 per cent in 1988 (U.S. Office of Personnel Management, 1990*a*). The downward trend is also evident in the bonuses paid to staff who receive an outstanding rating, the only group for whom bonuses are mandatory. During the period from 1986 to 1989, the average value of bonuses to these staff decreased from 2.99 per cent to 2.75 per cent of base pay. In 1989 less than 3 per cent of staff rated outstanding received a bonus greater than 5 per cent of base pay, even though the maximum bonus payable is 10 per cent. This drop in the size of bonuses paid to outstanding employees was partly due to increases in the proportion of staff rated outstanding and partly due to the payment of bonuses to a larger proportion of staff who received fully successful or exceeds fully successful ratings and, therefore, were eligible but not required to receive bonuses. Between 1982 and 1989, the number of senior executives receiving performance bonuses (not including Presidential Rank Awards) increased by 32 per cent. In that same period the average value of bonuses dropped from $6 290 to $5 480, a drop of 23 per cent before adjusting for inflation (U.S. Office of Personnel Management, 1990*b*).

The pressure to distribute bonuses more widely and to avoid discriminating amongst staff will probably be greater at the more senior levels where managers are more dependent upon their subordinates and where the potential negative effects of denying a staff member an award are much greater. Where there is discretion allowed in the allocation of bonuses we would expect much greater discrimination at middle management levels than at the more senior management levels. In Spain, for example, approximately half of middle managers receive productivity bonuses. This proportion increases to somewhere between 94 per cent and 100 per cent at the most senior levels.

Chapter 6

THE IMPACT OF PERFORMANCE-RELATED PAY

How successful have performance-related pay schemes been when assessed against the commonly stated policy objectives mentioned in an earlier chapter of this report? It is difficult to draw any firm conclusions about the impact of performance pay schemes on performance in public sector organisations. The majority of the schemes that have been analysed have not been in operation long enough for their full impact to have occurred. In the case of the longer-running schemes, there has been very little systematic analysis of their impact on individual performance or organisational effectiveness and of whether gains in productivity offset the costs of the schemes. This is largely due to the lack of quantitative measures of public sector performance outcomes that can be used to assess the impact of performance-related pay or other management improvement schemes. Evaluations, when conducted, have tended to focus on the processes of implementation and operation of schemes. Data have also been collected on various attitudes and beliefs that are assumed to reflect the level of motivation of managers. These data can be used to infer the possible performance effects of schemes, based on motivational theory and research, and also to provide data on a range of criteria that could be used as indicators for the various policy objectives of the schemes.

The most extensive evaluation of performance pay schemes has been carried out in the United States where regular audits of schemes and controlled experimental projects are conducted. The latter provide the most rigorous data for drawing conclusions about the impacts of performance pay schemes. However, experimental projects are limited in the number of design features from the complex range of options that can be studied at any one time. Audits, in which data are collected through surveys, interviews or analyses of secondary data sources, can provide insights on a much wider range of scheme features. When conducted on a regular basis, audits of a wide range of variables can provide useful data for analysing the impact of performance pay schemes.

In the remainder of this section we will review available audit data from a range of schemes, relating to a variety of different indicators of a scheme's success, relative to the stated policy objectives of schemes, as outlined in Chapter 1. These indicators include perceived links between pay and performance, costs of schemes, managerial attitudes, implementation processes and turnover of high performing staff. We will then discuss the findings from several experimental projects in the United States.

Perceived pay-to-performance relationship

A commonly stated objective for performance-related pay schemes in both the public and private sectors is to strengthen the belief amongst managers that rewards are linked to performance and thereby to make them feel more accountable for their individual contributions. According to the theory that underpins performance-related pay, a perceived relationship between performance and pay awards is a necessary condition for employees covered by performance pay schemes to be motivated to higher levels of performance (Vroom, 1964; Milkovich and Wigdor, 1991). The assumption is that the stronger and more widely held the perceived relationship between pay and performance, the greater the effect of pay awards on individual motivation and performance will be. At the same time, there is evidence to show that ambiguity regarding the relationship between pay and performance leads to diminished performance effects at the organisational level (Konrad and Pfeffer, 1990). Ambiguity about the determinants of performance pay also leads to lower levels of perceived pay equity and lower levels of satisfaction with pay (Wallace and Fay, 1988).

Therefore, the relationship which staff perceive between performance and pay awards provides a measure of the likely effects on performance of a pay scheme. A range of factors can undermine the perceived links between pay and performance. On the performance appraisal side these include poorly defined performance criteria, inconsistency and bias in performance ratings, and a lack of discrimination in the ratings. On the pay side, the use of quotas or forced distributions which require arbitrary discriminations in the allocation of pay awards, and a lack of dispersion in awards can undermine the perceived relationship with performance. The importance of the perceived link between pay and performance as an indirect measure of the performance effects of schemes has been recognised in the United States, where legislation has established a Pay-for-Performance Labor-Management Committee to develop recommendations for strengthening this link. This emphasis reflects the widespread use of expectancy theory as the source of logic for the introduction of performance pay schemes in the public sector in the United States (Milkovich and Wigdor, 1991).

Evidence regarding the effects of various schemes on the perceived relationship between pay and performance is limited but, on the whole, is not encouraging. The most encouraging support comes from an experimental project conducted in the United States at two U.S. Navy research organisations. The introduction of a performance pay scheme produced a significant improvement in the perceived link between pay and performance at the experimental sites but not at other, similar organisations that were used as control sites. After nine years of operation of the project, 61 per cent of the staff covered by the performance pay scheme at the experimental sites believed that there was a significant relationship between pay and individual performance (U.S. Office of Personnel Management, 1991). The results of this scheme indicate that the introduction of individual pay awards that are based on performance appraisal can significantly strengthen the perceived relationship between pay and performance and, therefore, be expected to enhance individual performance. However, as will be discussed later, this scheme was quite expensive to operate in terms of pay costs and the results cannot necessarily be generalised to other organisations.

In other schemes for which data are available, the clear perception of a link between pay and performance has not been established for a majority of employees covered by performance pay, even when schemes have been running for many years. Surveys of managers in the Canadian public service in 1986 and 1989, found that only 21 per cent and 16 per cent, respectively, believed that job performance was reflected in pay (Zussman and Jabes, 1989). In the United States, only 43 per cent of managers covered by the Performance Management and Recognition System in 1989 believed that better performance would result in a pay increase (U.S. Office of Personnel Management, 1990*a*). In Australia, only 40 per cent of the senior managers covered by the Victorian State scheme felt that pay was based on performance (Public Service Board of Victoria, 1989).

While it is difficult to pin-point the exact reasons for these results, they do highlight the difficulty of establishing a clearly perceived link between pay and performance in the minds of a majority of managers covered by performance pay schemes, and they call into question the impact of the schemes on employee motivation. The three schemes mentioned in the previous paragraph had all been operating for at least seven years at the time of the reported surveys. In the Canadian and Australian schemes, the problems appear to be related to the use of quotas and the rapid progression of a majority of managers to the top of the pay range where they can no longer receive merit increments. Both of these schemes have recently introduced more liberal bonus payments to deal with this problem. In the United States scheme, salary increments may include a standard increase, a merit increment and a bonus payment, each paid at a different time of the year. Added to this is the fact that the largest part of the pay increments has been the standard increase, which is received by almost all managers, while the merit increments and bonuses have both been quite small. At the time the scheme was introduced, standard increases and merit increments were meant to be paid concurrently. However, these are now paid at different times in most agencies. A 1989 report by the General Accounting Office revealed that most employees did not understand how the performance pay system worked and that the system was generally not succeeding in motivating and rewarding employees.

Further evidence on the effect of performance pay on staff motivation comes from a recent study of a performance pay scheme in the Inland Revenue Service in the United Kingdom civil service (Marsden and Richardson, 1991). This study surveyed staff on their views concerning the impact of the scheme on their own behaviour and that of others. The survey was conducted when the scheme had been running for approximately three years. The scheme covers the majority of staff in the Service, including staff at management levels, and takes the form of merit increments. The study found that although a majority of staff (57 per cent) accepted the principle of relating pay to performance, only a small minority (12 per cent) felt that performance pay had raised their motivation at work. Staff at the more senior grades reported the least positive motivational response towards performance pay. Officers responsible for carrying out performance appraisals (about 20 per cent of the total sample) were also asked how performance pay had affected their staff. Only a small minority reported any perceived improvement in the quantity or quality of work of their staff, or in staff commitment to their work.

The study identified two main reasons for the apparent failure of the performance pay scheme to motivate staff. One was that the allocation of performance payments was seen as being unfair. Many staff believed that there was an implicit quota system in operation and that this frequently distorted the assessment of performance. The perception that a quota was being applied came from the cost ceiling applied to the scheme, which assumed that the proportion of staff in receipt of merit increments at any given time would not exceed 25 per cent. A second reason for the lack of motivation was that staff felt the performance pay awards were not sufficiently large to justify a change in behaviour. The maximum reward for sustained outstanding performance was a pay rise over time of 12 per cent for senior staff, 15 per cent to 20 per cent for intermediate grades and 22 per cent for junior grades.

It is possible that the trend towards bonus schemes and the use of bonuses in conjunction with merit payments will have a more pronounced impact on the perceived relationship between pay and performance. However, this may depend upon how widely bonuses are dispersed. As mentioned previously, several countries have reported concerns about how to recognise the performance of the 60 to 70 per cent of managers who are rated as fully satisfactory in most schemes. Clearly the proportion of staff who perceive a relationship between pay and performance will be related to the proportion who receive awards. However, distributing awards more widely requires either reductions in the size of the awards or increases in budgets.

Approximately 35 per cent of the senior executives covered by bonus schemes in the United States civil service received awards in 1989. However, a 1990 report by the Merit Systems Protection Board showed that only 18 per cent of respondents believed that there were enough bonuses to ensure that they had a good chance of receiving one if they performed well. Only one in four senior executives believed that the bonuses provided strong incentives. In the United Kingdom, awards paid under an experimental bonus system with a 20 per cent quota on the proportion of staff who could receive awards were seen as being unrelated to performance by the vast majority of managers (see Annex 1). Therefore, while bonus schemes may offer greater flexibility than merit schemes in the allocation of performance pay awards, they are equally likely to fail to create a perceived link between pay and performance, depending upon rules governing the allocation of awards.

In summary, the goal of strengthening the belief that rewards are related to performance, and thereby enhancing individual motivation and accountability, has apparently not been achieved with any great degree of success in the schemes for which data are available. Most promising are the results of the Navy Demonstration Project in the United States where an evaluation has shown significant improvements in the perceived relationship between pay and performance at the demonstration sites as compared with the control sites. Against this must be set the rather disappointing results for long-running merit schemes in several countries, where the proportion of managers who believe that rewards are linked to performance appears to stabilise well below 50 per cent and often slips back the longer the scheme runs. The initial results from the United Kingdom Inland Revenue Scheme also indicate a failure to motivate the majority of staff. These results from a range of schemes in different countries appear to be related to design faults, including quotas and rapid progression through the merit range. Bonus schemes, with their greater flexibility, offer the promise of a stronger perceived link between pay and performance. However, this may depend upon how widely bonuses are distributed.

Overall pay costs

Given the frequently stated policy objective of containing salary costs, the impact of performance-related pay schemes on overall costs is an important issue. The two main sources of direct costs are those related to administration of a scheme and changes in the overall salary bill of staff covered by a scheme. In addition, there are the indirect costs of implementing and monitoring performance pay plans. The impact of performance-related pay schemes on these costs must, of course, be considered in the broader context of any performance improvements that the schemes produce, and their influence on other factors related to organisational productivity, such as staffing levels and staff turnover.

Unfortunately, there is very little information of sufficient detail to draw any firm conclusions about the overall costs of schemes or whether these are partially or fully offset by performance gains and cost savings in other areas. None of the schemes considered in this study has been the subject of a rigorous cost-benefit analysis, nor is there satisfactory information from other sources. A recent study on behalf of the United States Office of Personnel Management, which examined research findings from both private and public sector schemes, found that research on cost regulation and the cost-benefit tradeoffs associated with performance-related pay is sparse and limited to production jobs and manufacturing settings (Milkovich and Wigdor, 1991). That study concluded that there is at present no evidence that any particular performance pay scheme is superior to another or to no performance pay scheme in regulating direct labour costs.

There is evidence from several schemes covered by this study that performance-related pay has resulted in increased pay costs. The Canadian Treasury Board Secretariat has assessed the impact of performance-related pay schemes in the federal public service on costs in four areas: *i)* pay rates, *ii)* in-range merit increases, *iii)* performance bonuses, and *iv)* administration of the pay plans. A comparison of employees covered by performance pay with those who are not covered by performance pay revealed that performance pay is not associated with higher pay rates and that in-range merit increases for performance pay employees do not, on average, exceed the increases that would have been awarded as lock-step increments. However, the performance bonuses available to employees, above the pay rate for the job, do increase the cost of performance pay plans over pay plans with lock-step increments and fixed pay rates for the job. In the case of the Management Category in 1990, all performance bonuses averaged 4.3 per cent of basic pay. No judgement was possible on whether the total administrative costs associated with performance pay plans are greater than for groups that collectively bargain their rates of pay.

The merit pay range for Assistant Secretaries in the Irish public service is estimated to have increased pay costs for this grade by about 5 per cent. This was a calculated increase resulting from the recommendations of the pay review body for senior civil servants. There is estimated to be no significant cost associated with the administration of the scheme. In New Zealand, preliminary analysis suggests that the introduction of performance pay has contributed to wage drift above the collective pay settlements, averaging 1.5 per cent per year. However, because progression within the pay ranges is linked to recruitment and retention criteria as well as performance, it is difficult to disentangle the impact of performance pay from other factors.

In the United States, evaluations of the Navy demonstration project revealed that employees at the demonstration sites were paid salaries that were 6 per cent higher than those received by similar employees at other laboratories that were used as control sites for evaluation purposes (U.S. Office of Personnel Management, 1991).This increase in pay costs was attributed primarily to higher starting salaries paid to entry-level scientists and engineers at the demonstration laboratories, and larger then average salary increases given to employees at all levels both within pay bands and through promotions between bands. It was estimated that salary costs at the two laboratories involved in the pay experiment had increased at a rate of approximately 1 per cent faster than at the control laboratories since the project was established in 1980.

It would be tenuous to generalise the partial and tentative results from the four schemes discussed here to other schemes, and differences between the four schemes mean that no clear association between the design of schemes and the cost implications can be discerned. Moreover, no assessment has been made of whether the increased pay costs under these schemes were offset by productivity gains. What these data do show is that much more analysis is needed of the direct payroll costs of schemes as well as the indirect costs and the cost-benefit tradeoffs associated with performance-related pay schemes.

Performance planning processes

Another policy objective of performance-related pay schemes is to strengthen the relationship between individual job goals and organisational goals and to ensure that individual outputs contribute to the overall effectiveness of the public sector. Reward systems can, of course, reinforce ineffective performance as well as effective performance. The degree to which performance pay reinforces one or the other depends upon the performance appraisal system, and particularly the performance criteria used and their links with organisational outcomes.

The use of objective-based appraisals and their linkages with other planning systems, such as programme budgeting and corporate planning, are claimed to have strengthened the relationship between individual job goals and organisational goals across a range of public sector performance pay schemes. This is one of the benefits identified in reviews of performance-related pay schemes in the United Kingdom. In Australia, evaluations of the performance pay scheme for Senior Executive Service officers in the state of Victoria have shown that implementation of individual performance planning and its integration with departmental planning systems have been the most successful outcomes of the scheme (Wood, 1991). In the United States, four out of five agencies report that all or most managers are involved in the development of performance criteria and standards for their jobs and, for employees covered by the Performance Management and Recognition System, 88 per cent of agencies conduct progress reviews of performance with all employees (U.S. Office of Personnel Management, 1990*a*, pp. 25-26).

However, while individual work planning and potential links with departmental planning systems (*i.e.* through participative goal-setting and progress reviews with supervisors) appear well established in the United States civil service, there is no evidence or claim that this has led to improvements in organisational effectiveness. In fact, among members of the Senior Executive Service, only about one in ten believe that the individual work planning and appraisal system used to determine their bonus payments has improved organisational effectiveness (U.S. Merit Systems Protection Board, 1990). By way of contrast to the experience in the United States, several other countries claim that performance pay has led to the improvements in planning identified in the Australian scheme mentioned above, but without the supporting evidence of formal reviews of their systems (see Annex 1). An initial evaluation of the performance pay scheme in the Netherlands civil service found that both managers and other staff thought the scheme had contributed to improving performance management processes and organisational effectiveness.

These benefits might of course have occurred as a result of performance appraisal schemes, without the link to performance pay. However, there is some evidence to suggest otherwise. A frequently mentioned benefit of performance pay schemes is that they have led to significant improvements in the planning activities on which appraisals are based. The pressure of pay allocation decisions has focused the attention of managers and staff on the development of better performance indicators. Several countries report greater integration of performance appraisal processes with programme and corporate planning processes. Because these performance appraisal and performance pay schemes are often introduced concurrently it is difficult to separate out the true nature of these effects. However, in countries with long-running performance pay schemes, such as Canada, the United Kingdom and the United States, there is evidence that dissatisfaction with performance pay schemes has provided an impetus for improvement of the planning and appraisal systems on which pay allocation decisions are based.

A related policy objective for performance pay schemes is to provide managers with greater flexibility in recognising and rewarding individual performance contributions, and thereby to allow them greater discretion in their use of resources to achieve their goals. This objective is consistent with the principle of ''letting the manager manage'', mentioned in Chapter 1 in relation to a range of reforms that were intended to provide greater delegations of authority to lower levels of public sector organisations. There are no direct data on the achievement of this objective. However, the highly standardised approaches in some schemes, such as in Canada, could be usefully contrasted with schemes such as those in Denmark, the Netherlands, and New Zealand that have fewer centrally imposed rules. On the surface, schemes in these latter countries appear to provide greater decentralisation of authority to departments and to managers within departments. An evaluation of the Netherlands scheme has found that managers feel they have more influence over pay since the scheme was introduced. It is possible, however that informal norms, or other aspects of organisational culture in departments may more severely curtail a manager's autonomy in pay allocation decisions than centrally imposed standard rules. The imposition of quotas also seems to curtail severely the flexibility of managers to allocate rewards amongst their staff as they might otherwise choose.

Job satisfaction and staff turnover

The policy objectives of enhancing job satisfaction and reducing the turnover among higher performing managers are interrelated in that satisfaction with pay, and other aspects of one's job, is a key predictor of staff turnover (Steers and Mowday, 1981). Unfortunately, there is very little evidence on job satisfaction and turnover from the schemes examined, and there is no evidence that enables us to link job satisfaction to performance. Data from the Navy demonstration project in the United States suggest that job satisfaction has increased and turnover among high performers has decreased since the scheme was introduced in 1980 (U.S. Office of Personnel Management, 1991). However, evaluations of the scheme indicate that pay alone does not explain the positive attitudes found among employees. Moreover, the evidence on staff turnover must be viewed as tentative because of weaknesses identified in the evaluation of the scheme (U.S. General Accounting Office, 1988). Audits of performance pay schemes in Canada and the United Kingdom show that dissatisfaction with pay is generally higher among those managers who are rated fully satisfactory but receive no performance pay due to quotas or budget constraints.

Demonstration projects

In the United States, the Civil Service Reform Act of 1978 that established performance pay schemes for senior and middle management levels included provision for up to ten demonstration projects intended to determine whether specified changes in personnel management policies or procedures would result in improved personnel management. These experimental projects were to be approved by the Office of Personnel Management and to be subjected to systematic evaluation. Three of these projects have addressed performance-related pay issues.

The Navy demonstration project

The Navy demonstration project is the longest running project, introduced in 1980 to coincide with the implementation of the Civil Service Reform Act. The timing of the introduction allows evaluations to be made against the baseline data collected in 1979, prior to the introduction of the reforms. The project was originally planned to run until 1985 but has been extended twice and will now run until at least 1995. It covers some 7 600 employees at two Naval research laboratories in California, and has instituted changes to position classification, performance appraisal and pay. The objectives of the project are to enhance the effectiveness of the laboratories, provide greater managerial flexibility to assign work, and improve recruitment and retention of employees. Two similar research organisations, one in Pennsylvania and one with locations in Virginia and Maryland, did not introduce changes in their personnel management systems and were used as control sites for purposes of evaluating the project.

Under the project, performance pay was introduced for all white-collar employees at the two demonstration laboratories, with merit increments and bonuses of up to 10 per cent of basic salary. Pay allocation decisions are based on performance ratings from an appraisal scheme which uses an objective-setting approach. The appraisal scheme is considered to be less rigorous than the government-wide system based on job elements and performance standards, and supervisors have more discretion in their ratings of staff against agreed objectives. Thus the performance measurement system is similar to the appraisal schemes used in several other public sector schemes across OECD countries.

The project has been extensively evaluated by the United States Office of Personnel Management (OPM) and has also been reviewed by the United States General Accounting Office. The OPM's report on the results of the project for the ten-year period from the baseline measures in 1979 to 1989 (U.S. Office of Personnel Management, 1991) show that:

a) The perceived link between pay and performance, critical to the effective operation of performance pay schemes, has been significantly strengthened at the two demonstration laboratories but did not change at the control laboratories; 61 per cent of eligible staff at the demonstration laboratories versus 47 per cent at the control laboratories saw a link in 1989. These figures were down from 65 per cent and 50 per cent respectively in 1987.

b) Support for performance pay among staff has grown during the life of the project, increasing from 29 per cent in 1979 to 70 per cent in 1987, where it has remained. Supervisors at the demonstration laboratories are almost unanimous in their support for the performance pay system.

c) Turnover among high performers is lower at the demonstration laboratories than at the control laboratories.
d) Average salaries at the demonstration laboratories are about 6 per cent higher than at the control laboratories. This reflects pay increases due to changes in the pay structure as well as more generous performance pay under the experimental scheme.

These results suggest that performance pay based on an objective-setting performance appraisal scheme can have a positive effect on several of the key policy objectives of performance pay schemes. Of particular interest are the observed effects on the perceived link between pay and performance and on turnover of higher performing staff. Difficulties in obtaining objective and inclusive measures of performance have meant that no firm conclusions can be drawn about the impact of the project on productivity. At the same time it is not possible to say whether the additional salary costs of the demonstration project have been offset by any resulting productivity gains.

Evaluations of the Navy demonstration project have also identified several factors relating to its implementation and operation that are believed to have contributed to its success (U.S. Office of Personnel Management, 1991):

a) All white-collar employees are covered by the same performance pay scheme. This has avoided invidious comparisons between employees covered by different schemes and has made it easier to create a performance-oriented culture.
b) At the time the scheme was introduced, the Navy compensated staff for expected step increases and promotions when converting from the old to the new salary structure. This created a climate of perceived fairness and enhanced acceptance of the new scheme.
c) The system was designed, in consultation with staff, by the organisations in which it was implemented. By contrast, other performance pay schemes in the United States civil service, such as the Performance Management and Recognition System and the scheme for the Senior Executive Service, are centrally imposed and relatively standardised across government departments. The local development of the Navy demonstration scheme resulted in a greater level of acceptance and commitment by staff.
d) Supervisors have considerable flexibility in choosing both the range of payments for a given performance rating and the combination of bonus and merit increments in individual awards. This flexibility allows supervisors to reward high performers who are at the top of the pay range.

Whilst these results are encouraging, it must also be noted that a review by the General Accounting Office (GAO) of the project and of the evaluation by OPM concludes that although the project shows that a performance pay system can be implemented to the general satisfaction of many managers and employees, the outcomes of the project are unclear and the results cited by OPM must be treated with caution. The GAO review points out that because of missing data and differences between the demonstration and control laboratories, it is not possible to assess whether the major outcome benefits cited by OPM are attributable to the change in personnel practices, to pre-existing differences between laboratories, or to outside factors. The review emphasises that even if the evaluation data had been conclusive, this would not necessarily mean that the project would be workable in other locations and with other types of staff. A key feature of the

Navy's project, which it might not be possible to replicate in other settings, is that it provides for an increase in salary costs (approximately 1 per cent each year since the project was established) and has, therefore, been quite expensive.

The Air Force Pacer Share project

The Air Force Pacer Share project initially covered 1 800 employees working in the warehousing and distribution organisation in the Air Logistics Centre, McClellan Air Force Base, California, with equal proportions of blue-collar and white-collar employees. Four other equivalent organisations around the country serve as comparison sites. The Pacer Share project includes a productivity gainsharing programme in which performance pay is linked to organisational performance, with savings in labour costs being shared equally between the Air Force and the employees. Other changes include a simplified job classification system, a new pay structure, and the elimination of individual performance appraisals that had previously been used to determine annual pay increases. Under the demonstration project, all employees receive the government-wide general increase as well as an annual increase related to their position in the salary structure. Each employee also receives an equal share of the organisation's labour cost savings. These performance payments are made quarterly.

The Pacer Share programme has been affected by a variety of changes that were not part of the original plan for the demonstration project. These have included budget cuts and hiring freezes, as well as changes in budgeting procedures and the gainsharing formula. Most importantly, the gainsharing programme has not provided the expected payouts. Prior to the commencement of the demonstration project, it was estimated that performance payments would total $1 200 per person per year. Actual payouts from gainsharing have been zero for 1988, $502 for 1989, and $362 for 1990. In order to make up for the lack of gainsharing payouts, management gave all employees incentive awards of $128 in 1988 and $200 in 1990. The payment for the first 2 quarters of 1991 was $475, the highest annual rate so far, and was due to the unexpected effects of the war against Iraq in the Middle East.

Evaluations of the Pacer Share project have highlighted several of the features of the scheme that are relevant to other performance pay schemes (U.S. Office of Personnel Management, 1991).

a) Productivity gainsharing and other schemes that base performance pay on organisational or programme measures of performance are difficult to operate during periods of cut-backs and full workloads;

b) The elimination of performance appraisal further weakened an already weak perception that there is a link between pay and individual performance;

c) According to external evaluations, there is no evidence that the demonstration site has reduced its costs relative the comparison sites or relative to its own baseline;

d) Average salaries have increased more at the demonstration site than the comparison sites, but total payroll costs did not increase because of attrition and lower staffing levels.

These initial evaluation findings are not encouraging. However, the unanticipated changes affecting the environment in which the scheme has to operate, such as budget cuts and staff reductions, make it virtually impossible to disentangle the effects of the scheme from other causal factors. Moreover, the scheme was only two years old at the time of this evaluation.

The NIST project

The National Institute of Standards and Technology (NIST) project was implemented in January 1988 and included performance pay as one of a series of changes to personnel management systems at two sites. The project covers approximately 3 000 employees in four different job classifications (scientists and engineers; technicians; administrative employees; and support staff). An interesting feature of the NIST scheme is that although the legislation authorising the project does not require budget neutrality it was designed by the agency head to be budget-neutral. The performance pay increases come out of funds formerly used for within-grade increases, quality step increases, merit pay increases and promotions between grades.

The initial performance pay scheme was based on a five-point performance appraisal rating for each of several job elements or performance criteria. Each rating was then multiplied by an importance weighting to give a summative score ranging from 100 to 500. A forced distribution was then applied to the scores to give each employee one of five levels of summary ratings (outstanding, commendable, fully successful, marginal, satisfactory) that were used in the allocation of pay awards.

The initial evaluations of the scheme, conducted during the first two years of its operation, (U.S. Office of Personnel Management, 1989; 1990*c*) found that:

a) The performance pay scheme has significantly altered the distribution of salary increases. NIST employees at higher performance levels receive larger salary increases than their counterparts in comparison organisations and NIST employees on lower performance levels receive smaller average salary increases than their counterparts in the comparison organisations.

b) Within NIST there is a strong positive relationship between performance ratings and salary increases.

c) Performance awards to NIST employees were generally higher than within-grade increases to their counterparts in comparison organisations.

d) The scientists and engineers covered by the scheme felt that the labels used in the performance appraisal system were derogatory of the standard of work done by qualified staff. Many employees felt that being designated as "fully successful" indicated that their work was judged to be mediocre.

e) NIST met its budget neutrality target by maintaining a small staff and keeping the average cost per employee down. The latter was partly a result of a drop in the mean age of the NIST workforce since the project began.

These results must be viewed with caution. An assessment by the GAO of the design and implementation of the evaluation on which they are based concluded that it was flawed (U.S. General Accounting Office, 1991). The GAO review also noted that NIST underwent significant organisational changes after the demonstration project was initiated which made it difficult to interpret the results of the project. Moreover, the scheme has undergone changes because of dissatisfaction on the part of both employees and managers with the performance rating system. A new system, initiated in October 1990, eliminates the appearance of a forced distribution of ratings and allows managers to rank employees for compensation purposes without labelling them or inferring that their work is inferior. Managers are also allowed more flexibility in deciding on the distribution of performance pay increases among eligible employees (U.S. Office of Personnel Management, 1991).

Data from the new system are not yet available at the time of writing, but preliminary observations by the OPM emphasise the importance of organisational culture in the design of a performance appraisal system. The NIST is a scientific organisation whose mission is precise measurement and whose managers want to make finc distinctions among employees to support distinctions in pay. The OPM notes that it remains to be seen whether such a complex system is transportable to other organisations.

Evaluation models

Despite the problems encountered, the demonstration projects in the United States provide models of how to design the evaluation of performance-related pay schemes. The use of baseline measures (*i.e.* measures taken before the introduction of the new schemes) enables assessments of the magnitude of change in the variables studied. Comparisons with control sites, where the performance pay schemes are not introduced but which are similar to the host organisations in most other ways, provide an additional means of observing changes following the introduction of a new pay scheme, although the experience with the demonstration projects described above shows that it is not always possible to determine that the observed changes were due to the new pay scheme and not other factors. It is not always feasible to identify control sites for comparison purposes and to gather data that cover periods before the introduction of the new scheme, particularly survey data on managerial attitudes and perceptions. However, historical data on the distributions of pay awards and staff turnover, and even productivity and cost measures, are often available in existing records of departments with performance-related pay schemes and those without schemes. These data, if collected, can be analysed in an experimental design to establish the impact of the performance-related pay scheme on the associated variables.

Even without experimental designs, regular audits and surveys of performance pay schemes can provide longitudinal data on a wide range of variables that can be used to interpret changes in the effectiveness of schemes across time. Surveys and other audits need to focus on the impact of schemes on motivational variables, costs and, where possible, performance measures, and not just evaluate the processes of implementation and operation. Whilst data on these latter variables are important for the redesign and improvement of schemes, they provide insufficient justification for their continuation. Measures of motivational variables that have been shown to be related to performance can be used as surrogate measures for performance where direct quantitative measures of performance are not available. These could include measures of the perceived link between pay and performance, perceived equity of pay distributions, goal commitment, self-reported efforts in response to pay incentives and pay satisfaction. If standardised data were collected on these variables for different schemes across a range of OECD countries, it would enable much stronger and more specific recommendations regarding the design of public sector performance pay schemes.

Chapter 7

FINDINGS AND CONCLUSIONS

We began this report by noting the significant growth of performance-related pay schemes in the public sector in recent years. We have reviewed and analysed material from a range of such schemes covering senior and middle managers in central government organisations in OECD countries. Most of the schemes discussed have not been in operation long enough for a thorough assessment. Moreover, even for the longer-running schemes, there has been very little systematic analysis of their impacts on the effectiveness of public sector organisations. Therefore, it is not possible to say whether or not the costs of performance-related pay schemes in the public sector are justified by performance gains or cost savings. This state of affairs is, at least partly, a reflection of the lack of objective performance indicators that can be converted to productivity measures or cash values for public service outcomes. Evidence for the impacts of performance pay on performance indicators for other policy objectives mentioned in Chapter 1 is similarly sparse.

Despite the lack of evidence for the positive effects of performance pay schemes, the principle of linking pay to performance has strong support among elected officials and public sector managers in a wide range of countries. This support, it was argued, is due to the perceived consistency of performance-related pay with the rationalist economic principles and policies that were in the ascendancy across OECD countries during the 1980s. Given the continued push for reforms that enhance the cost effectiveness of public management, it seems likely that the use of performance-related pay will continue to spread in the public sectors of OECD countries during the 1990s. For governments in many OECD countries the question is not so much whether to adopt or to continue applying performance-related pay schemes, but rather how these schemes can be made as effective as possible.

The popularity of performance-related pay appears to be based on several factors. As outlined in Chapter 1, governments expect it to deliver a range of benefits, including: strengthening accountability for performance; strengthening the belief that rewards are linked to performance; forging a closer link between individual job goals and organisational goals; helping to contain salary costs; enhancing job satisfaction and the belief that rewards are distributed fairly; and reducing turnover among high quality staff. Managers who support the principle of performance-related pay for themselves appear to do so from a belief that individual effort and initiative should be recognised and that it is equitable to base some portion of pay on performance. Managers also hope that performance-related pay will give them more discretion in rewarding their own staff.

Despite the limitations of the data, we have tried to analyse the extent to which these objectives have actually been realised and to identify problems affecting schemes. This analysis has been supplemented by an assessment of the schemes surveyed against the key requirements for effective performance-related pay schemes. Given the uneven and fragmented nature of the information available, the findings and conclusions of our study must necessarily be treated as partial and tentative. A more thorough assessment must await the completion of the second phase of the research programme in 1993.

In presenting our findings and conclusions, we shall begin by reviewing the main features of the performance-related pay schemes examined, covering managers in central government administrations. We shall then summarise our conclusions concerning the extent to which these schemes appear to satisfy the requirements for effective operation of performance-related pay schemes, and the degree to which the schemes appear to have met their stated objectives. We shall conclude by drawing some lessons from the analysis concerning the operation of performance-related pay schemes in the public sector.

Main features of the schemes

The following main features and trends can be identified in the schemes examined:

- **Coverage of schemes is extremely varied.** Where performance pay has been introduced in the central administration, it generally applies to all or most management level staff. Among the countries included in this study, Ireland is the only one where performance pay applies to only one management grade. It is quite common, however, to find that different schemes apply to managers at different levels (*e.g.* Canada, New Zealand, United Kingdom, United States), and that separate schemes apply to managerial and non-managerial staff. Nevertheless, schemes in Denmark, France, the Netherlands, Spain and Sweden cover staff at all levels. Many schemes exclude the most senior management level.
- **Performance pay awards are typically based on an annual appraisal rating on a five-point summary rating scale which, in some cases, may be supplemented by other considerations.** The most common form of appraisal is a management-by-objectives system in which managers are rated for their achievements against previously agreed goals. Standardised criteria, known as job accountabilities, job responsibilities or critical elements, are also widely used, usually in conjunction with job goals (*e.g.* in Australia, Canada, the United Kingdom and the United States). In some of the less standardised schemes, trait criteria are still used in performance appraisals (*e.g.* Denmark, France and the Netherlands) and in Spain the number of hours worked is used to allocate bonuses.
- **The most common forms of performance payments are a combination of merit increments and lump-sum bonuses.** The combinations of the two forms of payment include a scheme in the Netherlands, where managers may be paid either a bonus or a merit increment, schemes in Canada and the United Kingdom where bonuses are paid in place of merit increments for managers at the top of the salary range, and a scheme in the United States where mid-level managers may receive both bonuses and merit increments. Only Ireland among the countries surveyed has a pure merit scheme. There appears to be a preference for bonuses over merit increments in recently proposed schemes (*e.g.* Australia) and in revisions to established schemes, such as in Canada and the United Kingdom.

- **The potential sizes of merit increments and bonuses vary widely across the schemes surveyed but maximum awards payable tend to be greater for bonuses than for merit increments.** Maximum merit increments range from 3 per cent in the United States scheme for mid-level managers to 10 per cent in the Canadian Management Category scheme. Bonus schemes with upper limits of 20 per cent and higher are not uncommon, although bonuses above 20 per cent are usually only awarded to a small proportion of staff in the top three or four levels of the management hierarchy.
- **The degree of central control and standardisation of schemes across different departments and agencies also varies considerably across countries.** For example, schemes in Canada, Ireland, the United Kingdom and the United States are more standardised and exhibit a greater degree of central control than schemes in Denmark, France, the Netherlands, New Zealand and Sweden. In Canada and Ireland the levels of bonuses and merit increments are specified for each level of performance rating. However, there have been moves recently in several of the more standardised schemes towards a more decentralised approach. In Australia and the United Kingdom, for example, appraisal schemes are standardised and the maximum awards payable are centrally determined but the specific levels of awards given to individuals are left to the discretion of individual agencies. In most countries, budgets are centrally determined and individual agencies have very little discretion in supplementing them. In Denmark and the Netherlands performance pay budgets can be supplemented with salary savings from unfilled positions within individual agencies. In New Zealand performance pay must be paid out of the departmental budget.
- **Although performance pay schemes have spread rapidly in recent years, their introduction has not always significantly modified traditional public service pay systems.** Automatic salary increments are still the major component of pay increases in Denmark, France and Spain. And with the exception of schemes covering senior managers in Canada and the United Kingdom, the scheme for middle-level managers in the United States, and schemes in New Zealand, annual general increases in pay rates are not dependent on performance. However, even in these schemes it is usually only the one or two per cent of managers who are rated as performing unsatisfactorily who do not receive the full annual general adjustment. Throughout the 1980s, annual general increases in salary rates averaged around four per cent in several of the countries surveyed. This meant that for many of the schemes the large majority of managers rated as performing fully satisfactorily were receiving bonuses and merit increments that were equal to or less than their general annual increase and their automatic annual increment. In private sector organisations, the amount of pay at risk under performance pay schemes is usually a much more significant proportion of a manager's salary.

Findings concerning the effectiveness of performance-related pay

In Chapter 2 we noted three key requirements for effective performance-related pay schemes: a significant positive relationship between performance and pay awards and a clear understanding of this relationship on the part of staff; equal rewards for staff who perform at the same level so that rewards are perceived as equitable; and, rewards of sufficient value to motivate the recipient. The importance of a good fit between performance pay schemes and the values, goals and strategies of organisations was also underlined as being critical to the long-term effectiveness of schemes. Schemes which satisfy these requirements are more likely to be effective than those that do not and therefore, in the absence of direct measures of the outcomes of performance-related pay schemes, the degree to which schemes satisfy these requirements can be used as a surrogate measure of their effectiveness.

Underlying these requirements is a set of assumptions that are implicit in the simple logic which claims that performance-related pay schemes, along with other managerialist reforms, will enhance the performance of public sector organisations. These include the assumption that organisations can accurately measure individual outputs; that individual outputs contribute to organisational performance; and that rewards, including pay, can be administered in a way which captures their expected incentive value for potential recipients. The validity of these assumptions for the areas of public sector management covered by the schemes surveyed, along with the design of the particular schemes, will determine whether such schemes satisfy the requirements for effective performance-related pay schemes.

How well are the key requirements identified being met? The available evidence suggests that, for many of the schemes surveyed, not very well. There have been recurring problems with the operation of performance-related pay schemes. These have included:

- a lack of discrimination in performance ratings, due mainly to inflation over time in the ratings given. In most schemes more than 95 per cent of managers are rated as fully satisfactory or better, including 60 to 70 per cent who are rated as fully satisfactory;
- a clustering of managers at the top of the salary range in merit pay schemes where they are no longer eligible for merit increments;
- dissatisfaction among staff who are rated fully satisfactory but who, under quotas and other restrictive guidelines for some schemes, either receive a smaller performance pay award than their colleagues or no award at all in a given year;
- relatively low levels of funding which make schemes highly competitive and, in some countries, cut-backs in funds during times of economic restraint; and
- a narrowing of the range and reduction in the average size of bonuses paid.

Individually and collectively, these problems have meant that performance-related pay schemes have failed to establish a clear relationship between pay and performance in the minds of many of the managers who are covered by them. In several of the schemes surveyed, significantly less than half of the managers eligible for merit increments or bonuses believe that pay awards are determined by their performance or that they have the chance to obtain an award if they perform better. The impact of quotas, clustering at the top of salary ranges and the lack of discrimination in the performance appraisals on which pay awards are based have all contributed to a weakening of the actual and perceived links between pay and performance. They have also meant that managers who are perceived to perform at the same levels receive different performance pay awards.

The limited budgets for performance pay, and instability in the availability of funds due to political decisions, have also contributed to the negative perceptions of performance-related pay among public sector managers in longer-running schemes in Canada and the United States. Experience in the United States has shown that instability in the funding for performance pay schemes leads to cynicism and undermines the perceived link between pay and performance amongst managers covered by the schemes. In schemes in Canada and the United Kingdom quotas ensured discrimination in the allocation of the limited funds available but also resulted in a perception of arbitrary distinctions between staff, thus weakening the perceived link between pay and performance. Quotas have also created situations where managers who have received the same performance rating or are perceived to be performing at the same level have received different awards, thus failing to satisfy the equity requirement of equal pay for equal performance.

The United States experience has shown that in the absence of quotas, the limited funds may be dispersed so widely that the size of awards received by individual managers becomes too small to satisfy the requirement that rewards be of sufficient size to be motivating for the recipients. In several schemes, the value attached to the performance awards has also been diminished by comparisons with annual cost-of-living adjustments which, during the 1980s, were greater than the performance awards received by many of the public sector managers in the schemes surveyed.

On the positive side, results from the experimental demonstration projects conducted in the Navy and at the National Institute of Standards and Technology in the United States show that, compared to other pay schemes, performance-related pay schemes may lead to significant improvements in the perceived relationship between pay and performance and distributions of salary increases that are more closely related to performance. It is further encouraging to note that performance appraisals based on objective setting, similar to those used in several OECD countries, were also used in these demonstration projects. However, as noted in an earlier section of this study, these schemes had several distinctive features that need to be taken into consideration when generalising the results to other settings. And, although the projects represent the most rigorous evaluation of public sector performance-related pay schemes conducted thus far, reviews by the United States General Accounting Office have highlighted several methodological flaws which challenge the validity of the findings.

There is no evidence that individual agencies use performance-related pay to implement their corporate strategies or to shape the culture of their organisations. In countries with highly standardised schemes, such as Canada and the United States, agencies have little flexibility in tailoring schemes to their specific organisational needs despite the wide ranges in the sizes and functions of different government agencies. In countries with more decentralised systems, such as Denmark, the Netherlands and Sweden, the involvement of unions and the lack of highly developed corporate planning systems has mitigated against the strategic uses of performance pay. The use of individual performance awards in all of the schemes surveyed, and the corresponding lack of team or corporate bonus schemes, is indicative of the common logic that has motivated the design of schemes. If individual agencies were using performance pay strategically to support and shape corporate values and to implement corporate goals we would expect greater variation in the approaches adopted.

Based on the data available for this study, we conclude that many of the schemes surveyed have failed to satisfy the key requirements for effective performance-pay schemes. Whether this is due solely to the design and operation of particular schemes, and therefore could be improved upon by better designs, is difficult to establish at this stage. Most of the data that are available are for more standardised schemes, particularly from Canada, the United Kingdom and the United States. An early evaluation of the more decentralised scheme in the Netherlands did identify several similar problems to those mentioned above, although the conclusion reached in that case was that the problems were due to inappropriate applications of the scheme by managers.

An alternative explanation for the apparently widespread failure of the schemes surveyed to satisfy key requirements for effective operation is that the assumptions regarding performance pay are simply invalid for the public sector, particularly for central government agencies. In Chapter 2 we discussed some of the difficulties of reliably measuring the work of public sector managers and of establishing a clear relationship between the outputs of individual managers and the performance of an agency. Public sector organisations and individual public sector managers pursue complex outcomes that incorporate aspects of cost-effectiveness, equity, community needs, and professional standards. Much of what a public sector manager does is of a service nature. The difficulties of measuring the marginal contributions of individual managers to the performance of an agency are obvious, but not easily accommodated by performance pay schemes that require regular assessments of individuals against verifiable indicators. The comparability required in competitive schemes further begs the question of whether the standards achieved in different jobs are amenable to such comparisons? When one begins to consider the diverse range of constraints that can selectively affect different public sector programmes, it is hard to reject the frequently mentioned criticism that standards are applied unequally, and therefore inequitably, when determining performance pay.

The widespread use of performance appraisal schemes and annual appraisal ratings to decide on performance pay awards is a reflection of the difficulty of objectively assessing the contributions of individual public sector managers. Annual ratings on a single scale do provide the necessary basis for comparing managers and for deciding on the allocation of performance pay awards. However, the process of quantification does not remove the inherent sources of uncertainty about the value of the contributions tapped by performance indicators and the relative standards of those contributions. The use of annual performance ratings to decide allocations of performance pay is based on the assumption that the measurement problems mentioned can be adequately dealt with through the proper design of a subjective appraisal process. Further data are required to test the validity of this assumption.

The assumption that performance pay has some incentive value for public sector managers is one aspect of the logic of performance pay that, contrary to the expectations of many critics, does appear to be supported. Public sector managers are strong advocates for the adoption of performance pay, even when they are critical of particular schemes. What the available data do not tell us, however, is whether the available awards are sufficiently motivating to lead to higher levels of effort by public sector managers or whether performance pay is viewed as a form of salary increase without much risk attached.

Lessons from experience

One of the lessons to be learned from experience so far is that the design and development of performance-related pay schemes is a continuous process. Schemes, particularly merit increment schemes, appear to have an effective life cycle of up to five years before requiring major changes. The regular monitoring of schemes, including annual audits of managerial attitudes and of the distribution of salary increases, appears essential in this process. Any new scheme, no matter how well planned in advance, will experience problems as salary distributions and staff profiles change over time. Experience in the longer-running schemes suggests that a continuous process of experimentation and revision is needed.

If performance ratings and pay awards are to be linked formally, then the performance appraisal system must give a valid distribution of performance ratings that provides sufficient discrimination for the purposes of allocating pay awards. Many of the problems experienced with performance-related pay appear to be a joint product of the low levels of discrimination in performance appraisal schemes and restrictions on the number and sizes of awards that can be given. Performance appraisal schemes effectively provide a three-level rating of managers, with 60 to 70 per cent rated at the fully satisfactory level. As a result, performance ratings can effectively only be used to allocate two levels of performance-related payment, with a smaller, across-the-board payment to the vast majority who fall in the fully satisfactory performance category.

Another lesson is that performance-related pay schemes must provide adequate funds for a sufficiently large number of staff to receive rewards worth striving for. There are no hard and fast rules for determining the size of awards. However, the impact of the budget on the distribution of awards should be taken into account when setting the maximum levels of awards that can be paid. If the objective is to raise the general performance level of staff, then the budget should provide a level of funding per eligible staff member that allows awards to be both widespread and a reasonable proportion of the maximum payable. Most schemes are currently under-funded relative to the maximum performance awards payable. As a result, quotas have been applied that make arbitrary distinctions between staff, thus weakening the perceived relationship between pay and performance and creating the impression that schemes are elitist. Less competitive schemes in which a larger proportion of staff can receive significant bonuses are the norm in private sector organisations. If governments are not willing to increase the budgets for performance pay then a wider distribution of smaller payments would be necessary to achieve this goal. This, of course, must be balanced against the motivational effects of a drop in the average value of awards paid to higher performers.

The different approaches to performance-related pay schemes in OECD countries represent a range of different solutions to a common set of problems and pressures for reform. Inherent in the different approaches chosen are tradeoffs between the standardisation of centrally imposed schemes and less standardised, decentralised approaches. The standardisation of appraisal schemes and of the relationships between performance ratings and pay awards offers the potential advantages of increased incentive value for rewards and greater consistency and equity in their allocation. Less standardised approaches which allow departments greater latitude in the design of their own schemes within budget constraints offer the potential benefits of flexibility in the determination of awards and their distribution among staff. This flexibility will allow departments to better tailor schemes to their own cultures and strategic goals. Data are not yet available on the relative effectiveness of the different approaches to standardisation. Decentralised schemes have typically been adopted by those countries that have introduced performance pay schemes in recent years. The longer-running schemes have adopted more standardised approaches across the whole of government. However, it is worthy of note that many of the problems experienced with these latter schemes have been related to the standardisation of awards and of the links between performance ratings and awards. This has led to a relaxation of the rules governing the allocation of awards in several countries.

Performance-related pay schemes continue to offer promise for improving the efficiency and cost-effectiveness of public sector organisations. Continuous monitoring and evaluation of the processes of different schemes and of their impacts on managerial attitudes, motivational variables, and performance will be needed to determine the effectiveness of different schemes. Not all will be successful. At the present time, performance-related pay schemes are one of many such managerial systems that are shifting the culture of public service organisations toward a stronger performance orientation.

Annex 1

SUMMARY DESCRIPTIONS OF PERFORMANCE-RELATED PAY SCHEMES FOR SENIOR AND MIDDLE MANAGERS IN CENTRAL GOVERNMENT

Australia

Overview

- The scheme described below is yet to be implemented. It may need to be presented to the Australian Industrial Relations Commission.
- Statutory authorities and government business enterprises (*e.g.* Telecom, Qantas) have several performance pay schemes covering senior managers.
- In the State of Victoria, a centrally administered scheme has covered all members of the Senior Executive Service since 1984. In 1990, this scheme was changed from merit increments to lump-sum bonuses and the maximum awards increased to 15 per cent of total employment costs.
- The states of New South Wales and South Australia both have provisions for performance pay but neither has schemes operating in central departments at this point.

Coverage

- It is envisaged that all members of the Senior Executive Service in central government departments of the national government, approximately 1 700 managers, representing 1 per cent of the civil service, will be covered by the scheme.
- Departmental secretaries (Heads of Departments) are excluded from the scheme.

Performance appraisal

- Objective-based appraisal.
- A five-point summary rating of annual performance is recommended, but in designing their own schemes, individual departments can choose to develop different rating scales.

Performance payments

- There are three SES levels, for which the 1991 salary rates are as follows:

SES Level	Salary rates
1	$59 121 - $66 387
2	$70 928 - $81 954
3	$82 745 - $99 005

- The proposed performance pay scheme will provide for payment of annual lump-sum cash bonuses in addition to basic salary. The size of the maximum bonus has not yet been confirmed.

Flexibility and controls

- Budget set at 50 per cent of maximum performance payments for total number of SES positions in departments.
- It is recommended that, on a five-point performance rating scale, officers must receive a level three rating (*i.e.* fully effective) to receive a bonus. There are no other constraints on distribution of ratings or pay allocation decisions, except for maximum bonus levels.
- Performance appraisal systems must be endorsed by the Public Service Commission.
- Plans to monitor effectiveness of programs through surveys and audits across departments.

Experience

- System yet to be implemented.
- The merit pay system in the state of Victoria experienced problems due to inflation of performance ratings, compression of salaries at the top of the merit range and quotas that limited payments available for high performers. These problems led to dissatisfaction and a widespread perception that pay was not related to performance. In response to these problems the Victorian government shifted to a bonus system. The Australian national government bonus scheme is similar to the new Victorian scheme but is much less standardised.

Canada

Overview

- Pay increments based on formal appraisals of performance and competence rather than automatic progression were first introduced in 1964. It was this original scheme, the Senior Officers Pay Regulations (1964-67), that evolved into the Management Category Salary Administration Plan described below.

- A separate performance pay plan covers the Deputy Ministers, who are the heads of departments in the Canadian public service. This scheme, the Governor in Council Performance Pay Plan, is also described below.
- Other occupational groups in central government agencies covered by specific pay plans, and the estimated number of staff covered by each scheme, include:
  • Professional staff in medical and defence science areas (n=36)
  • Non-management staff in the senior levels of the Administrative and Foreign Service categories (n=968)
  • Mediation/conciliation officers (n=15)
  • Law group staff in the Scientific and Professional category (n=928)
  • Defence science service staff (n=564)
- These different schemes are all similar to the Management Category plan described below, although the specifics, such as levels of payment, quotas and budgets vary between schemes.

The management category salary administration plan

Coverage

- Covers 4 607 staff from the Senior Manager level through five executive levels up to, but not including, Deputy Minister level in all public service departments covered by the *Public Service Staff Relations Act,* for which the Treasury Board is the employer.
- The Management Category employees covered by this plan represent 2.2 per cent of the public service staff.
- Executive and senior managers covered by this scheme are appointed by the Public Service Commission, have tenure for an indeterminate period, and are excluded from union membership and collective bargaining.

Performance appraisal

- Since 1979 departments have been subject to Treasury Board policy on performance appraisal. Prior to that, departments developed their own performance appraisal schemes.
- Standardised scheme used across departments is objective-based appraisal, with an annual five-level rating of performance. Objectives cover job duties set out in job descriptions and departmental objectives.

Performance payments

- Progression through the salary range is on the basis of merit, with in-range increases up to the job rate, which represents the maximum base salary attainable for a manager whose performance has been fully satisfactory or better over a period of time. The maximum in-range merit increase is 10 per cent of base salary.

- Bonuses of up to 10 per cent of salary may be paid in place of a merit increment for managers whose salary is already at the job rate or who reaches the job rate through an in-range increase. Bonuses are in the form of pensionable lump-sum payments and must be re-earned each year.
- Annual salary increases also include a general adjustment to the pay range. This is normally awarded in April, at the same time as the merit increment or bonus, but in 1990 was awarded in June.

Flexibility and controls

- The system has a highly standardised approach to the pay allocation decisions within departments.
- The guidelines for determining merit increments and bonuses are as follows:

Performance Rating	Recommended Award
Outstanding	7-10 per cent of base salary
Superior	5-7 per cent of base salary
Fully satisfactory	3-5 per cent of base salary
Satisfactory	0 per cent of base salary
Unsatisfactory	0 per cent of base salary

- Budgets are limited to 5 per cent of the departmental Management Category payroll for 31 March of each year. This is calculated using the recommended guidelines for awards, thus encouraging departments to adopt the recommended standard awards for each level of performance rating. Small departments, *i.e.* those with fewer than 20 employees, are allowed slightly more than 5 per cent.
- No more than 30 per cent of Management Category employees in a department may be rated as superior or outstanding.
- Under a revision to the scheme in 1990, managers at the job rate who are rated fully satisfactory are eligible for bonuses of up to 10 per cent, along with those rated superior or outstanding. However, the budget and quota constraints mentioned above remain in place.

Experience

- Several surveys of the Management Category scheme have established that performance pay is not accepted by managers as either fair or effective as a monetary reward. Zussman and Jabes (1989) found, in surveys conducted in 1986 and 1988, that only 21 per cent and 16 per cent respectively of managers believed that job performance was reflected in salary increases.
- Research by the Treasury Board Secretariat in 1989 also found that:

- 94 per cent of the Category's salaries were at or within 5 per cent of the job rate, leaving little room for any *meaningful* performance-related increases for those rated fully satisfactory (66 per cent of the Category);
- only 30 per cent of managers, those rated superior and outstanding, remained eligible to receive any performance pay (through bonuses) once their salary had reached the job rate;
- there was quite a de-motivating effect when no additional reward was possible for fully satisfactory performers already at the job rate, even though the job rate was defined as the rate appropriate for fully satisfactory performance;
- 61 per cent of fully satisfactory performers at the lowest level of the Management Category would not receive any merit increase in 1989;
- departments were having difficulties administering performance pay increases for managers seconded to other departments or outside the Public Service. Their concerns related to the 30 per cent restriction on superior and outstanding performance ratings and funds available for awards.

Governor in council performance pay plan for Deputy Ministers

Coverage

- Covers 59 Deputy Ministers as well as 377 other Governor in Council appointees. These staff are appointed by the Governor General, acting on the recommendations of the Prime Minister. This method of employment places them outside the scope of the *Public Service Staff Relations Act.*
- The Deputy Minister classification comprises three levels:
  - DM-1, associate and junior Deputy Ministers;
  - DM-2, experienced Deputy Ministers, heads of small and medium sized departments;
  - DM-3, senior Deputy Ministers, heads of large departments.

Performance appraisal

- No formal appraisal scheme.
- Performance is appraised annually by a Committee of Senior Officials on Executive Personnel (COSO) that includes members of central agencies with service-wide responsibilities for staff (*e.g.* Treasury Board and Public Service Commission) along with other Deputy Ministers.
- The COSO's review of each Deputy Minister's performance is based on:
  - the Minister's assessment of his or her deputy's performance;
  - an assessment by the Treasury Board Secretariat of the performance of the Deputy Minister's department against corporate goals and financial indicators;
  - an assessment by the Public Service Commission of the performance of the Deputy Minister's department against corporate goals and staff management indicators;

• a voluntary self-assessment by the Deputy Minister.
- The COSO then compares the performance of Deputy Ministers at the same level and assigns each Deputy Minister a rating.

Performance payments

- Deputy Ministers are paid bonuses that must be re-earned each year. These bonuses have maximum limits of 15 per cent for DM-1s and DM-2s and 25 per cent for DM-3s. Prior to 1988 the maximum bonus payable for all three levels of Deputy Ministers was 10 per cent.
- The level of bonus paid is based on the evaluation grades assigned by the COSO. Once these are approved by Cabinet, Deputy Ministers are informed of their evaluation grade and pay award by letter.

Flexibility and controls

- Limitations on expenditure for pay awards for Deputy Ministers are at the discretion of the Prime Minister, on the advice of the Privy Council Office.
- The economic climate has constrained the payment of the maximum bonuses allowable since the new limits were introduced in 1988.

Experience

- None reported so far.

Denmark

Overview

- Two performance-related pay schemes were introduced in the Danish public service in 1989 as part of wider changes aimed at modernisation and reduction of bureaucracy in the public sector.
- The first steps towards delegation of pay decisions to departments were taken in 1985/86 with decentralisation of salary pools for university graduates. In 1987-89 there was further decentralisation of agreements that gave departments limited ability to pay performance-related awards.
- The two schemes introduced in 1989, one covering all public servants and the other limited to senior managers, are similar in several ways and, therefore, will be described together.

Coverage

– The Ministerial scheme is available to all public servants.
– The senior managers' scheme is limited to:
  • Heads of Divisions;
  • Heads of Central Customs and Tax Administration;
  • Colonels;
  • Chief Physicians;
  • Post and Telegraph Services;
  • Danish State Railways.
– The senior managers' scheme was introduced to provide greater flexibility in rewarding public servants in leadership positions.
– Permanent Secretaries (*i.e.* heads of departments) are not covered by the schemes described here. A Board Committee, whose membership includes the Prime Minister and the Minister for Finance, reviews the salaries of Permanent Secretaries.

Performance appraisal

– There are no requirements for formal appraisals to be used in allocating awards.
– Central guidelines recommend, but do not require, that the following criteria be used in pay allocation decisions in the Ministerial scheme:
  • efficiency;
  • willingness to change;
  • creativity.
– For the senior managers' scheme the recommended criteria are:
  • job evaluation score;
  • future tasks;
  • willingness and ability to establish a motivated, results-minded work team;
  • resource conscious leadership;
  • active participation in management development.
– Although not highly standardised, these criteria reflect the organisational culture that the Danish public service is trying to move towards.

Performance payments

– There are three types of performance payments:
  • one-off lump-sum bonuses (these are preferred because they allow maximum flexibility);
  • temporary salary increases;
  • merit increments (which are permanent and were expected to be limited in number).
– Allocation of funds under the Ministerial scheme is subject to the agreement of the unions.

Flexibility and controls

- The Danish system is highly decentralised. There are very few guidelines and no constraints on allocations of awards to individuals. The Ministry of Finance did issue guidelines on the allocation of awards; these stressed that funds should mainly be used for one-off lump-sum bonuses and not permanent merit increments to ensue future flexibility in pay allocations.
- Budgets for the two schemes were 0.3 per cent of the total salary budget for the Ministerial Scheme and 0.1 per cent of the total salary budget for eligible staff in the senior managers' scheme.
- Allocation of performance pay funds is subject to public scrutiny and union involvement in the negotiations of awards.

Experience

- Unions support the performance evaluation of senior managers and believe it should be extended to other groups of managers.
- There is a belief among managers that too much time has been spent on negotiations as a result of union involvement.
- The use of performance criteria and their weighting has been found to vary across departments.
- An evaluation of the Ministerial scheme by the Ministry of Finance in 1990 found that:
  - one-off bonuses were used more frequently than merit increments;
  - awards were allocated with preference for seniority;
  - there was increased local freedom and the opportunity to provide quicker solutions to individual pay problems;
  - budgeted funds were considered too small for effective performance-related pay allocations;
  - costs related to the introduction of the scheme were 100 weeks of full-time consultancy work plus DKr 125 000 for publications of guides and scheme materials.
- Feedback from a conference held to review the senior managers' scheme noted that:
  - departments' opinions were mixed on the effectiveness of the scheme but there was unanimous support for continuation of the program;
  - some departments were unwilling to use their autonomy in allocating performance-related pay awards;
  - a survey of managers is to be conducted to develop a performance appraisal system to be used in allocating pay awards;
  - central costs of implementing the scheme totalled about 90 weeks full-time work of one person. This does not include time and costs associated with implementation in departments.
- Success with the schemes to this point has led to an agreement to expand their coverage to more than 95 per cent of civil service employees. The schemes are to be divided into two. The first scheme will apply solely to civil service salary

grades one to thirty-four. The second scheme will apply only to managers in salary grades thirty-five and above. The total budget for the revised schemes is going to be increased to about 0.8 per cent of the total salary bill.

France

Overview

- The system of bonuses in the French civil service is highly complex and obscure. Among the most important bonuses for senior grades are productivity bonuses, overtime bonuses and fees bonuses, all of which have merit elements. Other important bonuses include payments to reward qualifications and expertise, which have no merit element.

Coverage

- The concept of a performance bonus has long been accepted in central government departments (Ministries), in technical organisations and in regional departments.
- Groups not covered by performance-related pay schemes include teachers.
- The number of civil servants earning high bonuses is believed to be quite small with only 10 per cent of civil servants earning bonuses of more than 30 per cent of basic pay and 50 per cent earning bonuses that represent less than 10 per cent of basic pay. The high bonuses are concentrated in the senior management group.
- Bonuses represent a higher proportion of basic pay for senior than for junior grades. There are also wide variations between Departments and occupational categories.

Performance appraisal

- Regulations covering performance bonuses do not include any specific mechanisms for performance appraisal.
- Performance appraisal schemes are the subject of experimental studies but have not gained wide acceptance in the civil service.
- There is scepticism regarding the application of performance appraisal schemes to senior management jobs where the largest bonuses are paid.
- Staff can request an appraisal interview and ask their manager to justify their performance bonus ranking. This may or may not include a performance rating.

Performance payments

- Performance bonuses are not included in basic salary and do not enter into pension calculations.
- In 1990, benefits, including all bonuses, accounted for 12 per cent of the total wage bill; of this, approximately one quarter, or 3 per cent of the wage bill, was performance-related.
- Among the senior grades, bonuses accounted for an average of 33 per cent of base salary. This varies across agencies. For example, in prestigious corps such as the Inspectorate General of Finances, bonuses are thought to average around 45 per cent of base salary.
- Variations among occupational groups are also quite marked. After 5 years, the range is from 3.5 per cent of basic pay for social workers to 64.3 per cent for civil engineers.
- Performance bonuses are generally paid as quarterly or half-yearly advances. Advances are based on payments for previous years and are adjusted for performance in February each year.
- Some agencies have introduced performance bonuses linked to specific activities of a civil servant's job. Examples are found in the accounting services of the Ministry for Economic Affairs and the Postal Service. These may include commissions on savings or sales of products.

Flexibility and controls

- Annual budgets for bonuses are allocated by the Finance Ministry to departments and corps. The budget is based on an average rate for each occupational group multiplied by the number of staff in that category within a department. The budget is indexed against general wage increases. There is very little control over how the budgets are used. Individual departments decide on how to allocate bonuses amongst their staff. Departments can supplement budgets from their own resources.
- Audits by financial controllers, the General Financial Inspectorate and parliament are the major forms of control against abuse of the system.
- There is a rule that bonuses should not exceed 100 per cent of an officer's salary; however, it is believed that bonuses do exceed this limit on occasions.

Experience

- Surveys have apparently shown that most staff are sympathetic to the use of performance bonuses but that they are not always sure how they work.
- Criticisms of existing schemes include:
  - the low variation in the rates of bonuses paid to staff within the same service;
  - lack of transparency of the bonus system;
  - disparities between ministries and corps.

- Nevertheless, in recent years there have been efforts to render the system more transparent (including discussions in the bi-partite consultative bodies of ministries and publication of bonus rates in some ministries) and experiments aimed at improving the link between pay and performance.

Ireland

Overview

- The Merit pay scheme for Assistant Secretaries was introduced in 1990 as part of a broader management improvement programme that has included introduction of corporate planning, more decentralised administrative budgets and greater emphasis on personal responsibility for results, costs and services.
- The introduction of performance pay included a revision of the existing pay scale so that a merit range, instead of a fixed incremental scale, covered the Assistant Secretary positions.

Coverage

- The scheme to be described presently covers 95 Assistant Secretaries, the second most senior position in most government departments.
- Permanent Secretaries in central government departments are not covered by performance pay.
- Schemes have been introduced for management grades in some non-commercial state bodies, such as the Industrial Development Authority, and for the chief executives of commercial state bodies. These two schemes cover 400 and 23 staff, respectively. In commercial organisations, managers below the chief executive are paid against personal contracts that typically include some performance requirements.

Performance appraisal

- Objective-based appraisal with an annual four-point rating of performance. Unlike the more common five-point scales, this scheme only includes one rating below the fully satisfactory level.

Performance payments

- Awards are paid as merit increments to base salary on an annual basis.

– The merit pay range for Assistant Secretaries in 1991 was £35 212 to £43 701.
– Merit increments are linked to annual performance ratings as follows:

Rating	Increment
Outstanding	£ 2 830
More than satisfactory	£ 1 415
Satisfactory	£ 943
Unsatisfactory	£ 0

Flexibility and controls

– The system is non-competitive and there are no quotas or other restrictions on the number of increments given at each level.
– Application of the system is left to departments. The Department of Finance will monitor the numbers and levels of increments paid.
– The overall costs of the scheme are considered part of the normal salary bill and are not budgeted separately

Experience

– No formal evaluation has been conducted; however, the general impression is that the scheme has been implemented successfully.
– It is anticipated that the scheme will have to be revised in a few years as a majority of staff reach the top of the pay range.
– The maximum additional cost of the scheme is expected to be 5 per cent because the maximum point on the new salary range is 5 per cent above the old scale.
– Criticisms of the scheme by the unions have included:
  • the merit pay range is too narrow for worthwhile rewards;
  • salary earnings within the range are below what staff would have achieved under a straight revision of the old scale;
  • payments for satisfactory and more than satisfactory ratings are too low.

Netherlands

Overview

– Performance-related pay schemes were renewed in 1989. A previous system of performance bonuses was considered ineffective.

– The new system is intended to be more "management friendly"; the rules are easier to apply; there is a bigger budget; and managers were given training as part of the implementation process.
– The system allows individual departments considerable freedom in deciding on the size and distribution of awards.
– Major goals of the schemes were to improve the motivation of staff, reinforce managerial accountability and align individual job performance with organisational goals.

Coverage

– All central government employees are covered by performance pay.
– There are no separate schemes for managers.

Performance appraisal

– There is no standardised appraisal scheme. Individual departments develop their own schemes and may link performance payments to ratings. Decisions concerning merit increments or temporary salary increases are usually made at the same time as the annual performance appraisal, which may be informal.
– There is no central requirement for a formal appraisal, unless the supervisor and employee fail to agree on an (informal) assessment. In this case, the formal appraisal can be made by the supervisor or by the manager two levels above the appraisee.

Performance payments

– Performance payments to staff can be one of three types:

  • a merit increment of one or more steps on the salary scale for their position. Each step is equal to an increase of around 3 per cent.
  • a temporary salary increase for a period of up to one year; the maximum increases payable depend upon a person's position in the salary scale, as follows (Note: Scales 14 and above are managerial positions).

Scales	Maximum
1-5	3%
6-9	6%
10-13	9%
14-15	12%
16-18	15%

- a bonus for special achievements. This may be given at any time following a special achievement. There is no maximum on the amount of bonus paid, departments establish their own rules. A bonus might typically be 20 per cent or 25 per cent of one month's salary (*i.e.* 1.6 per cent – 2.0 per cent of annual salary). Higher awards (*e.g.* above 50 per cent of a month's salary) are less common and, in some departments, may require the permission of the head of the Ministry.
- a token for special achievements. This may be given at any time during the year and could be in the form of a bottle of wine or some other token.

Flexibility and controls

- Since 1989, the additional budget allocated to departments for performance pay is about 0.25 per cent of the base salary budget. Departments are also allocated 1.5 per cent of base salary for normal increments and 0.5 per cent for merit increments.
- There are no limits on the number of awards paid. Limits on the sizes of individual payments are mentioned above, under Performance Payments.
- Departments can supplement this budget with funds from other areas, such as training budgets.
- The departments are responsible for the implementation and management of the schemes. There are no central agencies involved in the running or auditing of schemes.
- Staff who are dissatisfied with a payment can appeal to the Civil Service Tribunal for a review.

Experience

- At the time of introduction, it was agreed that an evaluation of the scheme would be undertaken after two years. This evaluation was done in 1991. The findings included the following:
  - there is a good deal of diversity in the way performance pay has been implemented in different ministries;
  - many employees are unclear about how the performance pay system works;
  - most employees who received performance pay were satisfied with the size of payments;
  - the proportion of employees receiving performance pay awards was substantially higher at more senior levels than in lower grades;
  - more use is made of bonuses than of the other forms of performance pay;
  - although increments are no longer automatic, the provision for withholding increments from poor performers is rarely used;
  - both managers and employees expect that the system will improve organisational effectiveness, make staff more performance oriented, give managers more influence and make the pay system more equitable;

- managers and employees feel that the system may demotivate employees who do not receive performance pay.

New Zealand

Overview

– Since early 1988, the New Zealand public service has undergone considerable change through restructuring and creation of a new legislative framework covering public service management. A key aspect of the changes introduced was that every department has become an employer in its own right. The aims of this legislation were to improve the effectiveness and accountability of public sector management.
– Performance pay schemes were introduced as part of this general set of reforms.
– There is no standardised system. For staff covered by voluntary agreements (which excludes Chief Executive Officers, the Senior Executive Service (SES) and other contract staff), there is a similar set of provisions inserted into each departmental agreement. However, within these broad provisions, departments are free to design their own systems and they must fund them from their own budgets.

Coverage

– A range of pay schemes apply to middle and senior managers in central government departments. The merit scheme described below is that operated in the State Services Commission and is given as an example only of one of these diverse performance pay schemes.
– Chief executives and a limited number of senior managers, including those in the SES, are covered by individual employment contracts. The SES covers about 150 positions throughout the public service.

Performance appraisal

– Objective-based appraisals with an annual five-point rating of performance.
– Factors to be taken into consideration in determining annual performance ratings are:
  - achievement against agreed objectives;
  - contributions to the wider departmental goals.

Performance payments

- The public service has introduced ranges of remuneration rates for most staff, including middle and senior level managers. These ranges fix upper and lower limits, expressed as a percentage of the median. The ranges are open and do not have fixed incremental steps.
- Merit increments and other movements within the pay range are decided by individual departments. The specific criteria used to place a person within the range are decided by the department, within the boundaries set out in voluntary agreements, and may include labour market considerations (*e.g.* skills or recruitment difficulties) as well as performance.

Flexibility and controls

- There is no centralised oversight of the operation of departmental performance pay systems.
- The broad provisions of performance payment schemes that are included in the voluntary agreements of individual departments are similar across the core public service departments.
- Within the framework outlined in the voluntary agreement, departments have discretion as to how they operate the systems and the levels of payments.
- Control is through the overall financial accountability of the Chief Executive Officer who must ensure there is adequate budgetary provision for approved performance payments.

Experience

- An evaluation of the performance pay scheme is currently being undertaken.
- Impressions gained so far suggest that:
  • the schemes have led to clarification of job goals and greater accountability of staff;
  • the schemes have been more successfully implemented in small departments where they can be more closely monitored;
  • the schemes have not led to the expected reduction in wage drift.

Spain

Overview

- The introduction of performance-related pay was part of a general set of reforms introduced in 1984. These, in turn, have been influenced by the opening up of the

Spanish economy and a push for greater productivity in both the public and private sectors.

- The introduction of the new system involved extensive consultations with the unions and extensive job evaluation studies.
- Productivity bonuses were one of several forms of supplementary pay adopted in 1984. Other merit-related bonuses that were adopted included:
  - position bonuses (there are 30 categories of posts or positions);
  - special bonuses, depending on individual job circumstances (*e.g.* risks, responsibility, technical requirements).
- *Ad hoc* bonuses, which predate the 1984 reforms, are also paid on occasions, but are not a regularly used system of performance-related pay.

Coverage

- Productivity bonuses are available to staff at all levels. However, their payment has become more widespread among middle and senior management grades. Percentages of recipients are 13.5 per cent at grade 10, 49.0 per cent at grade 24 (the bottom of the management range) and 94.3 per cent at grade 30 (the top of the management range). The average percentage of staff receiving bonuses across all levels is 24.9 per cent.
- Director-Generals, who are the heads of departments, are also covered by the productivity bonus scheme. All staff at that level are paid bonuses, although the size of the bonuses varies.
- The size of the bonuses varies quite markedly across departments. For all government departments, the productivity bonus represents around 7.2 per cent of total fixed salary (11.2 per cent of base salary). In the Department of Social Security, for example, the average productivity bonus represents 12.8 per cent of total fixed salary and 28.19 per cent of base salary.

Performance appraisal

- There was no general system of performance appraisal when the performance pay scheme was introduced. Different departments have adopted their own approaches and criteria, and their own links between performance assessments and bonuses.
- The different approaches have resulted in the use of two types of performance assessment, or some combination of the two approaches. The most common is to base bonuses on quantitative criteria (these are known as fixed productivity schemes). The most common quantitative criteria used are hours worked, type of activities, and grade of the post. These types of assessments do not directly link pay to performance. Examples of quantitative criteria used in government legal services include:
  - number of cases processed;
  - number of cases with "A" importance rating.

– A less common approach is to base bonuses on performance appraisals (*i.e.* more subjective assessments of job performance). Examples of performance appraisal criteria used in government legal services include ratings of:
  • the outcome of cases;
  • quality of communication.
– The Ministry for Public Administration has proposed a model objective-based appraisal system with a five-point annual rating of performance for central government departments. This is currently being pilot tested in different agencies (National Institute of Meteorology; the Sports Council).

Performance payments

– There are no centrally established rules or guidelines concerning the levels of bonuses. Different departments decide on their own rules and guidelines and the maximum size of bonuses paid varies among departments.
– Bonuses are usually paid quarterly. In some cases (*e.g.* the National Institute of Health) managers receive an advance payment that represents 50 per cent of the maximum bonus that could be paid.
– Under the proposed scheme for central government departments (mentioned in the section on Performance Appraisal above), the recommended payments for different rating levels would be as follows:

Rating	Percentage of Fixed Pay
Exceptional	15 per cent
Excellent	10 per cent
Very Satisfactory	5 per cent
Fair	2.5 per cent
Unsatisfactory	0 per cent

– The actual amounts paid would depend on the available budget. However, the ratio of payments (*e.g.* six to one between the exceptional and fair ratings) would be maintained.

Flexibility and controls

– Up to now, the system has been highly decentralised. Departments are able to implement their own performance appraisal system and establish their own approach to performance payments.
– Budgets are allocated by the Ministry of Economic Affairs and Finance. This is done by applying a percentage to the total gross salaries bill for each department. In this way, performance pay is indexed against general salary increases. Budgets for individual departments differ and may be adjusted to reflect levels of performance against departmental objectives.
– Adjustments in the overall allocation for performance can be the subject of collective bargaining negotiations with the unions. Operation of the system is not

necessarily subject to collective bargaining; however, some departments do involve unions in the process.

- Reporting and review of the systems implemented provides several levels of indirect control.
  - financial aspects of the system are subject to annual audits;
  - non-financial aspects (*e.g.* criteria used and distribution of awards) are reported to the Ministry of Economics Affairs and Finance and the Ministry of Public Affairs;
  - individual bonuses are published within departments;
  - review boards help ensure consistency in appraisals and bonus payments within departments.

Experience

- Current experiments with objective-based appraisal schemes and standardised distributions of bonuses may lead to greater standardisation of the system.
- The most contentious issues for the unions have been the appraisal criteria chosen in departments, because of their fundamental influence in determining bonuses. There was an increase in conflict in some departments following the introduction of performance appraisal.
- Unions have been opposed to objective-based appraisals. Management support for such schemes is strong.
- The introduction of performance pay led to an improvement in public service pay and, as a result, an overall increase in staff costs. Performance pay has come to be viewed as part of their fixed salary by many staff.
- The flexibility in the present scheme is seen as providing the possibility of future refinements.

Sweden

Overview

- In Sweden, wages and other terms of employment are regulated by collective agreements with unions, which are well organised and have large membership. Up to the late 1970s, salary was related to function and difficulty of work, with automatic annual increases.
- In 1977, the most senior government officials, including university professors, Director-Generals, Under-Secretaries of State (who are heads of government departments) and others, were taken out of the collective bargaining system. Their salaries are now set by either a Review Board (with three government representatives and three union representatives) or directly by the government.

– In 1985, the pay structure for these top officials was replaced by a system of individual pay setting. This decentralised approach was meant to link pay more closely to performance and other merit criteria.
– During the 1980s the wage trend in Sweden was high compared to other OECD countries and this has led to wage stabilisation agreements, with low wage increases planned for the period 1991-1993.

Coverage

– The salaries of Director-Generals and Under-Secretaries of State are set, on an individual basis, by the government. The salaries of other top officials are determined by the Review Board mentioned earlier. Salary reviews include performance considerations.
– Workers at all levels may be covered by bonus systems as part of their local collective agreements.

Performance appraisal

– There are no centrally required appraisal systems. However, individual salary increases are based on merit ratings, along with other factors such as job level. Merit ratings are typically based on tasks undertaken and identified job outputs and outcomes. Different departments have developed their own performance appraisal schemes.
– Wage agreements establish the basic criteria for salary differentiation. These include difficulty of work and level of responsibility, as well as skills required and actual levels of performance.
– Supervisors are required to inform subordinates of their individual wage increase and to explain it in terms of job performance.

Performance payments

– Under the individual salary systems, each official gets the general wage increase but there is no guarantee of a merit increase. Each individual is placed within a salary range and movement within that range is based on assessments against the criteria mentioned above.
– For levels below the top officials, the salary ranges and the average increases to be paid are established in negotiations with unions.
– Where applicable, bonus payments are more directly linked to efficiency measures or cost savings.

Flexibility and controls

- The individual salary setting system is a highly decentralised one. Each department establishes its own wage policy and wage structure, in negotiation with unions, and the necessary performance appraisal schemes for individual merit or bonus payments.
- Budgets are the result of central wage agreements plus annual or biannual decisions by the government or the Review Board.
- A statistical monitoring system is currently being developed as a means of monitoring payments across departments.

Experience

- Bonuses are believed to have ranged from zero to over 30 per cent of base salary in agencies with bonus schemes.
- Recruitment and retention of good managers is believed to have improved under the individual salary setting scheme.

United Kingdom

Overview

- The use of performance-related pay schemes has increased substantially in the public sector in recent years, especially for senior and middle managers. Schemes are now operating in central government departments, government business enterprises, local government agencies and the National Health Service (NHS).
- Major motivations for the introduction of schemes have been the decentralisation of managerial and financial control and the fostering of a performance culture in which value for money and accountability are given greater emphasis.
- The need for greater flexibility in pay has been identified on several occasions in reports of review Committees, dating at least as far back as the Fulton Committee (1968).
- The experience with schemes in central government departments include:
  - An experimental bonus scheme that ran from 1985 to 1988;
  - A merit plus bonus scheme introduced in 1987. This covered senior management grades 2 and 3 (the grades immediately below the heads of ministries). A similar scheme was introduced for grades 5 to 7 in 1988. In 1991, the scheme for grades 2 and 3 (but not grades 5 to 7) was revised.
- The description to follow will cover the experimental bonus scheme and the merit and bonus scheme for grades 2 and 3. The description of the latter will note the 1991 revisions to the scheme in the appropriate sections.

The experimental bonus scheme (1985-1987)

Coverage

- Grades 3 to 7
- Permanent Secretaries (who are normally heads of ministries) and staff reporting directly to them (*i.e.* Grade 2s) were excluded.

Performance appraisal

- There were no formal requirements for appraisal.
- Bonuses were meant to be a reward for particularly good performance over a period of a year.

Performance payments

- The minimum bonus was £500 and there was no set maximum. Bonuses of more than 10 per cent of salary were unusual.
- The awards were based on the recommendation of the line manager and were confidential.
- Bonuses were paid as lump sums.

Flexibility and controls

- There was a quota of 20 per cent on the number of staff in a department at Grades 3 to 7 who could be paid bonuses in any given year.

Experience

- A consultants' review concluded that the scheme was generally not a success. Criticisms included:
  - Staff viewed the scheme as a "competition which only 20 per cent of people can win and where the rules are not clear". It was not clear what performance would merit an award;
  - The scheme had no impact on motivation, performance or management practices and was not integrated with other performance management processes in departments;
  - The objectives of the scheme were unclear and there were problems with both design and management of the scheme.
- On the positive side, the consultants reported that:

- most staff were in favour, in principle, of relating pay to performance, including team performance;
- the bonus scheme had promoted discussion of issues relating to performance pay among senior managers.

The merit and bonus scheme for grades 2 and 3 (1987)

Coverage

– Senior management grades 2 and 3. These currently number about 140 and 490 staff respectively. A similar scheme has covered grades 5 to 7 since 1988. Also there are several schemes in government organisations (*e.g.* NHS) that are broadly similar to this scheme.
– Permanent Secretaries were excluded because their assessment would have involved Ministers, who are outside the civil service.

Performance appraisal

– Performance appraisal systems have a long history in the United Kingdom civil service. For the most senior grades, including grades 2 and 3, these were traditionally informal. With the introduction of performance pay, performance appraisals for these levels have become more formalised and more similar to those for middle management.
– Appraisals are objective-based and lead to a five-point annual rating of overall performance.
– Performance appraisals remain the same following the revisions to the scheme that were introduced in April 1991.

Performance payments

– The introduction of the merit pay scheme required the introduction of a pay range, in place of the single pay points, for both grades 2 and 3.
– Initially the salary range included two salary points below the job rate or ''normally maximum attainable salary'', which a new appointee moved through semi-automatically. Above the job rate were several discretionary salary levels. The individual manager was placed at one of these levels, based on his or her performance rating.
– In 1990, the points below the job rate were removed and the pay scales for staff in London were as follows:

	Grade 3	Grade 2
Job rate	47 000	54 900
Merit levels	49 300	57 600
	51 800	61 000
	54 000	64 300

- The placement of staff at the merit levels (known as discretionary pay points) was based on performance ratings but there was no mechanistic link between the two.

- Annual general increases in pay scales, which everyone received, were normally paid from April, whilst awards of merit increments were made in October. Merit increments were fully pensionable.

- In addition to the merit increments, departments could make pensionable bonus payments to staff.

- Under the revised scheme, introduced in April 1991:
  - The merit steps have been replaced by an open range. Permanent Secretaries therefore have greater discretion in the choice of amounts that they award to individual staff.
  - Annual increases in the pay range are no longer paid automatically to all staff. Those with ratings of less than fully satisfactory can be paid less than the general increase at the discretion of the Permanent Secretary.
  - The salary grades were revised to reduce disparities with the private sector. This resulted in increases of up to 15 per cent for grades 2 and 3.

Flexibility and controls

- The main budgetary control for the merit scheme was a quota on the number of staff who could be paid merit increments or discretionary pay levels. This was initially set at 25 per cent of staff in each of the grades within a department. After criticism from management and staff that the quota was unduly restrictive it was raised to 35 per cent in 1989.
- For the bonus part of the scheme, the additional payments were limited to 0.2 per cent of the wage bill.
- In the revised scheme, introduced in April 1991, there are no quotas on awards. Control will be through the budget.
  - A fund of 2 per cent of the basic pay bill for each grade will be available for merit increments or bonuses.
  - Added to this will be the annual increase in the salary range. Every staff member who receives a fully satisfactory rating or better must receive the full standard increase.
  - Funds can be carried over from one year to the next.
  - Performance pay awards can be paid as merit increments or bonuses.

Experience

- The 35 per cent (formerly 25 per cent) quota system was the major problem under the old system. This meant that the majority of staff received the standard increase and no performance pay.
- The scheme helped to sharpen job goals and link them more directly to departmental goals.
- Major concerns with the system were:
  - how to tailor schemes to the needs of different departments;
  - how to contain costs and, at the same time, reward the fully satisfactory performers;
  - how to measure performance objectively.
- Under the revised scheme there is a risk that practices will diverge between departments; however, central monitoring of this and other aspects is planned.

United States

Overview

- Performance pay is found in different forms in all departments of the Federal Government. Forms of payment include small cash awards, merit pay, bonuses, and productivity gainsharing programmes.
- Following the Civil Service Reform Act (CSRA) of 1978, there were several changes to the pay structures of the United States civil service.
  - Most managers in grades 16-18 were converted to a six level Senior Executive Service (SES). Managers in the SES are covered by a bonus scheme, as well as special Presidential Rank Awards, which are described below.
  - Virtually automatic increases for managers and supervisors in grades 13-15 were abolished and replaced with a performance-related pay scheme with open pay ranges known as the Merit Pay Scheme. This scheme was revised in 1984 and became the Performance Management and Recognition System (PMRS), that is also described below.
- The reform of civil service pay structures was aimed at improving the quality of public service through better individual performance, motivated, in part, by performance-related pay.
- All performance pay decisions are based on performance appraisal schemes that have been developed according to laws and regulations specifically related to performance appraisal.
- Regular reviews of different schemes have provided extensive data on the attitudes and motivational beliefs of managers covered by performance pay. These data include the analyses of several experimental projects that have been established under the authority of Title VI research and demonstration provisions of the CSRA of 1978. Results from three of the Title VI Demonstration Projects were described in the body of the main report.

Performance Management and Recognition System (PMRS)

Coverage

PMRS covers:

- Approximately 140 000 white-collar managers and supervisors in grades 13, 14 and 15, who represent about 8 per cent of the total white-collar federal workforce.
- In 1991, the salaries for grades covered by PMRS were as follows:

Grade	Salary Range
13	$44 348 – $57 650
14	$52 406 – $68 129
15	$61 643 – $80 138

- There are 110 federal departments covered by PMRS and 36 that are not. Departments that have their own pay schemes (*i.e.* are not covered by the General Schedule) are excluded. Examples include intelligence and banking organisations.
- Non-managerial and non-supervisory positions in grades 13, 14 and 15 are not covered by PMRS. This provides a basis for comparison with staff at the same level who are not covered by the scheme.

Performance appraisal

- The performance appraisal system for the PMRS is specified in legislation and implementing regulations.
- Managers are appraised once a year and assigned a summary performance rating on a five-point scale. Appraisals are against either job-specific goals or standardized critical elements criteria.
- The development of standardized critical elements criteria and their validity must conform to legislation and implementing regulations. These include the use of job analyses to establish the definitions of criteria and the standards for different rating levels, as shown in Figures 4 and 5 of the main report.

Performance payments

- Each grade is covered by a merit pay range of approximately 30 per cent, defined by the maxima and minima shown above. The pay ranges have no fixed steps and so are open ranges.
- PMRS consists of three merit pay components, an annual general increase, a merit increment and cash bonuses.
- Annual general increases, based on comparisons with private sector pay, are used to adjust the maximum and minimum rates of the three merit pay ranges for grades 13, 14 and 15. The size of this general increase varies from year to year. In 1991 it was 4.1 per cent.

- Managers who are rated "fully successful" or better receive the full general increase. Managers rated "minimally successful" receive half the adjustment; and managers who are rated "unacceptable" receive no general increase.
- Merit increments are based on the manager's annual performance rating and current position in the pay range. The formula for determining the size of a merit increment for a manager is shown in Table 7 of the main report. A full merit increment is equal to one-ninth of the difference between the minimum and maximum pay rates for the range, or approximately 3 per cent of the average pay rate for that grade.
- Cash bonuses or performance awards of up to 10 per cent of base pay can also be paid to PMRS managers. In the case of unusually outstanding performance, a department head may pay an individual a larger bonus, but not more than 20 per cent of base pay. Up until April 1991, managers who were rated "outstanding" had to receive bonuses of at least 2 per cent of their base pay. This requirement has now been removed in order to give agencies greater flexibility in managing their bonus funds. Managers rated below "fully successful" are ineligible for bonuses. The size of actual bonuses paid in a department, therefore, depends upon the distribution of performance ratings.
- In most departments the three components of performance-related pay are awarded at different times during the year. It is believed that this undermines the impact on managerial attitudes and motivation, particularly as the full general increase is the largest, most consistent and most widely received increment in most years.

Flexibility and controls

- The performance appraisal and performance payment systems are highly standardized. However, some departmental discretion is exercised in the operation of performance appraisal systems and, within the defined limits, in the distribution of cash bonuses. The distribution of general increases and merit increases, according to the formulae mentioned above, are fixed in law and apply uniformly across all agencies.
- The law forbids the use of forced distributions or quotas in the annual performance ratings.
- The budget for cash bonuses may not exceed 1.5 per cent of total PMRS salaries for the department. Merit increments and general increases are not budgeted separately for departments and their costs are controlled through the formula mentioned earlier.
- The PMRS is audited annually by the Office of Personnel Management (OPM) and a report prepared for the President and the Congress. These reports are based on data about performance ratings, salary adjustments and awards as well as surveys and other data collection activities. On the basis of the reports Congress may adjust the laws that regulate the operation of the PMRS.
- When PMRS was established in 1984, the legislation specified that the system should expire in 1989, effectively requiring a thorough assessment at that time. PMRS was extended by Congress and a committee established to study ways of strengthening the link between pay and performance.

- Other evaluations of PMRS have been carried out by the General Accounting Office (GAO), the Merit Systems Protection Board (MSPB), and the management associations representing PMRS employees.
- Within departments, Performance Standards Review Boards are required to review PMRS performance plans and to make recommendations for improvements.

Experience

- From the extensive array of data on the PMRS it appears that the system has been successfully implemented within departments. The vast majority of managers are receiving regular appraisals against job relevant criteria and their pay is being adjusted as a result of the performance ratings they receive. The majority of staff (86 per cent) believe pay should be based on individual performance.
- A major weakness in the PMRS system in many departments has been a steadily rising average, and resulting lack of distribution, in the annual performance ratings of managers. As a result, there has been little discrimination in the allocation of the general increases and merit increments and smaller average bonuses are being paid to a larger proportion of managers.
- Surveys have found a significant percentage of managers expressing the following dissatisfactions with PMRS:
  - Better job performance does not lead to more pay;
  - The five-level summary rating is too rigid, too complex, and demotivating;
  - Some departments are using arbitrarily forced distributions of ratings to enable discrimination in bonuses;
  - There are not enough funds to provide significant enough awards to motivate managers;
  - The system is not adequately linked to organisational goals and does not include measures and rewards for group performance;
- There are no data on the impact of PMRS on departmental productivity and performance.

Senior executive bonus scheme and presidential rank awards

Coverage

- Members of the Senior Executive Service (SES) number approximately 7 300 career and non-career staff across the federal government. The majority of these staff are in professional occupations, the major job categories being engineers (15 per cent), administration (35 per cent), attorneys (11 per cent) and physical scientists (10 per cent).
- The SES has six levels. Appointments in the SES are to a position at a defined SES level. Each position has a salary rate defined by the SES level of the position. The pay scale in effect since January 1991 is as follows:

SES Level	Pay
1	$87 000
2	$91 200
3	$95 300
4	$100 500
5	$104 600
6	$108 300

– An SES officer's pay rate may be adjusted, up or down, on the basis of performance or position responsibilities.
– Annual bonuses and Presidential Rank Awards are available for career SES officers only. Non-career and limited term appointees are not eligible for either type of award.

Performance appraisal

– Objective-based appraisal, similar to the PMRS scheme, with annual rating of performance that must include at least three levels by law (unsatisfactory, minimally satisfactory and fully successful). Departments may include up to two additional levels of ratings above the ''fully successful'' level.
– Initial ratings, and any additional information provided by the senior executive or a higher level executive, will be reviewed and evaluated by a Performance Review Board that will make a written recommendation concerning each senior executive's performance appraisal.

Performance payments

– Annual bonuses or performance awards are paid as a lump sum. The bonuses can be between 5 per cent and 20 per cent of base pay.
– Staff must receive a rating of fully successful or better to be considered for a bonus.
– All bonus nominations are reviewed by a department's Performance Review Board which then prepares a set of recommendations for the distribution of bonuses within the department.
– There are two levels of Presidential Rank Awards:
  • Distinguished Executives receive a lump-sum payment of $20 000 and a gold pin;
  • Meritorious Executives receive a lump-sum payment of $10 000 and a silver pin.
– These awards are traditionally presented to the recipients by the President in a formal ceremony. SES officers are nominated by their departments for Presidential Rank Awards. To be considered for an award an SES officer must have performed at an exceptional level for at least three years. A central review panel

composed of leading individuals from government and the private sector, and the Director of OPM, recommends candidates for awards to the President.

Flexibility and controls

- Budget limits and quotas for the different awards are as follows:
  - total bonuses paid within a department cannot exceed 3 per cent of the departmental payroll for career SES officers;
  - no more than one per cent of the career SES may receive a Distinguished Executive award each year;
  - no more than 5 per cent of the career SES may receive a Meritorious Executive award each year;
  - an individual SES officer may be awarded the same Presidential Rank award only once in five years.
- The SES bonus schemes are subject to regular reports based on audits and surveys by a variety of departments, including the OPM, the MSPB and GAO.

Experience

- As with PMRS, experience with the SES bonus scheme has been mixed. The major problems include:
  - ratings inflation;
  - a drop in the average size of bonuses paid due to a wider dispersion of bonuses;
  - a widely held belief that improved performance is unlikely to lead to increased pay and that available awards are weak incentives for improving performance.

Annex 2

CASE STUDIES OF PERFORMANCE-RELATED PAY SCHEMES

CONTENTS

INTRODUCTION

This Annex contains case studies and descriptive notes relating to performance-related pay schemes in the public sector in different OECD countries. The cases and descriptive notes are not restricted to central government departments and include examples and analyses of performance pay schemes in government business enterprises, statutory authorities, state government departments, and local government departments. The schemes described also cover a diversity of positions and occupational groups, including lawyers (Canada), postmasters (Denmark), university faculty (Spain) and health employees (Canada, Spain). There are schemes that cover staff at all levels of public sector organisations (e.g. Sweden), as well as those that are restricted to managers and other specific occupational groups. Through the materials presented, readers should obtain a feel for the diversity of approaches taken to performance-related pay in public sector organisations. The cases and notes also provide insights into performance appraisal judgements and performance pay allocations and how these are handled in different schemes.

The schemes covered in this Annex illustrate several points about performance-related pay schemes that either reinforce or supplement points raised in the main report.

- The pay allocation decision process is often conducted by a representative committee. In cases where quotas are applied, this may mean that the final decision is not based solely on a manager's performance rating or, alternatively, a performance rating is revised by the committee. Examples of how this process is handled are provided in the Canadian Department of Transport case study.
- Schemes may include the use of grievance procedures for appeals against pay awards. Examples are provided in North Carolina (United States), Shepway (United Kingdom) and the Law Group scheme in Canada. In the majority of schemes, particularly those covering managers, there are no rights of appeal against pay awards. It is often assumed that grievances are resolved as part of the performance appraisal or pay allocation processes. The appeals against the Canadian Law Group scheme mentioned provide useful data on the scheme's shortcomings.
- Related to the issue of grievance procedures is union involvement in development and management of performance-related pay schemes. The adoption of performance pay for managers in several countries included their removal from collective bargaining processes. An example of how this was done in response to union resistance to a performance pay scheme is provided in the British Rail (United Kingdom) case study. The Swedish Telecommunications scheme, by way of contrast, illustrates the involvement of unions in the performance pay scheme.

– Problems of funding raised in the main report are further highlighted by the experiences of several of the state and local government schemes in the United States that have had either diminished budgets or no performance pay funds for several years.
– As a contrast to the emphasis on individual rewards for individual job performance in schemes discussed in the main report, several schemes described in this Annex use team and corporate criteria to allocate bonuses. This reduces the political risk of rewarding managers when an organisation or work unit is performing poorly. Other benefits of corporate and team performance criteria may include a stronger team orientation plus the use of quantitative performance indicators, the latter being more typical at the aggregate levels of team and corporate performance. In the Irish Electricity Supply Board, the proportion of a manager's bonus that is determined by corporate performance varies with his or her level in the organisation. In British Rail, low profits in poor economic times have meant that top management have received no bonuses. In the Swedish Telecommunications organisation, individual bonus rates are based on performance within regional organisations.
– Another feature of schemes described in the cases and notes is the use of contracts for managers, (e.g. Danish Railway, Irish Electricity Supply Board). Contracts, like performance pay, reflect another of the reforms to public sector management that have grown out of the rationalist economic policies of the 1980s. In some cases, bonuses are paid to contract staff to offset the loss of tenure that is typical in most public sector organisations.
– A final issue raised by the materials in this Annex is the use of performance-related pay as a strategy for changing or reinforcing a particular corporate culture. In the United Kingdom local government schemes, the introduction of performance pay was intended to create stronger customer-service and performance oriented cultures. In the Canadian Health and Welfare Department, performance is related to the "corporateness" culture, and the role of the reviewing committees includes a consideration of other human resource management strategies.

STATE OF VICTORIA, AUSTRALIA PERFORMANCE-RELATED PAY SCHEMES FOR THE SENIOR EXECUTIVE SERVICE[1]

A merit pay scheme for senior executives was introduced in Victoria in 1982 as part of a wider package of organisational reforms. The scheme was replaced with a performance bonus system in 1990. This case study examines both schemes.

The merit pay scheme

The 1982 reforms included new organisational structures, planning and accountability systems, and selection processes. The reforms built on a clear set of goals and management principles, emphasising a strategic outlook focused on achievement of results; development of flexible and responsive senior management; more responsive and effective agencies; continuing improvement of agency performance; negotiation of results to be achieved between managers and agencies; and assessment of the contributions of managers to the agencies. Within this framework, merit pay was expected to contribute to a strategic outlook, flexible and responsive management and the improvement of agency performance.

Performance appraisal

The planning and appraisal system that provides the link between management performance and pay is formalised in an annual performance improvement plan (PIP), which includes jobs goals, performance indicators and verifiable performance standards for each of three broadly-defined key results areas (KRAs): Program Delivery, Program Support and General Management. Each manager is expected to identify around four more specific KRAs within each of the three broadly-defined groups, for inclusion in his or her performance plan. For each KRA included in his or her plan, the manager develops a number of verifiable performance standards that define what is considered effective performance over an agreed time period for the KRA. To ensure their contribution to agreed organisational objectives, performance plans are developed as subsets of corporate plans and in discussion with other senior managers.

The verifiable performance standards provide the objective base for annual appraisals. Performance indicators must be directly observable or recorded by some measurement system, but it is not deemed necessary that indicators be quantitative and many of those included in performance plans are descriptions of behavioural processes or deadlines for the completion of specified tasks.

Managers are assessed annually, on or around 30 September, against their performance plans and their pay levels are adjusted accordingly. The assessment of performance leading to the performance pay decision is a two-stage process and at each stage there are two optional methods of assessment. The options chosen are applied to all management positions within an agency.

The first stage in the assessment process includes a discussion of the manager's achievements against the agreed standards and a rating of overall performance for each of the KRAs in his or her improvement plan by a supervisor. Two options are available for rating performance:

a) Direct application of an eleven-point performance rating scale in which all factors relating to the manager's performance against the agreed performance standards are combined in a single judgement;

b) Use of a three-factor method in which the rating on the eleven-point scale is based solely on results achieved against agreed performance standards. This is then weighted by the "degree of difficulty" and "degree of assistance received" to arrive at a final rating for the KRA.

The second stage of the assessment process converts the ratings for the individual KRAs into a single summary rating which is then submitted to the Chief Administrator for approval before being used to determine the manager's performance pay. The two options for deciding the summary rating of a manager's performance are:

a) A whole-of-job assessment in which the supervisor uses the KRA ratings and other qualitative information about the manager's performance to rate his or her performance on the same eleven-point performance scale used for each of the KRAs;

b) A weighted average assessment in which the individual KRA ratings are each weighted by an importance factor, agreed when the improvement plan is negotiated, and then combined arithmetically to give an average score. If all KRAs were given the same importance rating the overall performance score would be the simple average of the KRA ratings.

Under the merit pay scheme, the summary eleven-point performance ratings were then converted to a five-point scale and matched to a five-level pay range for the manager's grade, as shown in Table A2.1. In principle, every Senior Executive Service (SES) officer received the level 1 or base pay for his or her position. Payment at levels 2, 3, 4 or 5, was intended as bonuses which depended upon a manager's performance score for the year. This "bonus" was paid as part of regular salary over the year following the award. If the manager's performance score dropped in later years, then his or her salary would drop to the lower performance pay level. Therefore, the salary increment above the base rate for each position was, technically, at risk each year. However, very few managers actually had their performance pay level decreased as a result of performance appraisals.

In agencies with ten or more SES managers, the salary budget was set at the midpoint for all SES positions within the agency. Therefore, the performance pay levels had to be maintained at an average level of 3. If the performance payments based on the ratings of managers' performance took the agency above an average level of 3, the Chief

Table A2–1. **Performance pay levels for SES, prior to October 1990**

	Annual performance appraisal rating				
	1	2	3	4	5
	Base pay		Performance pay range		
	Australian dollars				
SES-1	48 992	50 920	52 850	54 778	56 709
SES-2	53 269	55 373	57 475	59 578	61 681
SES-3	57 079	59 336	61 593	63 851	66 108
SES-4	61 182	63 606	66 029	68 454	70 877
SES-5	65 662	68 221	70 781	73 341	75 900
SES-6	71 217	74 008	78 798	79 590	82 379
SES-7	76 807	79 819	82 829	85 843	88 855
SES-8	82 389	85 626	88 861	94 433	95 331

Administrator had to alter the relationship between the performance scores and the pay levels to maintain the average and meet the salary budget. A 1989 survey by the Victoria Public Service Board found that more than a quarter of managers had missed pay increments because of the averaging requirement, and over a third of these had had an initial assessment reduced more than once.

Evaluation of the performance pay system

Two surveys of senior managers in the Victorian Public Service, one conducted in 1986 (Hede and Cook, 1987) and one in 1989 have provided some measures of the effectiveness of the merit pay scheme. The 1989 survey, conducted by the Public Service Board of Victoria, was the basis for a redesigned bonus scheme, described below. The 1989 survey also provides a base-line for assessing the impact of the new bonus scheme on the attitudes and work planning processes of managers.

The results of these surveys reveal that the performance planning system which underpins performance pay has been successfully implemented and has been integrated with the corporate planning systems in most agencies. From this evidence it could be inferred that the goal of developing a focus on strategies and outcomes has been achieved and, to the degree that performance standards focus on these issues, senior management has become more flexible and responsive. No data were collected which could be used to establish the impact of the system on agency performance.

A weakness of the system is the lack of regular review of plans and feedback against goals during the annual cycle. Widespread difficulty in the development of verifiable performance standards is another major weakness in the system, which undermines the perceived objectivity of performance ratings used to allocate bonuses.

Turning to the pay-for-performance system, the results are less positive. The clear perception of a link between performance and pay has not been established in the minds of many managers, although the perception has become more widely spread since 1986. The complexity of the scoring system and the averaging requirements to meet salary budgets both created ambiguity in the perceived relationship between performance and pay. The percentage of staff who fully understood the system remained relatively low for a system that had been in operation seven years. The percentage of managers either fully or partially satisfied with the performance pay system was a low 41 per cent in 1989 and had dropped since 1986. A major cause of the dissatisfaction with performance pay was the averaging requirement which limited the number of increments that could be paid in any agency.

In the absence of direct measures of performance and experimental controls for factors other than performance pay, it cannot be stated with any confidence that performance pay has had any impact on the effectiveness of public sector agencies in Victoria. Confidence in any claims regarding the performance benefits of the scheme is also undermined by the clear failure to establish an unambiguous link between performance and pay in the minds of participating managers.

The problems and dissatisfaction with the performance pay system were, at least partly, due to a lack of discrimination between different levels of performance in annual appraisal ratings. The survey results for 1989 indicate that there was a steady, almost automatic, progression from level one to level three and then, because of the budget constraints of a level three average, more limited opportunities for progression beyond that point.

It is quite possible that the failure of the system to discriminate effectively between different levels of performance was related to the difficulty experienced in establishing verifiable performance standards. Without objective measures of performance, supervising managers are less confident in their relative judgements about different managers and are more likely to adopt a lenient, non-discriminatory approach when rating overall performance. Among supervising managers included in the 1989 survey it was widely believed that assessment standards were applied inconsistently by different supervisors within agencies.

New bonus system

Despite the problems with the existing system, the overwhelming majority of managers surveyed in 1989 (83 per cent) felt that there should be some link between their performance and pay. Added to this was the acceptance of the performance-planning system and links between individual management plans and organisational goals. Therefore, on the basis of the 1989 review, the Victorian Public Service Board decided to revise the performance pay scheme and replaced merit increments with annual cash bonuses equal to either 0 per cent, 5 per cent, 10 per cent or 15 per cent of total employment costs. The relationship between annual appraisal ratings and bonuses is shown in Table A2.2. Under the new scheme, there are four, instead of five, levels of reward and managers who receive an appraisal rating of either 1 or 2 will get no bonus. Under the old scheme managers who obtained a rating of 2 received an increment above base salary.

The revision of the performance pay scheme was accompanied by an upgrading of the SES pay scales and a move to total employment costing for the purpose of calculating bonuses. The total employment costs used to establish the base for calculating bonuses

Table A2–2. **Bonus system for Victorian SES, commencing October 1990**

Performance rating	Descriptive anchors	Bonus levels: % TEC[1]	Bonus levels: Cash[2]
1	Unsatisfactory	0	Nil
2	Marginal/Development required	0	Nil
3	Fully Effective	5	$ 3 367-$ 5 155
4	Superior	10	$ 6 735-$ 10 310
5	Outstanding	15	$ 10 102-$ 15 465

1. TEC = Total Employment Cost
2. Australian dollar equivalents for the lowest and highest SES classes.

include base salary, expense of office allowance, cost of a private motor car where provided, and the employer contributions to superannuation.

In the transition to the bonus scheme all managers were placed on one of two salary scales based on their performance appraisal rating for the final appraisal period under the old scheme. Managers who received a performance appraisal rating of 1 (unsatisfactory) were placed on a salary scale which was 3.4 per cent lower than the scale for managers who received ratings of 2, 3, 4 or 5. Following full introduction of the new system, all managers will be transferred to the new higher salary scale. Managers whose existing performance pay levels were above the new salary scales were guaranteed continued payment at that level for three years if their total remuneration, including performance bonuses, does not exceed their existing pay levels. This, of course, is a further acknowledgement that the previous system was a merit increment system and not a bonus system as intended.

The averaging requirement for the distribution of bonuses is retained but in a different form. Each agency will have an annual performance bonus budget set at 7.5 per cent of total SES employment costs. Within this budget limit, chief executives will have the discretion to distribute bonuses among their managers at the levels shown in Table A2.2. The joint constraints of a 7.5 per cent budget limit and fixed bonus levels will force a minimum discrimination of at least two levels of bonuses (e.g. 50 per cent at 5 per cent and 50 per cent at 10 per cent) for managers within an agency. However, with the lump-sum payment, it is hoped that bonuses will be more clearly viewed by managers as being at risk each year and that chief executives will have more latitude in awarding a range of bonus payouts in any given year.

Other changes relating to managerial pay that were introduced along with the changes to the performance pay scheme will reduce the pressure for a central tendency in bonus payments under the new scheme. These include:

a) Recruitment and retention loadings of up to 15 per cent, or more with the approval of the Remuneration Review Committee, for approved occupational categories or positions. These loadings will be based on market assessments of the comparative worth of the occupational category or position. They will run for up to two years and will be renewable through additional applications to the Remuneration Review Committee. Previously, chief executives had to use merit increments for recruitment and retention of staff in positions covered by the new loadings;

b) Limited-term appointments can be used for special projects and positions with reporting relationships to the Minister. The employment contracts for these appointments can run for up to five years and include a loading of up to 10 per cent. Managers on limited-term contracts can still qualify for bonuses. Up to 15 per cent of the SES positions within an agency can be appointed to limited-term contracts;

c) Appraisal process reforms which may help to strengthen the relationship between pay and performance include a greater emphasis on the use of quantitative and qualitative indicators that provide measures of efficiency, effectiveness or equity outcomes. A second change which should help strengthen the perceived link between pay and performance is replacement of the old eleven-point rating scale used for overall appraisals of performance with the five-point scale used in determining bonus allocations.

Note

1. This case study was prepared by Professor Robert Wood, Head, Department of Management, University of Western Australia. A longer version of the study appears in *Performance Pay and Related Compensation Practices in Australian State Public Sector Organisations,* Public Management Occasional Papers, Paris, OECD, 1991.

DEPARTMENT OF HEALTH AND WELFARE, CANADA MANAGEMENT CATEGORY PERFORMANCE PAY PLAN

Background

The Department of National Health and Welfare is responsible for the promotion and preservation of the health, social security and social welfare of the people of Canada over which the Parliament of Canada has jurisdiction. A significant amount of departmental activity involves collaboration with provincial and territorial authorities. The need for joint activity in certain areas arises from the constitutional division of responsibilities and the existence of federal programs that assist provinces and territories to maintain their own health and social service programs. The policy environment of National Health and Welfare is highly complex due to the diversity of the department's interests, the multiple clienteles, the emergence of new clienteles and the need to keep up with changing societal needs.

The Deputy Minister (head of the department) provides strong leadership and one of her primary objectives within the performance review process is to foster a greater sense of "corporateness" within the department while focusing efforts on continuing to improve operational effectiveness. The Deputy Minister recognises the importance of people in achieving performance and treats them in a way that makes them feel valued; she gives high priority to "managing downward" and places as much authority as possible in the hands of front line employees and managers.

Ninety per cent of the total departmental budget and approximately 45 per cent of person years are allocated to regional operations. Various programmes are delivered from 1 200 regional locations of which approximately 600 belong to the Medical Services Branch. In most regions there are seven distinct programme operational units, each reporting independently to Ottawa. The geographical districts covered by the seven programme areas vary from region to region.

Within Health and Welfare Canada, 163 employees are covered by the Management Category; 22 of these managers are in the regions. The ratio of Management Category to total staff is 2 per cent. This case study describes how the Management Category performance pay plan is operated in the Department of Health and Welfare. It should be read in conjunction with the description of the Management Category Salary Administration Plan contained in Annex 1.

Performance appraisal

The internal performance criteria used for assessing senior managers are a combination of operational and corporate objectives. The corporate objectives have been established by the Deputy Minister and are communicated by her to all managers. Managers are rated on a five-point scale, according to the following global rating definitions:

Outstanding – exceeds all job requirements (1)

Consistently demonstrated exceptional performance in all areas of his/her own responsibility and enhanced both the contributions and quality of working life of others. Results far exceeded normal expectations and were achieved in an exemplary manner. Showed outstanding personal effort, creativity, initiative and leadership (where applicable) as well as very sound decision making and reasonable risk taking. Created and took advantage of opportunities to make some very significant contributions to the organisation, at times setting new standards of excellence.

Superior – meets all job requirements and exceeds most (2)

Excelled in most key job activities and required skills. The employee also demonstrated a very high level of quality and judgement in decision making and leadership. Made significant contributions to the success of the organisation.

Fully Satisfactory Plus – meets all job requirements and exceeds some (3)

Has consistently performed better than the accepted standards for the job, showed excellent qualities on occasion and good, solid performance at all other times. Has made use of strengths to very good advantage.

Fully Satisfactory – meets job requirements (4)

Good solid performance. Has achieved the requirements of the position. Demonstrated sound judgement and responsibility and can be counted on to perform tasks effectively, on time and to required standards. Made a solid contribution to the success of the unit/organisation.

Needs Improvement (5)

Although performance in many areas of the job was adequate, there were significant areas in which the job requirements were not effectively met. Specific improvements are required to come up to acceptable standards of performance. Management believes that this employee is capable of making the necessary improvements in his/her performance.

In line with Treasury Board policy, each branch of the department has a quota of 30 per cent for ''Superior'' ratings, based on branch population of Management Category and equivalent employees entitled to performance pay. The Deputy Minister holds in a reserve some of the quota. There is also a limitation of 20 per cent for ''Fully Satisfactory Plus'' ratings.

Two departmental committees are involved in administering the performance appraisal system. The Branch Executive Committee (BEC), composed of all those reporting to the branch head and including representatives from Communications, Finance, and Personnel, reviews the performance appraisal reports completed by supervisors, and confirms the global performance ratings to be sent to the higher committee for approval. The Departmental Executive Committee (DEC), chaired by the Deputy Minister and composed of the Senior Assistant Deputy Minister, all Assistant Deputy Ministers, the

Director General of Personnel Administration, the Director General of Communications and the Chief Counsel, approves the ratings and reviews issues relating to management of the senior cadre.

The performance appraisal cycle in 1990 was as follows:

November 1990, DEC approved the following:

i) modified global rating definitions to incorporate a definition for ''Fully Satisfactory Plus'';

ii) a determination as to how performance pay will be awarded, including the distribution of quotas for ''Fully Satisfactory Plus'' and ''Superior'' ratings.

8 February 1991 – Call letters explaining the modifications and process for this year go out to all Management Category employees and equivalents entitled to performance pay with an April 15 1991 due date.

Phase I – BEC review committees

15 April to 10 May 1991 – Branch level committees review the performance appraisal reports and confirm the global rating to be approved by the DEC. Employees concerned can be informed of their proposed rating once the Phase I level committee review has been completed. BEC review committees will also confirm the recommended training needs and career planning for executive and feeder group employees. This information will be summarised for discussion at the DEC review committee in Phase II.

Phase II – DEC review committee

15-16 May 1991 – Ratings for Management Category and equivalent employees that report to branch heads are confirmed. If required, requests for ''Superior'' ratings from the reserve are considered. An overview of where we are in terms of the age of the population, language proficiency, corporate training priorities, promotability and reassignment plans are reviewed for this group.

Career development and training needs for employees in feeder groups to the Management Category that are ready for a promotion or in need of additional developmental assignments will also be reviewed.

30 May 1991 – Branch heads' performance ratings are confirmed and 1991-92 objectives provided. Letters are sent to employees. Feedback is provided to employees and their appraisals are returned for final sign off. Pay action is initiated.

30 October 1991 – A review of progress made on our human resources plans for all Management Category and equivalent employees will be conducted. Dependent on the evaluation process of this exercise other options for changes will be reviewed, along with any impact of Treasury Board decisions regarding the distribution of performance pay.

Concluding remarks

An evaluation of the departmental performance management process revealed that whilst the vast majority of our managers felt the departmental system worked well from a corporate perspective, they received insufficient feedback about their performance.

The insertion of ''Fully Satisfactory Plus'' as a global rating seems to have alleviated the previous problems caused by the Treasury Board Secretariat's 30 per cent limitation on ''Superior'' ratings. There is still, however, an internal practice of rotating ''Superior'' ratings. ''Outstanding'' is rarely utilised.

The introduction of a lump-sum bonus for ''Fully Satisfactory'' ratings was well received by employees, but some concern was raised at the DEC that the bonuses might become disguised economic adjustments. For this reason the amount of the bonus attached to a rating of ''Fully Satisfactory'' was reduced.

DEPARTMENT OF TRANSPORT, CANADA PERFORMANCE PAY FOR EXECUTIVES AND SENIOR MANAGERS

Background

Transport Canada is a large decentralised department. Four groups within the department administer airports, aviation, marine and surface transportation operations. The department's headquarters organisation in Ottawa includes groups responsible for security and emergency planning, policy and co-ordination, and review, finance and personnel programmes. A number of crown corporations report to Parliament through the Minister of Transport.

There are approximately 19 500 employees at Transport Canada, 4 500 of whom are located at headquarters. Of the 285 Management Category employees, 90 are located in the regions. The ratio across the department is one Management Category employee to 68 employees. This case study describes how the Management Category performance pay plan operates within the Department of Transport. It should be read in conjunction with the description of the Management Category Salary Administration Plan contained in Annex 1.

Performance review

In Transport Canada, the Performance Review and Employee Appraisal System for members of the Management Category covers the period 1 April to 31 March.

Performance reviews are carried out by Assistant Deputy Ministers (ADMs) of the groups in question. These reviews are held during the month of May in Ottawa and cover all regional and headquarters senior managers (SMs) and executives (EXs) except EX-3s and those EXs reporting directly to the ADM. EX-3s and EXs who report directly to an ADM are reviewed by the Deputy Minister (DM) in June.

Group review committees, comprised of the group's executive management team, are responsible for:

- ensuring that the employee and supervisor have correctly interpreted and fulfilled their obligations in the application of the performance review and appraisal system;
- ensuring that procedures established for the program have been followed and correctly applied;

– evaluating the objectivity and relevance of the supervisor's observations, comments and recommendations;
– ensuring that the supervisor's observations, comments and recommendations are supported by documentation and/or specific examples;
– ensuring that training and developmental recommendations are justified, realistic and capable of being followed up in the next review period.

Following the group review committee stage, the appraisals are reviewed by the DM and a committee consisting of EX-4s and above reporting to the DM.

In order not to exceed the Treasury Board Secretariat's (TBS) 30 per cent limitation on the award of ''Superior'' and ''Outstanding'' ratings, it has been necessary to stipulate to the ADM of each group the number of performance reports that can be appraised at ''Superior'' and above. As each group carries out its review in isolation from the others, complete figures of the number of ''Superior'' and above ratings across the whole department are not available until the DM's review, which is the last one held. If the 30 per cent limit has been exceeded, the DM's review will look more closely at the ''Superior'' and ''Outstanding'' ratings. In cases where the review committee disagrees with a performance rating or finds insufficient justification for it, it will return the appraisal report to the supervisor for additional justification of the rating. Should the committee still disagree, it will change the rating and provide a written rationale for so doing.

Ratings are lowered or raised only if there is a clear indication that the employee's performance warrants such a decision. In Transport Canada no rating has ever been lowered just so that the department can remain within its 30 per cent limit.

Performance appraisal criteria

Up to 1991 employees had their performance rated on a seven-point scale, divided into three sectors.

iii) Performance exceeds overall requirements:
7 Exceeds all requirements;
6 Meets all requirements and exceeds most;
iv) Performance meets requirements:
5 Meets all requirements and exceeds some;
4 Meets all requirements;
3 Meets requirements but needs improvement in some areas;
v) Performance does not meet requirements:
2 Does not meet some requirements;
1 Does not meet most requirements.

A four-point rating scale (Superior, Fully Satisfactory, Satisfactory and Unsatisfactory) has been in operation since the Spring 1991 appraisal period.

For the purposes of assessing performance, ''requirements'' means goals which have been agreed to by the manager and the supervisor at the commencement of the appraisal period.

In determining an employee's performance rating, the supervisor takes into account how well the employee achieved the established goals, as well as any unusual situations or circumstances which arose during the assessment period. The assessment of performance also reflects the manager's contribution in carrying out such managerial functions as getting things done through others, formulating policy, planning and designing programs and evaluating their impact and effectiveness.

Administrative process

The performance appraisal process and the performance pay process are separate events. The overall administration of the performance pay exercise is carried out by the department's Compensation Division, under the general direction of the Assistant Deputy Minister, Personnel. The performance pay process is discussed each year with the DM and the members of her senior management team (*i.e.* group heads). Recommendations for group head performance pay awards are made to the DM for approval.

The administrative process begins with the determination of the size of the eligible population, the calculation of the departmental budget (based on TBS guidelines) and the allocation of a summary performance rating for each Management Category employee. The rating is provided to the Compensation Division upon completion of the performance review exercise. As the formula for determining the departmental performance pay budget is based, in part, on the principle that not more than 30 per cent of the eligible population will be rated above ''Fully Satisfactory'', and given that at the time of the performance appraisal review process steps are taken to ensure that the department has not exceeded its 30 per cent limitation, the performance pay exercise becomes a largely mechanical process.

The philosophy of the department is to grant employees the greatest percentage award possible while remaining within the prescribed TBS guidelines for performance pay levels and within the fixed departmental budget. For example, if the TBS guidelines suggest a performance pay range of 6 to 8 per cent for ''Superior'' performance ratings, the department will attempt to provide an 8 per cent award to all employees rated as ''Superior'', regardless of their group or classification level. Consequently, group heads have the flexibility to reduce the size of the awards for their employees, but not to increase them.

The size of performance payments is reduced when the departmental budget limitations will not permit the maximum performance award or where, in the opinion of the group head, there should be a monetary distinction made between employees with the same global performance rating. Where the departmental budget will not permit the allocation of the maximum performance pay awards to all eligible employees, the practice is to reduce the size of payments until the total value of the performance awards comes within the allocated departmental budget, although this has proved to be unnecessary for the past two performance pay exercises.

Group heads may reduce the performance awards of their employees and reallocate the balance of their budget to one or several individuals, so long as the awards do not exceed the TBS guidelines. Another alternative is for the group head to reduce the size of an individual's award without providing for a corresponding increase in the value of the awards for employees with similar global performance ratings. These two practices did occur during the 1989-90 performance pay exercise, but the size of the differentials is so small that it is not considered to be a significant motivating factor to encourage exceptional performance. The administrative performance pay practice is made public, but the value of individual awards is kept confidential.

Payment of performance awards for the Management Category is considered a top priority by senior management and every effort is made to have the performance pay exercise completed and employees paid as quickly as possible. Once the recommended performance awards have been approved by each group head, regional personnel offices are informed by the Chief of Compensation of the value of the performance award and are requested to take payment action. The regional personnel offices are not informed of the employee's performance rating.

The introduction by the Treasury Board in 1990 of a lump sum bonus for "Fully Satisfactory" performance is considered a positive step by senior management. Within Transport Canada, a number of the employees entering the senior management cadre at the SM level come from professional/technical groups with pay bands that are competitive with or exceed the SM job rate. As a result, many of these employees enter the SM classification at, near or exceeding the job rate and in previous years, unless rated as "Superior" or "Outstanding", were not eligible for performance pay. The SM population at the time of the 1989-90 performance pay exercise was 166 employees, 72 per cent of whom were rated "Fully Satisfactory". Of these employees, 83 per cent reached the job rate prior to the allocation of performance pay. As a result of the additional flexibility built into the plan, these employees were eligible to receive a performance award. Had changes to the performance pay plan not been made, most would not have received any performance pay.

Evaluation and monitoring

There has not been a formal internal evaluation of Management Category performance pay since its inception.

The performance pay plan, up until 1990, was applied in a mechanistic fashion with very little discretion being exercised. The addition of bonuses for "Fully Satisfactory" performance in 1990 increased the scope for discretion. Even so, this additional discretion results only in recognising varying degrees of performance with salary increments of less than 1 per cent. The continued application of the "30 per cent rule" is viewed as an unnecessary barrier on management's ability to exercise discretion in the way performance awards are allocated. The benefits of the plan are uncertain.

The cost to management staff of administering the plan can be measured in hours per annum. The cost to the Personnel Branch is less than one person-year. There has been an additional investment of perhaps $50 000 for computer equipment and programs to perform the calculations and produce reports.

In the view of the department, Treasury Board monitoring and evaluation should be directed at determining the extent to which the plan allows performance to be recognised and compensated and the degree to which it serves to encourage exceptional performance and commitment from employees.

DEPARTMENT OF JUSTICE, CANADA
LAW GROUP PAY PLAN

Background

Performance pay has applied to senior counsel from 1963. In 1981, a performance pay scheme was introduced for the entire Law Group. This plan recognised three classification levels and five pay levels. In 1986 it was amended to recognise six pay levels, since when it has remained unchanged. The possibility of aligning the Law Group pay plan to the Management Category pay plan is currently under study within the Department of Justice. This case study should be read in conjunction with the description of the Management Category Salary Administration Plan contained in Annex 1.

The objectives of the pay plan are to provide performance incentives to members of the Law Group and to attract and retain capable legal talent within the government.

Description of the pay plan

Each of the six pay levels corresponds to a salary range defined by a minimum and a job rate, which represents the maximum attainable. Progress through the range is based on performance. For lawyers at the lowest pay level (LA1), performance increases are implemented twice a year. For all other levels, increases are implemented once a year. Individual performance pay outcomes are not made public.

The Law Group generally receives an annual economic range adjustment which is passed on to each lawyer. As of 1990, the cost of living increase was not implemented at the same time as the performance adjustment (1 April for performance and 1 June for the economic increase).

Whilst it is not formally part of the pay plan, the Treasury Board has insisted that the Law Group adhere to a 30 per cent limit on the awarding of ''Superior'' and ''Outstanding'' ratings. Those who are at the job rate (maximum) and who receive a ''Superior'' or ''Outstanding'' rating are given a cash performance bonus. Those who are rated below the ''Superior'' level and who are at the job rate do not receive a cash bonus. Approximately 35 per cent of lawyers are currently at the job rate.

Performance appraisal

When the departmental performance review and employee appraisal (PREA) system was amended in 1988, the department decided to establish objectives for the system which related specifically to the goals of improving employee performance, motivation and communication between employees and their supervisors. The link to the performance pay system is not referred to in the PREA policy and this has been identified as a weakness of the policy. The policy is currently under review within the department to correct this deficiency.

The global rating awarded on the appraisal form is used as the basis of the performance award. The link between this global rating and the performance award is mechanistic (*i.e.* a ''Superior'' rating yields a 7 per cent performance pay increase or bonus).

Employees have the right to appeal their performance ratings.

Flexibility and controls

Structural changes to the pay plan must be approved by the Treasury Board. The Board is also able, as noted previously, to impose limitations that are not formally in the pay plan (the application of the 30 per cent quota).

Apart from reporting requirements, central agencies are not involved in the implementation of the performance pay scheme. In-house monitoring includes a review of the distribution of ratings to ensure adherence to the 30 per cent requirement. Additionally, an annual report containing all salary adjustments is sent to the Treasury Board, which sends an annual report to the Deputy Minister on the departmental implementation of the performance pay plan.

The current pay plan does not limit the amount which may be spent on performance awards. Amounts are limited by virtue of the application of the 30 per cent rule. In 1989, 2.54 per cent of base salary was spent on the scheme.

Costs and benefits of the performance pay plan

The performance pay scheme, particularly the application of the 30 per cent rule, causes significant problems for the department. Lawyers contend that the nature of their work makes it difficult if not impossible for management to assess adequately their performance. Following the annual performance review and employee appraisal process (PREA) it is customary for approximately 3 per cent of the lawyers to formally appeal their ratings, with a further 5 to 10 per cent, while not formally appealing, to complain concerning their rating. There is a sizeable constituency who believes that the annual PREA exercise and the grief it creates is not worth the cost of the program and that the lawyers should move to a lock-step pay system. It should be pointed out that the promotion system for practitioners is fundamentally linked to the PREA system, (*i.e.* a lawyer must have two out of the previous five appraisals at the ''Superior'' or ''Outstanding'' level to be eligible for promotion).

The current scheme may have a positive effect on performance for the 30 per cent who receive increases or bonuses; however for the remaining 70 per cent, many of whom are at the job rate and receive nothing, the system is a major disincentive. During the two to three month period when ratings are being finalised and when performance pay awards are being delivered, there is an overall decrease in productivity. Time spent hearing the grievances at the four levels of the grievance process also detracts from productivity.

An additional problem with the grievance process is that if an employee presents a good case to have his or her rating amended to the ''Superior'' level, the manager is unable to make this adjustment without putting the Department's performance vis-a-vis the 30 per cent rule in jeopardy.

One of the features of the Management Category pay plan (described in Annex 1) is that it enables bonuses to be paid to ''Fully Satisfactory'' performers. It is felt that the addition of this feature would alleviate many of the problems associated with the current Law Group plan.

DEPARTMENT OF POSTS AND TELEGRAPHS, DENMARK
PERFORMANCE-RELATED PAY SCHEME FOR MANAGERS

Since 1 April 1989, a system of performance-related allowances has been in operation in the Posts and Telegraph Service. The scheme applies to all heads of services, including postmasters. This note provides a brief description of the scheme.

Criteria for granting allowances, or increasing existing allowances, are as follows:

i) Achievement of specified results with regard to service, quality, marketing, economy and productivity;

ii) Rational and economic organisation, including appropriate planning and distribution of tasks and responsibility;

iii) Engaging, motivating and developing staff; result-oriented and service-oriented management; fostering co-operation;

iv) Economic criteria;

v) Active management development.

On appointment, heads of service receive only the basic salary for the position. The question of allocation of allowances is evaluated after the person has been in the position for eight to twelve months. Allowances are paid for periods of between one and three years, and may be withdrawn if performance (*i.e.* achievement of specified goals) deteriorates. Unallocated allowances (due to vacancies or failure to achieve goals) are included in the performance pay pool and may be allocated to others, or to the same person later, when goals are reached.

In 1990, expenditure on allowances to postmasters, who number about 70 in all, amounted to about 1 million Danish Kroner.

Neither the managers concerned nor the unions have reacted negatively to the introduction of performance pay. In agreement with the unions, details are being worked out for applying the scheme to section leaders of district post offices.

In addition to the performance allowance system for managers, Posts and Telegraph services use bonus pools for sales consultants, related to achievement of good results (in quality and quantity).

FEDERAL POSTAL AND TELECOMMUNICATION SERVICES (DEUTSCHE BUNDESPOST), GERMANY EFFICIENCY BONUSES

Efficiency bonuses for the direct recognition of individual achievement were introduced in 1989, in the context of a reorganisation of the Postal and Telecommunication Services (Deutsche Bundespost) into a corporate legal structure. This note provides a short description of the scheme.

Efficiency bonuses were introduced because it was felt that the exposure to market competition resulting from the reorganisation of the Deutsche Bundespost made it necessary to offer additional pay incentives to staff. The individual bonuses provided under this scheme are intended to reward achievements which are considerably in excess of regular demands with regard to quality, economic efficiency and the amount of work done.

There are several types of bonuses:

a) Bonus for outstanding quality of work where an individual's clearly identifiable working results show that his or her achievements are considerably above average, as measured against standard assessment criteria, and better than the achievements of comparable civil servants;

b) Bonus for particular economic and managerial efficiency where previous results in terms of the revenue/expenditure ratio are exceeded significantly, (*i.e.* where outstanding sales increases and operating results are achieved);

c) Bonus for excellent results in negotiating contracts;

d) Bonus for outstanding work output where additional achievements are produced that are considerably above the average and can be quantified.

Such bonuses must not exceed the highest basic salary of the next but one salary scale. They are normally granted for a period of one year initially and may be retained for up to three years (in exceptional cases, for up to five years). At the end of this period the bonus payment must be suspended for at least one year.

Expenditure on bonuses must not exceed 2 per cent of the total pay expenditure for civil servants in the Deutsche Bundespost.

It is intended that the bonus system will be applied *mutatis mutandis* to office employees and manual workers of Deutsche Bundespost as well as to established civil servants.

In practice, the application of the scheme has proved difficult and up to now bonuses have only been granted in a few cases. It is therefore not possible to make an assessment of the scheme at this stage. However, the Federal Minister of Posts and Telecommunications intends to ensure that the implementation of the bonus system is accompanied by an evaluation exercise.

INDUSTRIAL DEVELOPMENT AUTHORITY, IRELAND PERFORMANCE-RELATED PAY SCHEME

Background

The Industrial Development Authority has national responsibility for the furtherance of industrial development in Ireland. The performance-related pay scheme was introduced in 1987, replacing an earlier variable increment scheme which had been in operation since 1970. The main objective of the scheme is to enable management to reward, and thereby further motivate, staff who make an above-average contribution assessed against predetermined criteria. The introduction of the new scheme was regarded as particularly important because of the rigidity of the previous salary system and the fact that a large number of staff were on the maximum point of their scales.

The performance assessment process

The assessment process commences in the Autumn when managers are required to carry out a performance appraisal of each member of their staff and to complete a performance record form, which is countersigned by the staff member concerned. The purpose of this formal, written approach is:

- To ensure that performance is reviewed and two-way feedback takes place in a formal way at least once a year;
- To assess the overall skill levels in the organisation and the areas where further development may be required;
- To provide a written input into the annual salary review and merit pay process and into the system for selecting staff for promotion and transfer.

Salary review boards meet in November/early-December to consider the performance of each staff member and to make decisions about merit payments. The review board for higher staff comprises the Managing Director and the executive directors. For more junior staff, the review board comprises the Executive Director with responsibility for personnel matters, the Personnel Manager and the relevant Divisional Manager.

The factors taken into account in deciding on whether or not a merit payment should be made are as follows:

- The extent to which specific results have been achieved as a direct consequence of the actions of the individual, given the difficulty of the tasks and the time scale for completion;
- Commitment and application displayed in the performance of work;

- Sustained performance which is considerably above that normally expected from staff members, having regard to their grade;
- Sustained contribution to the enhancement of quality and courtesy of the service provided to clients (internal and external);
- Sustained accuracy and reliability of work, coupled with demonstrated initiative and willingness to exploit the full potential of work situations;
- In relation to management grades, the competence displayed in managing people with maximum effectiveness, including leadership qualities, motivation and development of staff, delegation, clarity of work objectives, quality service to clients, financial control and use made of technology;
- The extent to which an individual co-operated with other people in the work group and across the organisation in order to achieve organisational objectives.

In the context of these criteria, the review boards base their decisions on:

- Recommendations made by division managers. Prior to making their recommendations, division managers consult with the other managers in their division;
- The annual appraisal forms;
- Details of salary points and length of service in grades, provided by Personnel Division.

When the review process is completed, Personnel Division writes to people awarded merit payments prior to the Christmas break, informing them of the board decision. Staff members may discuss the allocation of awards with their managers, who will inform them of merit payments being made at the staff member's level in the division.

Types of award

The review boards may grant merit increments, which become part of base salary, or lump-sum awards. Merit increments are available to staff who are not on the maximum point of their scale and who achieve the required level of performance. There is a set merit increment for each scale.

Lump-sum awards are paid to staff reaching the required performance standard, and may apply to not more than 20 per cent of staff at any level, subject to the overall cost of the awards not exceeding 1 per cent of the payroll budget. Awards of either 10 per cent or 5 per cent of base salary may be made, depending on level of performance, with the majority of awards at the 5 per cent level. All staff members are eligible to be considered for lump-sum awards. However, in view of the restricted number of awards that may be made, the review boards take account of other forms of recognition a staff member may have received in the recent past in the form, for instance, of a merit increment.

The number of lump-sum awards made in 1990 is shown in Table A2.3. The breakdown by value of the awards in 1990 was as follows:

Less than £1,000	20
£1,000-£2,000	52
£2,000+	24

Table A2–3. **Number of lump-sum awards by size and level of staff in 1990**

	Number of awards by size			Number of staff at level
	5%	10%	Total	
Senior management	4	8	12	57
Middle management	17	7	24	127
Executives	28	13	41	199
Secretarial/clerical	6	4	10	93
Services	1	–	1	14
Executives overseas	8	–	8	40
Total	64	32	96	530

General assessment of the scheme

The Authority is strongly convinced of the benefits of the scheme, particularly as a means of giving recognition and reward in a tangible and visible way to those who give above-average performance, thereby supporting and encouraging such performance in the future. They have observed a strong motivational impact on those who receive awards, but point out that this has to be set against some demotivational impact on those who also perform above average, but who do not receive an award solely because of the restriction on the number of awards that may be made.

ELECTRICITY SUPPLY BOARD, IRELAND PERFORMANCE-RELATED PAY SCHEME

Background

A performance-related bonus scheme for managers was introduced in 1990. The scheme, which is the only performance-related scheme in the company, is part of a move towards personal contracts for managers initiated in 1990, the objective of which is to emphasise the personal rather than the collective nature of managers' relationship with the company. It was also desired to introduce a new motivational tool, whereby each manager could achieve an element of his/her reward on the basis of personal performance against prescribed targets which feed into the goals of the business.

An additional factor was the introduction of performance-related pay for chief executives in all commercial State bodies in 1990, following acceptance by the government of a recommendation by the review body which advises on salaries of top public officials.

The performance pay scheme was devised by the Electricity Supply Board with some assistance from outside consultants. It applies to managers who have accepted individual contracts under which they have agreed to:

- short-term appointment
- new liabilities as to transfer
- restrictions relating to representation by unions
- a salary rate which is personal and confidential to each individual
- additional commitment in relation to extra attendance
- reduced holiday entitlement.

As 1991 was the first full year of operation of the scheme, it is too early to make an assessment of it. What follows is a short description of the scheme's main features.

Description of the scheme

Specific performance targets are set each year for, and in consultation with, the managers concerned. In this process the central principle followed is that targets must be challenging and provide for improvement in individual performance from one year to the next. A manager will be assessed as having met a target in full or not at all; there is no provision for coming close to target or for extraordinary situations limiting performance.

The eligibility of any individual manager to be considered for a bonus depends on *a)* corporate performance, *b)* team performance and *c)* individual performance. The criteria and targets against which corporate performance will be judged are established at the beginning of the year by the Chief Executive. In the case of directors, up to half of their bonus will depend on meeting the corporate targets, whereas for managers below director level one quarter of the bonus will be so dependent. For the remainder of the bonus, targets for directors are set by the Chief Executive, and for other senior managers by the directors. The Personnel Director has overall responsibility for the integrity of the scheme; everyone's targets must be agreed with that Director, as must bonus recommendations at the end of the year. The Internal Audit Service of the company is required to review and certify the whole process at the end of each year, so as to provide definitive and independent information with regard to actual performance against targets.

The bonus consists of a non-pensionable payment in the range of zero to 20 per cent of basic salary.

PRODUCTIVITY BONUS SYSTEMS IN THE SPANISH PUBLIC SERVICE

Productivity bonuses were one of several forms of supplementary pay adopted in the Spanish public service in 1984 (see Annex 1). What follows is a brief description of the operation of bonus schemes in the central government legal service, the health service and the university system.

Central government legal service

The productivity bonus is awarded every six months on the basis of the following factors:

a) The level of efficiency of the unit or the legal service as a whole.

b) Quantitative criteria relating to the workload of each lawyer:
- Number of cases of each type;
- Number of particularly important cases with an A rating;
- Total number of cases dealt with;
- Complexity of the procedure in these cases;
- Cases of major national importance.

c) Qualitative criteria relating to each lawyer's work, assessed as follows:
- The outcome of cases;
- A review of particular cases by central management;
- An assessment derived from communications between central management and the legal services;
- The obtaining of decisions setting new precedents which are considered to be advantageous from central government's point of view;
- An assessment by the central authorities or the agency of the work performed by the legal service in the unit or agency concerned.

The assessment of performance is the responsibility of the governing board of the General Directorate of the Legal Service of central government, made up of the Director-General and assistant directors. The Director-General makes an assessment of the assistant directors and submits the proposals concerning performance pay amounts to the Under Secretary of the ministry concerned, (in this case the Ministry of Justice) which adopts them.

There are no set rules concerning the size of bonuses, but a ratio of five to one must normally be maintained between the maximum and minimum levels. In exceptional cases the maximum level may be exceeded.

Public health service

For established staff working in health institutions controlled by the National Institute of Health (INSALUD), the Ministry for Health and Consumer Affairs has set up a variable system of productivity bonuses based on the assessment of performance or results.

INSALUD covers the entire health network under the control of central government, with the exception of the armed forces sector, and it acts as the management agency for the health services provided by the social security system.

The departmental directors of INSALUD are responsible for appraising the work of senior staff involved in the management of hospitals and primary health care centres located in their departments. The appraisal is based on achievement of specified objectives, and the percentage of objectives attained is calculated. Any activities not originally provided for in the programme of work, and their outcome, are also assessed. The appraisal may also contain comments on performance and suggestions for improvement. The final rating is divided into five categories ranging from exceptional to unsatisfactory.

Once the appraisals have been completed by the departmental directors, they are submitted to the general management sections of the Specialised Health Care Service or the Primary Health Care Service, as the case may be, for completion, and are then passed to the Directorate-General for Human Resources, which proposes what amounts should be paid in the form of a productivity bonus.

The appraisal is carried out during the last two months of the year and the final payment made at the end of the year, although a monthly advance is paid on this final amount.

The top management of each hospital and primary health care centre are assessed in a similar manner by their directors and they too receive an advance on their productivity bonus, the amount of which is again not finally decided until the end of the year.

The amounts of bonuses vary depending on the type and category of job, and the advance payment represents 50 per cent of the maximum amount that could be received in one year as a productivity bonus.

University teaching staff

The new system of remuneration for university teaching staff requires that the results of an appraisal of research activity should be taken into account in calculating the productivity bonus.

In 1990 the National Appraisal Committee, appointed by the Ministry of Education and Science and whose composition differs depending on the fields to be evaluated, was given the task of appraising university research activity. The identity of committee members is not made public nor are the results of each individual assessment. However, the appraisal criteria, the aspects covered and the overall results of the assessment are published.

The appraisal covers the previous six years and individual performance is rated simply as either satisfactory or unsatisfactory. The professors volunteer to undergo this appraisal, the outcome of which is, in the case of a satisfactory rating, the award of performance pay which varies in amount depending on their status (*i.e.* assistant university professors, assistant university-college professors, full university professors, full university-college professors). Performance pay is paid throughout the following six years and is adjusted regularly, until such time as a further assessment for the following six-year period determines whether it should be increased, maintained or possibly withdrawn.

TELECOMMUNICATIONS ADMINISTRATION, SWEDEN PAYMENT BY RESULTS AT THE TELECOMMUNICATION AREAS

A payment by results (PBR) system was introduced for the telecommunications areas of the Swedish Telecommunications Administration in 1984, as one of the means of improving service to customers and achieving greater efficiency. The system is based on group bonuses, which are intended to emphasise co-operation, good planning and economic consciousness. What follows is a short description of the main features of the system.

Employee participation

Employee participation is an important aspect of the PBR system. This involves, among other things, regular production meetings, where the management and the staff units give information concerning the performance measurements made in the context of the PBR system, and a detailed explanation of the connection between current production results and the PBR outcome. Regular reports are made on both the size of result bonuses and the factors which contributed to the bonus. The emphasis is on ensuring that the outcomes of the bonus system are easily understood by all, and that employees are thereby stimulated to improve the performance of their work units.

Another key feature of the system is the involvement of unions at both central and local levels in the design and operation of the scheme.

Description of the system

A central framework agreement with the union outlines the local agreement on PBR to be concluded in each telecommunication area. In the local agreement special emphasis can be given to adapting the central agreement to local conditions and possibilities in order to stimulate the achievement of good results. This means that the formulation and content of the local agreements can vary from one telecommunication area to another, depending on which activities are given priority.

All employees of a telecommunication area are covered by the framework agreement, with the exception of area directors and heads of sections, and sales staff who belong to a special bonus salary system.

A central agreement, stipulating that an annual result bonus can be paid to all employees, is concluded under the general salary agreement for civil servants within the telecommunication area. In addition, an increment relating to the annual result of the telecommunication area can be paid to area directors and heads of sections.

The central framework agreement on PBR

The central framework agreement stipulates that results in a telecommunication area should be measured for different sectors, and bonuses allocated within each sector. The framework agreement provides a basic model for the division into payment sectors, but it also allows considerable freedom for local area agreements to define how the division should be made. As a result, the composition of the PBR sectors may vary depending on the formulation of the local agreement.

Calculation of the result bonus

The size of the result bonus depends on criteria relating to levels of service, quality and general economic results. Within each PBR sector the size of the bonus is decided by means of an index based on both central and local criteria. In the framework agreement five central criteria are defined and these must always be included in local agreements. The central criteria give a maximum index of 320.

To these may be added local criteria, giving a maximum index of 80. If further local criteria are used in local agreements, the value of the central criteria is reduced. In this case the results of the local criteria will be the primary basis for the calculation of the index. Moreover, the use of further local criteria produces an increase in the maximum total index and creates the possibility of a higher result bonus than granted by the basic model defined in the framework agreement.

The criteria set out in the framework agreement for geographical telecommunication sections are as follows:

S — Fault clearing time;
F — Failure rate;
L — Delivery time;
I-U — Financial situation of the PBR sector (income and expenditure);
XT — Extra bonus (payable only when the other criteria show positive results).

For each criterion the result can be read from a table in the agreement and then translated into a certain index value. The index values of the different criteria are summed and this total, converted into the corresponding amount of money, indicates the result bonus for that particular PBR sector.

The results of the criteria S, F and L can be measured per month or per quarter, whilst the economy criterion I-U is measured every quarter.

For central sections, including the Central Telecommunication Section, the Manual Telecommunication Section, the Supply Section and staff units, the result bonus is calculated on the basis of an average of the total index for the central criteria attained by all the geographical telecommunication sections within the telecommunication area. In cases where local criteria have been given more weight and the weight of central criteria reduced accordingly, the average is still calculated on the basis of the non-reduced outcome of the central criteria. Results for the central sections may be measured either monthly or quarterly.

The rationale for basing the result bonus for central sections on the results of geographical telecommunication sections is that the planning and activities carried out by the various central units influence the results of the geographical sections.

Size of the result bonus

At present the bonus can reach a maximum of SEK 4.75 per working hour. The bonus may be paid monthly or quarterly, normally during the second month following the period for which the result is calculated. The amount of the bonus per employee is based on the number of hours worked within the relevant PBR sector. Time taken for medical examinations, information, training undertaken at the employer's request and so on may be counted as working hours for the purposes of calculation of the bonus. However, no bonus is paid for vacation time, compensatory leave or leave of absence which is not granted for trade union activities. Employees who are assigned to duties in a PBR section other than their own receive the bonus on the basis of the result index in their own sector.

In addition to this result bonus, an annual result bonus may be paid to employees in a telecommunication area, normally in December. The calculation of the annual bonus is based on a comparison between the economic results of the telecommunication area during the current budget year and the previous budget year. The economic results of the different telecommunication areas are then compared and the annual bonus, expressed in SEK per number of hours worked by the employee during the last budget year, is determined. The size of the annual bonus may, therefore, vary from one year to another, but the maximum is SEK 0.50 per hour.

An increment relating to the annual result of a telecommunication area can be paid once a year, normally in December, to the area director and the heads of sections. This increment is calculated on the basis of the average result bonus paid within the telecommunication area during that budget year.

BRITISH RAIL, UNITED KINGDOM
PERFORMANCE-RELATED PAY SCHEMES

Why "merit only" systems were introduced.

British Rail saw the move to entirely new "merit only" pay systems as one of the key planks of their human resources strategy, aimed at changing the culture of the organisation and reinforcing a "performance culture". In particular, by basing salaries entirely on merit, it was hoped to strengthen the process of performance review, and to make it more consistently well managed. In its turn, this could lead to greater involvement of managers as they played a more active part in the establishment of their objectives and the appraisal of their own performance.

There was also much dissatisfaction with the existing pay system, which was over-complex and inflexible. By 1988, over half of managers were already on the maximum of their salary scales, and this figure was expected to rise. Most managers therefore had little prospect of salary progression. At the same time, salary scales had deteriorated in relation to the market so that the scale maximum tended to represent the market worth of the job.

A further problem was lack of budgetary control over existing merit awards. The awards, which were in addition to a general increase, were made on the basis of a rating scale, and were semiautomatic, giving too little scope to line managers to reward performance, whilst giving central management no control over the size of the pay budget. It was possible for one head of department to give all or most of his managers high ratings and thus spend far more on merit pay than a colleague who assessed his managers less generously.

Finally, top management were aware of changes in pay systems elsewhere in organisations competing in the market for the same staff they wished to recruit and retain. Recruitment and retention considerations, especially for specialist staff, were accordingly important pressures for change.

Description of the performance pay system

The new scheme was introduced in 1987 for the 900 executives. It was extended to the 9 000 senior, middle and junior managers in 1988. The broad structure of the system is similar for both groups. The scheme applies throughout British Rail.

Under the scheme, staff are grouped in overlapping salary ranges with spans of 40 per cent to 50 per cent. Progression typically starts in the lower half of the range, and most staff are expected to move relatively quickly to a mid-point which represents the market rate. Beyond the mid-point, progress is possible for the better performers, with the best able to reach the top of the range. All increases are linked to performance: subject to their position in the range, staff who perform well will get above-average increases, whilst a small number of staff with poor performance may get no increase at all as there is no floor on the minimum increases which may be awarded.

For executives, there is no common date for increases in salary. Each executive has an individual contract, and pay increases are made on the anniversary of appointment to the current grade. For senior, middle and junior managers there is a single performance-related salary increase each year in July.

Performance appraisal

The possibility of moving away altogether from an appraisal system involving a formal system of classification was examined when the scheme was being introduced, but was not considered to be practicable. Appraisal is now based on a five-point rating system. The pay award to the individual is not however automatically linked to the performance rating, though that is one important factor which is taken into account.

The executives covered by the system are not considered to be typical of employees in the organisation as a whole. Most have progressed over a period of years through internal promotion, and their performance is above the average for employees generally. As a consequence, ratings are skewed to the upper end, with upwards of two-thirds receiving a level 2 rating of ''highly effective''. For the managerial groups, the proportion is much smaller.

Controlling costs

The size of the total increase in the pay bill is decided by the board of directors of British Rail. This includes the sum available for the ''merit only'' awards. Decisions on pay for individual senior, middle and junior managers are devolved through 15 regional co-ordinators who oversee 250 pay review groups across the country. (For executives, there are some 35 separate groups.) Each group may consist of a hundred or more managers or of only a handful. Discretion exists as to the amount which may be awarded to any individual, but the awards in aggregate must be kept within the budget for any department.

The process of arriving at individual awards is often complex, especially if there is a large number of managers in the review group. There are several variables, including the performance rating of the individual, the position of the individual in the salary range, and the overall ratings and positions of the other managers. To take account of these variables, a special computer software package has been developed which generates guideline recommendations for salary increases based on the unit's pay budget for the year. The local salary review manager can decide on either an increase within the guidelines, or a different increase. If the latter is suggested, the computer will adjust the other salaries within the review group to keep the aggregate cost within the budget.

Collective bargaining

The executives covered by the "merit only" scheme were previously covered by collective bargaining arrangements. However, the new scheme marked a decisive break, and the trade unions were not involved in any way in its preparation or in representing the interests of members. Executives were approached individually and asked to accept new, individual contracts. Nearly all agreed.

Negotiations started with the trade unions in 1988 to extend the "merit only" system to senior, middle and junior managers. The unions opposed the move and by the middle of the year the negotiations had broken down. British Rail then sent new individual contracts to all managers. All accepted and the new scheme came fully into operation in 1989. The unions no longer have a negotiating role. They are consulted about the increases to salary ranges, but not about the overall salary budget, which is not made public.

Implementation of the system

The new arrangements are underpinned by the Hay job evaluation system. This "scores" the weight of each job, and allocates it to a salary band. Through a central data base operated by Hay, jobs are also linked to external salary comparators. Such links into the external pay market are considered to be essential for a "merit only" scheme.

Monitoring and evaluation

The "merit only" schemes at British Rail have perhaps carried the concept of performance pay further than in any other schemes in public bodies in the United Kingdom. The schemes are still relatively new, and it would be difficult at this stage to make an overall assessment of their success. However, two clear advantages emerge: the previous unsatisfactory pay structure with individuals at the top of their ranges and no adequate cost controls has been removed; and the new pay ranges approximate more closely to rates in the market where British Rail is recruiting. A further, more intangible outcome is that staff at all levels are now obliged to talk with each other to settle common objectives.

Surveys have been undertaken in 1989 and 1990 of staff responses to the new schemes. In 1989, among general managers, 50 per cent thought the new schemes would motivate managers to improve performance, 20 per cent thought not, and 30 per cent thought it was too early to judge. In a later 1990 survey, the proportion who thought the schemes would improve motivation had increased to 58 per cent.

However, a trade union survey of 2 800 middle managers following the July 1989 pay review showed wide disparities in some of the increases awarded to managers on the same pay level who received the same performance rating. The union also argued that many of its members fared worse under the new system than they would have done under the previous negotiated system.

A further factor is a change in the economic environment in which British Rail is operating. The current recession has led to a sharp fall in overall profits, and a consequence has been the suspension of the bonus scheme introduced in 1989 for executives. This bonus scheme was directly related to achieving budgets in terms of income and costs, and whilst separate from the ''merit only'' scheme, was seen as part of the remuneration package, and intended to buttress moves towards a ''performance culture''.

British Rail is concerned to evaluate and monitor the success of the new ''merit only'' systems, and is joint sponsor of a research fellowship at a British university. Findings are not yet available.

CITY AND HACKNEY HEALTH AUTHORITY, UNITED KINGDOM, PERFORMANCE-RELATED PAY SCHEME FOR MANAGERS[1]

Background

Performance-related pay was introduced in the National Health Service (NHS) as part of a major reorganisation of its management. In 1984, general managers were appointed who were individually responsible and accountable for the management of each of the regions and districts throughout England. This entailed the creation of 14 regional manager posts, 191 district general manager posts and 612 unit general manager posts. In 1987 each health authority appointed between four and seven senior managers whose role is to assist general managers. The new corporate management team of each health authority, comprising general and senior managers, carries responsibility for ensuring effective delivery of health care services.

In the context of these reforms, incremental pay scales were replaced by a new pay and grading structure which aimed to reward added responsibilities and individual performance. The new arrangements included the introduction of a performance appraisal process, flat-rate salaries, performance pay and, for general managers, three-year or five-year contracts, rolled forward annually, continuance of which is subject to satisfactory performance.

Performance pay was, therefore, one of a series of measures aimed at improving management and encouraging a performance oriented culture throughout the NHS. The new reward package gives general managers greater autonomy in determining pay levels appropriate to individual responsibilities and local conditions; it aims at rewarding individuals for their contribution toward the organisation rather than length of service, and it seeks to provide greater flexibility for recruiting and retaining high calibre managers by enabling health authorities to pay over the national salary scale maxima for "hard-to-fill" vacancies.

Performance pay was introduced for General Managers throughout the NHS in 1987 and was subsequently cascaded to first and second tier senior managers in 1988 and 1989 respectively. In City and Hackney Health Authority some 40 managerial staff out of a total of 6 500 employees participate in the performance pay scheme.

Description of the scheme

Coverage of the performance pay scheme is compulsory for general managers. Senior managers were given the option of accepting new contracts, which place them within the revised pay and grading structure, or remaining on the existing incremental pay scales. All senior managers must participate in the individual performance review process, but only those who accept a new contract are covered by the performance pay scheme. The new contracts for senior managers specify that unsatisfactory performance may be regarded as grounds for disciplinary action or dismissal.

There was a financial incentive for acceptance of the new contracts since managers receive higher base pay within the new structure, plus the opportunity to earn additional performance-related pay. An additional incentive for moving to the new system is that it promises opportunities for faster career progression.

The new pay structure for senior managers consists of a single pay spine comprising 30 pay points. A manager's pay is set on one of the pay points, with increases based on performance. General managers are responsible for recommending the point on the pay spine at which each senior manager's pay is set initially, but the final decision rests with the Regional Health Authority and the Department of Health. The regional general manager is responsible for approving the unit and district general managers' pay levels.

For general managers there is a basic pay rate within a range, the possibility of a discretionary addition to reflect special factors such as responsibility for big projects, a performance-related pay element and a geographical allowance of up to 10 per cent of the range midpoint. A maximum salary is fixed for each general manager post throughout the NHS. The starting salary is based on ability and experience, whilst progression up the range is determined by performance.

Performance payments are made annually, together with cost of living increases, and are based on assessed performance, over the previous year. Performance is rated in five bands as follows:

Band 1 Excellent achievements – cannot be excelled
Band 2 Very good performance – excellent progress made
Band 3 Positive achievements – good progress made
Band 4 Some progress made – performance satisfactory
Band 5 No progress made – performance unsatisfactory

Managers whose assessed performance falls into Bands 1 to 3 receive a performance-related salary increase (see below), together with the standard cost of living increase. Those with a performance rating in Band 4 get only the cost of living increase, and Band 5 performers receive no increase.

Centrally prescribed limits on the distribution of performance ratings mean that no more than 20 per cent of senior managers within a region may be rated in Band 1 and no more than 40 per cent may be rated in Band 2. The maximum percentages for general managers are 20 per cent for Band 1 and not more than 60 per cent for Bands 1 and 2 combined.

Performance-related pay takes the form of a percentage increase in base salary, as follows:

Performance rating	Performance increase(%)	
	General managers	Senior managers
Band 1	4-6	3-4
Band 2	2-4	2-3
Band 3	up to 2	up to 1 ½
Band 4 and 5	no increase	no increase

There is a ceiling on the cumulative performance-related increases which individuals can receive over a five-year period. This is 20 per cent for Band 1, 14 per cent for Band 2 and 7 per cent for Band 3. The total remuneration of general managers is subject to a limit equal to the maximum salary for the post. Similarly, the total remuneration of senior managers is subject to a maximum equal to the flat-rate salary for the job plus 20 per cent. When these maxima are reached, a non-recurring bonus is paid.

Performance appraisal

Performance appraisal is based on achievement of job objectives agreed between managers and their immediate line managers each year. Regular monitoring of progress occurs throughout the year, and objectives may be amended. In determining the overall performance rating, factors such as the difficulty of the circumstances in which the appraisee has been working and the degree to which the job has changed are taken into account. The performance rating is established by the immediate line manager, but must be endorsed by the line manager at two stages removed from the appraisee. Performance ratings are ranked and sent to the Regional Management Executive for final approval. This may involve amending the original rating so that the quotas for each performance band are not exceeded.

Flexibility and controls

The design of the scheme, including the centrally determined performance rating allocations, was determined by an NHS and Department of Health working party and was subsequently imposed at individual Health Authority level. Whilst the proportion of managers who may receive performance awards is determined centrally by the Regional Health Authority, immediate line managers have some discretion, within imposed upper and lower limits, with respect to the size of the performance payment.

There are no formal grievance procedures for managers who are dissatisfied with their performance ratings, but they do have recourse to the line manager at two stages removed, who will help to resolve differences between the appraisee and their line manager if required. If the differences cannot be resolved in this way, then the issue may be referred to a higher manager. In practice, unresolved cases are unknown.

Whilst individual performance pay awards are not made public, there is regular reporting to inform the regions, and ultimately the Department of Health, of performance rating distributions.

Implementation

Implementation of the scheme was supported by training, provision of a reference manual and regular communication with staff. Further support was provided to staff during the implementation via an informal ''open door'' policy from the Personnel Director/Manager. The City and Hackney Authority were supported by the Regional Health Authority management services group, who performed job evaluations and assisted with training.

There was little consultation with unions during the implementation of the scheme. This was a result of their formal opposition to performance pay rather than any unwillingness on the part of the senior management to consult.

The introduction of the scheme was preceded by the implementation of the performance appraisal system, when General Manager positions were established in 1984. The provision of revised contracts was preceded by job evaluation of each post in order to determine its placement on the pay spine. This was controlled by the Regional Health Authority.

The acceptance rate of new contracts among senior managers was 85 per cent. Reasons for non-acceptance appear to relate to a perception by some managers that the new terms of employment represented an unacceptable break with their professional identity and to the fact that after the job evaluation exercise new conditions offered for some posts were less attractive. Moreover, senior managers were informed some eighteen months before the introduction of the new system that they would have the opportunity to earn performance-related pay, but the details of the scheme were not made available until just prior to its introduction. It is felt that this may have influenced staff acceptance of the new terms and conditions.

Monitoring and evaluation

There has been no formal monitoring of the performance pay scheme. However, a review is being conducted in order to make improvements to the objective-setting process within the organisation. It is felt that a mechanism is needed to cascade organisational objectives down through the system, instead of the present approach of setting objectives at the individual level.

Another initiative involves the development by the Planning Department of specific measures for monitoring organisational performance. There are plans to utilise these measures for the process of setting objectives and monitoring their achievement.

Assessment of benefits and costs

Despite the fact that no formal evaluation has been undertaken, it is felt that individual performance review and performance pay systems have made a major contribution to more effective management in the NHS and have underpinned the desired cultural changes. The objective-setting and appraisal process is viewed as an excellent management tool that has enabled the organisation to be more responsive to customers' needs, given managers a clearer idea of their role, provided a fairer basis for allocating rewards, and helped managers to deal more effectively with poor performance. It is felt that the scheme has had a positive impact on attitudes and motivation of managers and has aided recruitment and retention of high calibre managers.

The cost of assimilation into the new pay structure (including performance-related payments) across the health service, from 1 January 1990, is estimated to be an additional 2.5 per cent of the salary budget. The cost in terms of management time has been substantial, although it is felt that this has been balanced by improvements in management practices associated with the process of setting objectives and rewarding performance.

Problems

The quota system, which imposes rigid ceilings on the number able to receive performance pay awards, has not been well accepted by managers, who perceive it primarily as a means of cost control. Those interviewed for this case study acknowledged, however, that such negative views may be partially associated with a desire on the part of managers to increase salaries because base salaries are often not competitive, and also because they have problems dealing with poor performers. It is felt that the delay in extending the scheme to senior managers resulted in a lower acceptance rate than would otherwise have been the case.

Some of the impact of relating rewards to achievements is felt to be lost because there is a four to five month delay between assessing performance and allocating awards, and because performance awards are paid in monthly instalments consolidated into basic salary.

The unions remain formally opposed to both performance-related pay and the new pay spine, arguing that the cost of performance pay should instead be used to raise base pay. It is felt that such opposition may be a barrier to extending coverage of the scheme.

Difficulties have been experienced in setting specific, measurable objectives, measuring individual performance and assessing the effectiveness of the scheme. It is felt that these problems are attributable partly to the public sector service environment in which the organisation operates, but that they could be overcome by devoting more time and effort to perfecting the scheme.

Future changes

The difficulties experienced with the scheme are viewed as "teething troubles" which will eventually be resolved. It is felt that there is a learning curve associated with the introduction of such schemes such that they need to operate for a few years before the full benefits are realised.

Changes are planned at City and Hackney Health Authority to improve the monitoring of organisational performance by developing specific measures of effectiveness and a "top down" focus to objective-setting, whereby individual objectives reflect organisational goals.

Note

1. This case study was prepared by Gavin Adam, Price Waterhouse Management Consultants, London.

KENT COUNTY COUNCIL, UNITED KINGDOM PERFORMANCE PAY SCHEME[1]

Kent County Council has been at the forefront of change in local authority reward structures. In 1989, it became the first County Council to break away from national pay bargaining and to introduce local pay arrangements for senior managers. The new pay structure was preceded by the introduction of a performance-related pay scheme for senior managers in 1987. Coverage of the scheme has since been extended, so that by early 1991 all white-collar employees had an opportunity to be covered by the scheme.

Pay reforms were among a number of measures designed to promote a more strategic, customer-oriented culture in Kent County Council. Other measures included devolution of accountability and responsibility to managers of resources as close to the service delivery area as possible, a revision of the grading structure to produce fewer, broader, overlapping grades, introduction of a medium-term business planning process, and restructuring of the organisation.

The performance-related pay scheme was intended to facilitate the process of devolution by providing managers with a tool to manage their staff. At an organisational level, its purpose was to underpin the business planning process by allowing individual objectives to be set in the context of departmental goals. The scheme was also seen as a means of improving organisational productivity by rewarding high performers and clarifying individual objectives.

Unlike performance-related pay schemes in some other local authorities, Kent's scheme was not introduced as a means of addressing recruitment and retention problems. This problem was tackled through the introduction of more flexible local pay bargaining arrangements known as ''Pay Plus''.

Description of the scheme

The scheme initially covered all managers in the administrative, professional, technical and clerical groups throughout the organisation (over 1 000 employees). Coverage has been extended on a number of occasions, and by April 1991, all 11 000 administrative, professional, technical and clerical employees had been offered an opportunity to join the scheme.

The basic pay scales are structured around overlapping grades, and are divided into increments. Automatic progression through the scales has been replaced with pay progression linked to individual performance review. The performance-related pay scheme rewards above-average or ''Meritorious Performance'' by accelerated incremental progression and, in some cases, by a lump-sum payment in addition to base salary. Performance payments are made annually, and are normally paid together with cost of living increases.

Performance is assessed against specific objectives which are initially agreed in the form of a personal action plan twelve months prior to the assessment. There are five performance levels, as follows:

Level 1 (Exceptional performance)
Level 2 (High performance)
Level 3 (Good performance)
Level 4 (Incomplete performance)
Level 5 (Unsatisfactory performance)

To cater for exceptional cases in which assessed performance falls short of Level 3, but incomplete or unsatisfactory performance categories are considered to be inappropriate (for example where an individual has held the post for a short time) there is an ''Approved Performance'' category (Level 0).

Levels 1 to 3 are regarded as meritorious performance, and result in accelerated progression for individuals whose pay rate is below the maximum of their salary scale. Meritorious performers whose pay rate is at the maximum of the scale receive lump-sum payments. The performance awards for each performance level are illustrated in Table A2.4.

The majority of staff (for example, approximately 80 per cent in the Social Services department) receive a level 3 rating, which results in a progression of one increment for those who are not at the maximum of their salary scale.

Table A2–4. **Performance ratings and performance rewards**

Assessed level of performance	Below maximum of salary scale (Incremental progression)	At maximum of salary scale (Lump-sum payment – for managers only)
1	Scale placement at any point (with effect from previous October for managers)	Between 11% and 15% of base salary[1]
2	Two increments (with effect from previous October for managers)	Between 6% and 10% of base salary[1]
3	One increment in April	Between 0% and 4% of base salary[1, 2]
4	–	–
5	–	–
0	One increment in April	–

1. Calculated as % of salary point payable on previous 31 March.
2. Must be in their third year at the top of their salary scale; have been assessed at Level 3 for each of the three years; and have not received any lump sum award under the scheme in that three year period.

Performance appraisal process

The performance pay scheme is based on a comprehensive performance appraisal process. Each department, of which there are 19, is able to operate its own separate appraisal scheme. However, schemes must be based on certain core principles which have been determined at a corporate level. This approach ensures that the scheme design can be customised to suit the wide variety of jobs which exist in the organisation. For instance, the Department of Social Services scheme is designed for caring professions such as social workers, and reflects the culture of the department in that it focuses on the development of the individual rather than the reward element.

The appraisal cycle runs from April to March. An important feature of the scheme is that it supports devolution of accountability through the planning process. Objectives are agreed in April/May between individuals and their immediate line managers, and must then be agreed with the appraiser's line manager.

The objectives are developed in the form of specific, measurable targets with time deadlines for the following twelve months. Objectives reflect the core accountabilities of the job and are driven by annual departmental objectives which are, in turn, a reflection of medium-term business plans. Informal reviews are encouraged throughout the annual cycle, in order to cater for changes in the objectives.

A final review occurs in February, at which time a recommendation for salary progression is made. Whilst the responsibility for assessment of performance rests with the appraiser, the assessments must be ratified by the appraiser's line manager in order to ensure consistency and equity of ratings. There is no formal right of appeal against performance ratings. However, individuals do have recourse to their appraiser's line manager if they are unable to agree with the appraiser's assessment.

Individual assessments and performance pay awards are considered to be confidential.

Flexibility and controls

Although individual departments have some flexibility to customise their appraisal systems, the linkage between performance and pay is standardised across all departments. There are no formal restrictions or quotas on the percentage of staff who may receive particular performance awards. However, rating allocations must be justified at both departmental and corporate levels. The major cost control mechanism is that departments are required to fund performance awards from their own budgets.

Collective bargaining

The size of performance payments is not subject to collective bargaining, and because of initial union opposition to the principle of performance-related pay, it is not yet a feature of the joint consultation process. However, union opposition has begun to dissipate and the unions have commenced negotiating about details of the scheme rather than the broad principles underpinning performance-related pay. Unions are now also involved in discussions about the level of the "Pay Plus" award. This in turn affects the amount of performance pay awarded, as performance payments are based on salary scales.

Since the introduction of the scheme, joint consultation arrangements have been devolved from corporate to departmental level, and from departmental to area level. This change reflects the push toward devolution of management responsibility throughout the organisation rather than the introduction of the performance-related pay scheme.

Implementation

The performance-related pay scheme was initially introduced as a pilot project covering 120 managers in the three most senior tiers of the administrative, professional, technical and clerical groups in September 1987. At the same time, local fixed-term, renewable contracts were offered to Chief Officers and senior manager posts with salary structures related to that of Chief Officers. Coverage was extended on a number of occasions, first to all managers and subsequently to all employees in the administrative, professional, technical and clerical groups.

The introduction of the scheme was preceded by wide consultation, both within and outside the organisation. The views of county councillors, senior managers, a broad cross-section of employees, trade unions and public and private sector organisations with experience of performance-related pay were sought.

Important design factors were that the scheme should serve as a platform for assessment of training and development needs and a vehicle for employee feedback of problems and issues affecting achievement of their objectives, and should be easy to understand and use. Emphasis is placed on communication of the scheme's purpose and training of staff in using the scheme. Training in appraisal techniques is provided for both appraisees and appraisers.

As a result of carefully planned measures taken in implementing the scheme, there is a high acceptance rate (approximately 95 per cent) of local pay arrangements. The performance pay scheme is available only to those employees who voluntarily accept the local ''Pay Plus'' deal. Those employees who elect not to become part of the local pay structure remain within national pay and grading arrangements. Therefore, the performance-related pay scheme acts as an incentive for employees to move onto local arrangements.

In terms of financial support, in 1987 the Council provided an initial contribution of 3 per cent of the total salary budget for staff covered by the scheme toward the cost of implementing and operating the scheme. This support has been gradually scaled down so that the scheme is now funded totally from departmental budgets.

Monitoring and evaluation

The major techniques which have been used to monitor the effectiveness of the scheme include independently conducted employee opinion surveys and regular internal review by senior managers. The results of this monitoring have indicated a high level of acceptance, although there is greater acceptance of the appraisal process than of the linking of performance to pay. Whilst there is a general perception that the scheme has contributed to development of a more performance-oriented culture and to an improvement in organisational productivity, it is felt that a more rigorous evaluation of this contribution is required, along with a closer monitoring of the extent to which the objectives of the scheme are being achieved.

In the Social Services Department, planned initiatives to improve monitoring of the scheme include:

- establishing staff care groups in each of six regional areas to provide feedback on problems or areas for improvement;
- development of more quantitative performance indicators in the objective setting process;
- regular review meetings with senior managers to determine whether modifications or improvements could be made.

Assessment of benefits and costs

Many of the perceived benefits of the performance-related pay scheme at Kent relate to reasons for its introduction. Firstly, it is considered to have made a major contribution to changing the culture and management style of the organisation and is seen as an integral part of the new strategic, customer-oriented, accountable and efficient culture.

The scheme is also felt to be an important element of the organisation's business planning process. It has facilitated the translation of medium-term business plans into individual objectives and has provided an opportunity for employees to contribute to the planning process.

Thirdly, there is a clearer understanding by individuals of their role, responsibilities, objectives and how they contribute to organisational objectives. The latter is seen to be particularly important in a large, complex organisation such as Kent County Council. The scheme provides a mechanism to ensure that the efforts of higher performers are directed at achievement of organisational goals.

Linked to this, there is now an improved basis on which to measure the performance of individuals and to motivate the majority of staff by removing automatic increments. As a direct result of the scheme, the organisation is also better able to deal with poor performers. This is achieved by providing opportunities for improvement through counselling and training or, failing this, through separation. Finally, the scheme has resulted in an improved use of the salary budget as a managerial tool.

In addition to the financial cost of the scheme, its implementation and operation has required a great deal of managers' time. However, this is considered to be a worthwhile investment in good management. Because of the complexity of the organisation there are substantial costs associated with the development, monitoring and ongoing operation of the scheme. It is felt that the scheme must be "nurtured" to ensure continued commitment from managers, as well as an acceptance and understanding of the scheme's objectives.

Problems

Difficulties have been experienced in setting and measuring individual objectives which are truly output-oriented rather than focused on individual behaviour or attributes. However, it is felt that meaningful objectives can be set for any job through the use of more qualitative measures.

The level of resources provided for the scheme is seen as an issue both in relation to making improvements and extending its coverage. It is felt that improvements could be made in terms of training provided, in the support provided to departments from the central Human Resources area, and in monitoring the quality of the scheme.

In extending the scheme to cover non-management employees, lack of resources has precluded this group from receiving the same level of performance rewards as the management group. It is felt that this could be divisive and could create difficulties for managers in gaining their employees' acceptance of the scheme.

Problems have been experienced in gaining acceptance of the scheme among certain groups of employees and on the part of unions. Opposition has been strongest among staff working in ''caring'' occupations. The main union, NALGO, was fundamentally opposed to both the principle of performance-related pay and the appraisal process. The unions were formally opposed to the scheme throughout its introduction, but this problem now is diminishing.

As far as the design of the scheme is concerned, there is a perceived need for further refinement of the definitions and rewards for Level 3 performance (good performance). Because the vast majority of employees are awarded Level 3 ratings, it is felt that there should be a distinction between those who are almost Level 2 performers and those who are just better than Level 4. This problem has been partially addressed through the introduction of Level 0 (Approved Performance).

Note

1. This case study was prepared by Gavin Adam, Price Waterhouse Management Consultants, London.

SHEPWAY DISTRICT COUNCIL, UNITED KINGDOM PERFORMANCE-RELATED PAY SYSTEM[1]

Background

In 1988, Shepway District Council in Kent became one of the first local authorities in the South East to enter into local pay arrangements covering all its employees. As part of its new pay structure, a performance-related pay scheme was introduced for senior managers. The scheme has since been modified and coverage extended to all white-collar employees.

Pay reforms were part of a package of measures taken to address problems with recruitment and retention, low staff morale and performance, uncompetitive remuneration and poor employee relations. Other measures included a new job evaluation and grading structure, increased resources for training and development initiatives at all levels and a new departmental business planning approach.

Performance-related pay was specifically aimed at alleviating recruitment and retention problems, primarily by improving remuneration offered to senior employees, and improving performance throughout the organisation by making managers more accountable for their decisions and actions. It is perceived as a central element in the new local compensation strategy at Shepway District Council, which is based on the philosophy of "high pay for high performance".

Description of the scheme

The scheme covers all 430 white-collar employees, who comprise two-thirds of the total staff. Performance awards are paid annually, based on a formal assessment of performance for the previous year. They are treated separately from cost of living increases, which are negotiated through collective bargaining. Performance payments involve accelerated incremental progression and/or lump-sum payments, depending on whether the individuals are at the maximum of the salary scale for their grade. The amount of the performance award is derived from performance markings according to a predetermined formula.

Performance markings are established as follows. Each individual has a number of objectives which are assigned a weighting factor reflecting their relative importance at the time that the objectives are agreed. Objectives are weighted so that the sum of all weighting factors equals ten marks. An individual's performance against each objective is assessed using a six-point scale, ranging from 0 for unsatisfactory performance to 5 for exceptional performance. The weighting factor is multiplied by the assessed performance

Table A2–5. **Performance pay allocations**

Assessed marks	Performance pay award
5 or below	Minus one increment.
6-15	Nil.
16-25	One increment within grade.
26-35	Two increments within grade **OR** one increment to maximum of grade plus 3% **OR**, if already at maximum of grade, 6%.
36-45	Three increments within grade **OR** two increments to maximum of grade plus 3% **OR** one increment to maximum of grade plus 6% **OR**, if already at maximum of grade, 9%.
45 +	Four increments within grade **OR** three increments to maximum of grade plus 3% **OR** two increments to maximum of grade plus 6% **OR** one increment to maximum of grade plus 9% **OR**, if already at maximum of grade, 12%.

level to obtain assessed marks for each objective. Assessed marks are totalled and the level of performance pay is calculated as shown in Table A2.5.

There are no fixed quotas specifying the proportion of staff who may qualify for each level of payment. Instead, there is a predetermined budget for the scheme which is derived from a percentage of base salary.

There is an appeals procedure for dealing with cases where an appraisee loses an increment or receives no increment and wishes to contest the decision. The appeal is heard by a tripartite panel consisting of the Chief Executive, the Personnel/Management Services Manager and a union representative. The panel's decision is final.

Performance appraisal

At the start of the annual appraisal cycle, staff agree with their line manager their key objectives, the associated performance indicators and the weighting for each objective for the following twelve months. These may be adjusted at any time, but a formal review takes place half-way through the cycle. The final review of performance occurs at the end of the cycle and payments are awarded in the following month. The appraisal discussion focuses on accomplishments and areas for development rather than on the performance marking, which is the subject of a separate recommendation by the appraiser after the discussion. The marking is reviewed by the appraiser's line manager, whose role is to ensure equity of ratings. Any differences in opinion are resolved prior to advising the appraisee of the assessment.

Flexibility and controls

There is central oversight of the allocation of performance awards by the personnel function and the Personnel Sub-committee of the Council. The allocation is not governed by any limit on the percentages of employees who may receive a particular award. This policy is felt to encourage acceptance of the scheme because it indicates to employees that rewards are based on individual performance rather than the ability of the organisation to pay.

Managers are ultimately constrained by a salary budget for performance-related payments, which was approximately 5 per cent of the salary bill in 1990. However, at the time that assessments are recommended, individual managers are not aware of the size of this budget.

Collective bargaining

Salary scales are adjusted annually, following local collective bargaining. Performance payments are not subject to collective bargaining, but are affected by it as they are calculated as a percentage of base pay. Bargaining arrangements have not changed since the introduction of performance-related pay. However, union representatives are involved in the appeals process associated with the scheme.

Implementation

A pilot scheme covering the most senior staff, including the Chief Executive Officer, was implemented first, with a view to eventually extending performance pay to other white-collar employees providing that it was judged to be successful. The scheme was designed by the Personnel/Management Services Manager, taking into consideration the views of the Chief Executive Officer and members of the Council's Personnel Sub-committee. All these groups were aware of the objectives of the scheme and were supportive of its adoption. A group of senior managers was also consulted.

Once the nature of the scheme had been determined, staff were informed about the objectives. This process served to obtain their commitment to the scheme. Support provided to employees during the implementation phase included skills training, guidance and advice, as required.

The scheme was reviewed after a year and was extended to all white-collar employees. Consultants were used to improve the scheme's design. This resulted in changing from an input-based to an output-based framework, based on objective setting, and focusing on organisational requirements. Objectives now reflect the major accountabilities for each job.

Most employees received base pay increases as a result of the job evaluation exercise which preceded the introduction of pay structure changes. This encouraged acceptance of local arrangements, including performance pay.

Monitoring and evaluation

The Personnel Sub-committee of the Council is responsible for monitoring the scheme. This is done via structured interviews with senior managers, (including all departmental heads), and a random sample of employees. Random spot checks are also made by the Personnel/Management Services Manager on the quality of objectives set for employees and the allocation of awards. Individual managers are encouraged to take responsibility for monitoring the scheme's effectiveness and for feeding back their views to the personnel function. Central monitoring of the scheme includes oversight of the distribution of performance awards by gender and of equal opportunity issues.

Steps are being taken to identify internal and external indicators which could be used as a means of measuring whether the scheme has contributed to improvements in the quality and efficiency of the services provided to the public.

Benefits and costs

The extent to which the performance-related pay scheme at Shepway District Council has met its objectives is difficult to gauge precisely since the scheme was introduced as part of a range of measures to improve organisational performance. Furthermore, there were no baseline measures on which to assess the success of the scheme. Despite these factors, significant benefits are attributed to the introduction of the scheme.

Recruitment and retention problems have eased substantially, as evidenced by a reduction in the number of vacancies and rate of staff turnover. External factors such as the economic downturn and increased interest rates may have contributed to this.

Feedback from the Chief Executive Officer and senior managers, as well as indicators of service levels within separate departments and teams, suggest that productivity has improved since the scheme was introduced. There is a perception that the scheme has contributed to a shift toward a more performance-driven culture and has fostered "healthy" competition within the organisation.

The scheme is generally well accepted by employees, managers and councillors. The appraisal process has led to improved communication between managers and staff, resulting in better working relationships. Managers are more aware of problems faced by their staff in achieving their objectives and can take earlier corrective action where appropriate. Staff have a better understanding of departmental objectives, of their role and expected standards of performance.

The additional salary cost associated with the scheme in 1990 was equivalent to almost one more salary increment across the organisation than would have been the case under the old system of automatic progression through pay scales. This additional cost was budgeted for, on the basis of similar experience of other local authorities.

Implementation costs included significant management time to design and communicate the scheme and to provide skills training to employees, along with consulting fees for refining the scheme design and providing skills training.

Running costs include the ongoing management and staff time required to agree objectives and appraise performance. This is considered an essential part of the management process and is therefore regarded as an investment rather than a cost. In order to ensure that the load is manageable, there is a limit of six to seven appraisals per manager.

Problems

The major problem, which is also an obstacle to further enhancement of the scheme, is the lack of organisation-wide objective setting and planning. This problem is linked with the fact that the performance management system focuses on achievement of individual and departmental goals rather than overall organisational objectives. This has also made it difficult to assess the impact of the scheme on overall organisational performance. In order to improve measurement of the scheme's contribution to performance improvement more attention is now being paid to the development of specific, quantifiable performance indicators.

There have been problems with defining specific objectives and performance measures, especially in areas where outputs are difficult to quantify. However, it is felt that this problem will diminish with further experience and training in objective setting. It is felt that more resources could usefully be devoted to training.

Inflation of performance markings is an ongoing problem which is thought to arise partly from a tendency by managers to mark more leniently as a means of fostering staff acceptance of the scheme and avoiding stressful confrontations when reviewing performance. It is also linked to the difficulty of measuring performance against qualitative objectives. There are no plans, however, to impose limits on the allocation of performance awards as it is felt that this would create a negative perception of the scheme among staff.

A final problem relates to sustaining management commitment to the system in the face of other day-to-day pressures. Addressing this problem involves continually attempting to change attitudes so that time spent on objective setting and appraisal is seen as an investment and the process is seen as a useful management tool.

Future changes

The scheme at Shepway District Council is characterised by a process of continual refinement and modification and suggestions for improvements to the scheme are encouraged.

It is envisaged that the major change to the scheme will be to achieve a top-down approach toward objective setting through the development of council-wide objectives and plans. A potential obstacle to achieving this change relates to gaining the commitment of the council and top management to initiating the objective setting process.

Note

1. This case study was prepared by Gavin Adam, Price Waterhouse Management Consultants, London.

THE VEHICLE INSPECTORATE, UNITED KINGDOM PROFIT-RELATED PAY SCHEME[1]

The Vehicle Inspectorate became an Executive Agency on 1 August 1988. Its core business involves promotion of road safety, carrying out statutory testing on heavy goods vehicles and public service vehicles and administration of the car and motor vehicle (MOT) testing scheme. At the time of writing, it is the only Executive Agency in the United Kingdom to have a "profit-related" pay scheme, which rewards staff on the basis of organisational rather than individual performance. As the scheme is still in its infancy, what follows is a short commentary rather than a fully developed case study.

The scheme seeks to provide tangible recognition to employees for their contributions to improving the performance of the Inspectorate, and is one of a series of measures aimed at changing the culture of the organisation after it became an Executive Agency. Other initiatives which were taken with a view to changing the culture of the organisation included organisational restructuring to produce a flatter, more responsive structure; leadership training for middle managers; introduction of a health care package involving provision of private health screening and consultation on a voluntary basis; and initiatives to improve internal communication channels.

Description of the scheme

The scheme is a profit-sharing arrangement which provides a bonus to employees on the basis of savings made against a predetermined efficiency target, expressed as an annual percentage improvement in efficiency. An Aggregated Cost Efficiency (ACE) target is agreed with the Department of Transport and the Treasury for each year. Any savings made in excess of the agreed target, up to 1 per cent of the salary bill, can be retained in full by the Inspectorate to fund the scheme. Fifty per cent of the remainder of any savings can also be allocated to the scheme, but the total amount allocated must not exceed 4 per cent of the total salary bill. Savings must be sufficient to ensure that a minimum bonus of £50 can be paid; otherwise, no bonus payments will be allocated.

All full-time and part-time employees, except the Chief Executive, participate in the scheme. All participants receive at least one share or unit. In 1989/90, the first year in which payments were made, 1 750 staff received payments. Bonuses are paid annually, are separate from salary and are not pensionable. Payments under the scheme are intentionally small; in 1989/90 each employee received a bonus of £330 before tax for their single unit.

Employees who do not perform to expected levels are not entitled to receive any bonus units. This includes employees whose performance is assessed as requiring improvement (who may appeal the assessment) and those judged to be totally unsatisfactory. In practice, very few employees receive such assessments.

In recognition of the fact that managers have additional responsibilities for achievement of both financial and non-financial performance targets, additional shares may be provided to managers of key service areas if non-financial performance targets are met. Directors may receive up to five units and middle managers up to two units in respect of non-financial targets. The allocation of the additional shares is financed by a surplus of about 200 bonus units which remain unallocated after distributing the single unit to all employees.

Although there is no formal requirement to publicise bonus payments, the Inspectorate publishes details of the scheme, including the value of bonus units, in its annual report.

Implementation

Negotiations about the possible introduction of the scheme, and subsequently its design, commenced with ministers and senior public servants in the Treasury and the Department of Transport over two years prior to implementation. Whilst there was agreement with the principle of a bonus scheme, considerable discussion was required to work out the details. Consultations were subsequently undertaken with unions and employees, and staff were actively involved in finalising the details of the scheme.

Key design considerations were that the scheme must be:

- simple to communicate and understand;
- based on predetermined, profit-related payout criteria;
- self-financing;
- based on externally audited accounts prior to payout;
- fair and equitable;
- paid annually.

In addition, the scheme was not to affect conditions of employment in any way.

Careful consideration was given to the way in which the bonus was to be paid as this issue was considered to be extremely important. It was paid in a similar fashion to a dividend, with tax already deducted; employees received a cheque together with a personal letter from the Chief Executive, just before the summer holiday season.

Monitoring and evaluation

Because it is still in its infancy, formal monitoring of the scheme has yet to be undertaken. Evaluation is likely to focus on reactions of staff to the scheme and to be conducted by the Treasury via structured interviews with key managers. Feedback from employees would be included in this evaluation, possibly as part of a Total Quality Management System.

Benefits and costs

Many of the benefits arising from the bonus scheme are considered to be intangible. For instance, the credibility of those who initiated the scheme has improved and it has altered the commonly held view amongst employees and Treasury staff that it would be very difficult to introduce any radical changes, such as this initiative, into the civil service.

The scheme has contributed to the view that employees are part of a more dynamic organisation. There is also a belief amongst staff that their efforts now have a greater influence on organisational results. As a result, it is felt that staff are more likely to assess the costs and benefits of their decisions in terms of their impact on the profitability of the organisation.

There have been indirect benefits associated with the introduction of the bonus scheme which were not planned. For example, the process has highlighted weaknesses in human resources systems, which are now being addressed.

The provision of greater rewards to key managers has served as a means of recognising the importance of service-provider roles and has therefore contributed to the realisation of a long-standing desire throughout the civil service to alter the balance between policy roles and service-provider roles by improving the relative status of the latter.

Overall, it is felt that the scheme has contributed to changing the culture of the organisation, but it is not possible at this stage to judge whether it has led to a definitive improvement in performance at an individual or organisational level.

Because the scheme is funded from savings, it has not resulted in financial costs. However, there have been additional costs in terms of substantial management time required to plan and implement the bonus scheme. There are also ongoing costs involved in communicating with employees, unions and the Treasury, as well as administration costs.

Problems

Difficulties have been experienced in introducing the bonus scheme because the Vehicle Inspectorate was seen to be breaking new ground. As a result, cultural barriers and resistance to change had to be overcome. To an extent, this has affected the nature of the scheme, creating a preference for a standardised payment, as opposed to variable rewards related to individual performance, or a scheme where more than one criterion was used to assess performance.

The additional bonus allocations for managers and directors have created problems of divisiveness and it is felt that some of the good will generated by allocating equal rewards has been lost as a result.

The unions remain opposed to performance pay and still have not formally agreed to it. This stance is felt to reflect prejudices at the level of the national union organisation rather than the views of representatives at the grass-roots level, who have had more involvement with the scheme. This opposition has not directly hindered the scheme's implementation because union representatives have been supportive at the local level.

Future changes

Changes which may be made to the Vehicle Inspectorate's bonus scheme in the future include:

- providing, in addition to the agency-wide bonus, bonuses based on team performance of the seven main Districts within the Inspectorate. The aim would be to foster constructive competition between the groups;
- solving the problem of divisiveness created by introduction of additional bonuses for managers;
- introducing a more flexible pay and grading structure as the basis for employee reward to complement the bonus scheme.

Note

1. This case study was prepared by Gavin Adam, Price Waterhouse Management Consultants, London.

STATE OF ARIZONA, UNITED STATES PERFORMANCE ORIENTED PAY SYSTEM[1]

The current pay-for-performance system for the State of Arizona was adopted in 1984, replacing a merit pay plan that had been in place for approximately seven years. The state moved away from merit pay because both legislators and state managers felt that the system had essentially become the equivalent of automatic annual increases. Between 90 per cent and 95 per cent of eligible employees received merit increases in the last three years of the plan's operation.

The current pay-for-performance plan, called "Performance Oriented Pay System" (POPS), provides for performance awards of from 1.2 per cent to 7.5 per cent of base salary. Employees at the top of their pay range can receive a one-time special bonus of up to 5 per cent of base pay if they receive an "exceptional" performance rating. An employee who receives an unsatisfactory rating can receive a salary decrease of up to 2.5 per cent of base salary. When the POPS was created, within-grade step increases were abolished. As a result, pay-for-performance awards are the only way for employees to move within salary bands. With the exception of a 4.5 per cent cost of living increase in 1989, the POPS has been the only available avenue to increased compensation for those Arizona state employees covered by the system.

About 27 000 employees are included in the scheme. No unionised employees are covered. The Arizona Department of Administration is responsible for central co-ordination and oversight of the plan, but administration and many specific operating procedures are decentralised. Possibly as a result of this decentralisation, interviews with managers using the plan indicated some confusion about both guidelines and authority for issuing them. The Department of Administration, for example, was criticised by some managers for issuing guidelines and procedures (such as the percentage of employees in each organisation who could receive a bonus) which had actually been created by the manager's own department.

Performance appraisal procedures are centralised. The Employee Performance Appraisal System was created in 1987 and amended in 1988. It now contains three uniform performance standards: work habits, interpersonal relations, and familiarity with and adherence to policy and procedures. Additional factors are selected, as needed, by the employee and the supervisor. This is a joint process and one in which programme, department and state-wide goals are to be merged with individual development and achievement objectives.

The rating process uses a rating scale with four performance levels, each of which contains two numerical scores: Exceeds Standards (7,8); Meets Standards (5,6); Below Standard (3,4) and Unacceptable (1,2). The employee's final performance rating is a computer generated score based on these numerical assignments. Although payouts can range from 1.2 per cent to 7.5 per cent of base salary, the average is 2.5 per cent, for both performance awards added to base salary and one-time bonuses.

Technically, the pay-for-performance plan in Arizona is funded as a separate budget item by the state legislature. In 1987, the legislature set aside 1.2 per cent of the total personnel budget line for the plan. However, no funds have been available since that time and, as a result, the system has not paid out in three years.

The United States General Accounting Office (GAO) reported in 1990 that, in interviews with eight state employees in Arizona, overall satisfaction with the system was quite high (U.S. General Accounting Office, 1990). GAO noted that these employees indicated that certain refinements, such as changing the biannual appraisal requirement to annual, were improvements to the system, and that some thought that more money should be appropriated for the program, that higher increases should be awarded, and that subjectivity and favouritism still existed in the evaluation process at times.

Interviews and discussions for this report indicated quite different perceptions of the program. Reliance on pay-for-performance for essentially all salary increases has created serious discontent in years when the system does not pay out. Further, because Arizona no longer has within-grade increases, employees can become ''stuck'' very easily. One personnel official noted that ''We now have no end of probation increase; we have no promotional increases. We have people coming in at entry level salaries and staying there. We have many, many employees below the midpoint of their salary range.'' One mid-level manager observed that ''If there is no money, pay-for-performance is not pay-for-performance.''

In many respects, Arizona is typical of those governments in the United States that are struggling to cope with major budget deficits and cut-backs. It is often the case that personnel expenses are the first to be cut in such circumstances. Many pay-for-performance system designs, however, assume an expanding, or at least a steady, budget. In Arizona, the pay-for-performance system has been funded for only two of the five years of its formal existence. Even when the system was funded, the amounts were relatively low.

On the other hand, it is important to note that pay-for-performance was also viewed as one means of controlling personnel costs. The quasi-automatic nature of increases delivered by the merit pay plan was the primary reason for its abolition. Quite clearly, personnel costs are now being more tightly controlled. If the interviews conducted for this report are accurate, however, the pay-for-performance system is now contributing to a demoralised work force and is creating one that is quite possibly underpaid in comparative terms.

The Arizona State Department of Administration is currently searching for ways to improve the effectiveness of pay-for-performance. Many aspects of the system continue to be valued. Managers speak positively of improved communication and better understanding between mangers and employees. Some note the improved ability to deal with poor performers and problem employees. All are keenly aware, however, that, without funding, pay-for-performance may create more problems than it solves.

Note

1. This case study was prepared by Professor Patricia W. Ingraham, Maxwell School of Citizenship and Public Affairs, Syracuse, United States. A more extended version appears in Patricia W. Ingraham, *A Summary of the Experience with Pay for Performance in the United States,* Public Management Occasional Papers, Paris, OECD, (1991).

FORT WORTH, TEXAS, UNITED STATES PERFORMANCE BASED COMPENSATION PLAN[1]

The Performance Based Compensation Plan (PBCP) in the city of Fort Worth is a comprehensive, multilevel performance pay scheme. The plan currently applies to all city employees with the exception of Police and Fire personnel, who are guaranteed step increases through state legislation. The plan was first implemented on a very limited basis in October 1976, covering only 18 executive level positions. By 1982, it had been expanded to include 53 classes of personnel at the assistant department head and division head level; in 1985 it was extended to all professional and administrative employees, and in 1986 it was expanded to include all city employees except those mentioned above.

The PBCP comprises two pay plans, one applying to managers and the other to non-managerial employees. In both instances, pay increases are directly linked to individual performance scores. The pay plan for managers is shown in Table A2.6. The manager's immediate supervisor reviews and rates performance and decides upon the actual percentage increase within a variable performance score range. The salary increases become a permanent part of base salary and are not decreased for less than satisfactory performance. The plan thus emphasises performance evaluation, rewards for outstanding performance and management flexibility in evaluation and awards.

The management pay plan goals stress equity of salaries within the city, personnel motivation, salary competitiveness with other government units and with private industry, and effective salary administration (decentralised but guided by central precepts). The plan seeks to reward and retain high achievers in management level positions and emphasises competitive salary levels as the basis for the bonus program. The midpoint or

Table A2–6. **Pay plan for managers**

	Performance rating	Performance increase in per cent of midrange salary
Maximum	Distinguished (Outstanding)	112-120
	Commendable (Excellent)	104-112
	Competent	96-104
	Adequate	88-96
	Provisional	80-88
Minimum		80

average salary for level is determined by a nation-wide survey of similar positions. Each employee may receive from 80 per cent to 120 per cent of the midpoint salary depending upon individual performance. Salary increases are, thus, determined by the midpoint salary for each position, not the individual salary of each employee. No cost of living adjustments are budgeted under the pay plan. Market maintenance adjustments may be budgeted for the base salaries but these are not automatic from fiscal year to year.

A similar procedure exists for the non-managerial city employees. The pay bands are narrower but the concept remains the same. Base salaries are determined by job classification. Managers or supervisors rate the employee and choose a per cent increase of base salary within a discretionary range for each rating. The performance pay increase is also limited by the overall budget allocation for pay raises. The amount of money allocated for the compensation plan is influenced by the projections made by the compensation analyst but is, ultimately, determined by the projected amount of revenue available to the city.

The allocation process for performance pay is as follows. Each department, along with the compensation analyst, surveys salaries nation-wide and projects the total amount needed (per cent of existing salaries) to bring the base salaries in line with the national average. A percentage request is then presented to the city council. The actual budget for performance pay increases is based on general economic conditions and the city's ability to pay. The final amount available to the departments, thus, restricts the actual performance increases received. An employee, no matter how highly rated, cannot receive 120 per cent of the base salary if the funds are not available.

Individual pay increases are, of course, directly linked to the performance evaluation system. Managers are evaluated according to performance factors or target results formulated by the manager and his or her immediate supervisor. Specific goals, time schedules for completion, and quantitative or qualitative standards for evaluation are stated. Actual achievements are rated as above standard, standard or below standard and additional achievements are noted. Professional and technical staff also enumerate specific goals and standards of measurement. In addition, general work characteristics are rated on a five-point scale, corresponding to the performance pay scale (provisional to outstanding). Clerical, labour and trade employees receive a shorter, more general evaluation including quality and quantity of work, sick leave record, safety record, and work relationships. The evaluation is also conducted using a five-factor scale from unacceptable to outstanding.

In practice, the performance pay plan has suffered from a lack of funding. According to Fort Worth's compensation analyst, the plan, as developed, was thought to be "perfect" but it has never been fully funded by the city council. In theory, each department, along with the compensation analyst, should submit a proposed performance pay increase request. A total amount should, then, be budgeted to bring city salaries into line with the national average. In reality, the performance pay system receives left-over funds. For example, in FY 1990-91, 4 per cent of total city salaries was added to the salary budget for the performance pay plan; 8 per cent to 12 per cent was actually needed to bring city salaries up to national standards. A 7 per cent to 8 per cent increase will be needed for FY 1991-92 but no guarantees of any funding exist.

Because the plan has never been fully implemented, no formal evaluation of its effects has been undertaken. Generally, the plan generates less complaints than the previous step increase system. At the very least, employees feel that when the money is available for raises, it goes to the most deserving or hardworking employees. Some animosity has arisen from the guaranteed step increases for police and fire personnel but these increases are mandated by state law.

Does the plan work? Since employees perceive it to be a more equitable system, it may contribute to employee morale. Since it eliminates cost of living adjustments, it may limit salary expenditures. Until the plan is fully funded and until a more detailed evaluation is conducted, however, there is no concrete way to measure its success.

Note

1. This case study was prepared by Professor Patricia W. Ingraham, Maxwell School of Citizenship and Public Affairs, Syracuse, United States. A more extended version appears in Patricia W. Ingraham, *A Summary of the Experience with Pay for Performance in the United States,* Public Management Occasional Papers, Paris, OECD, 1991.

STATE OF NORTH CAROLINA, UNITED STATES PERFORMANCE MANAGEMENT SYSTEM[1]

North Carolina's Performance Management System was reinstated in 1990 after seven years without funding. It was generally conceded that the earlier system did not distinguish between performance levels adequately; most employees received increases. Supervisors and managers, in particular, were critical of the system. At the urging of many of these managers and the State Employees' Association (a quasi-union organisation) the state legislature created a legislative commission, whose purpose was to establish the broad outlines of a new pay-for-performance system. The product of that commission's report is the Performance Management System, which contains provisions for merit pay.

The system was piloted in FY 1989-90 and will be fully implemented by FY 1991-92. A total of 47 809 employees (64 per cent of the state employees subject to the State Personnel Act) received increases in FY 1989-90, ranging from 1 per cent to 6 per cent. The average increase was 2.8 per cent. All state employees continued to receive cost of living adjustments. The total amount of the annual cost of living increase is determined by the legislature. This increase goes to all employees and is intended to recognise satisfactory performance.

The Performance Management System and merit pay plan is intended only to recognise outstanding performance. As initially passed by the legislature, there were three "exceeds" performance levels. A revision in the first year (by the Office of State Personnel) decreased those levels to two.

All half-time and full-time employees below the maximum salary level for their position are eligible for merit increases. Each employee's job performance is rated according to individual performance plans and the following criteria:

a) an employee's value to the organisation;
b) an employee's placement in the salary range versus that for other employees in the unit with similar performance;
c) the length of time since the employee's last salary increase and the amount of that increase;
d) the total performance budget available for the work unit versus the performance ratings and salaries in the work unit; and
e) an employee's performance and disciplinary or work conduct history.

Employees who "exceed" minimum standards are awarded percentage increases in the following ranges: first level "exceeds" receive 1 per cent to 3 per cent of base salary; highest level "exceeds" receive 4 per cent to 6 per cent of base salary. This percentage increase is added to the salary to produce a new base salary. In FY 1990-91, employees who reached the maximum in their salary range were eligible to receive a one-time bonus for outstanding performance.

Employees may challenge their performance pay rating and may question the size of the salary increase, the lack of salary increase, or the performance rating itself. After review by a grievance committee, final resolution of the appeal rests with the agency head. No appeals are allowed beyond this point.

According to the enacting legislation, budgeting for performance salary increases is handled by the State Personnel Commission and the Office of State Personnel. The Commission surveys state salary needs and makes funding recommendations to the appropriations committees. The recommendations are based upon state budgetary constraints, labour market conditions, and the status of the state pay structure compared to the private labour sector. In practice, the amount of money available for merit increases is based on the monies left over after other appropriations are made, although each department submits requests to the Office of State Personnel which form the basis for the final requests forwarded to the legislature.

The Performance Management System is intended to promote both organisational goals and individual employee satisfaction. The process is fairly straightforward. The employee and manager set goals and standards of measurement. Employees develop day to day and long-term project oriented work plans. Each agency may develop its own system in this regard. Both plan development and appraisal implementation are monitored by the Office of State Personnel. This Office also monitors for equitable distribution of ratings within each agency, as well as for the general demographics of the pay-for-performance system.

North Carolina was forced to implement its pay-for-performance system less than one year after passage of the legislation. Partially because of the speed of implementation, but also because of lingering memories of the first pay-for-performance plan in the State, the Office of State Personnel is placing heavy emphasis on training. An outside consultant has been hired to assist in developing a training package for all supervisors and managers. The package, implemented in January 1991, emphasises not only the performance appraisal process, but the ability to make distinctions between employees, particularly those who exceed minimum (satisfactory) standards.

When the new pay-for-performance program was created, the North Carolina State Legislature allowed the Office of State Personnel great freedom in establishing specific guidelines and procedures. It is clear that expectations for the new system are high. It is also clear that employee access to the legislature is strong (as evidenced by passage of the new plan) and that any dissatisfaction with the new plan will quickly be communicated to that body. The system is structured to recognise only exceptional employees. If it is successful in achieving that objective without incurring dissatisfaction from the large majority of employees, it will be unique. The next two years are critical for the North Carolina system, in terms of both employee and legislative acceptance.

Note

1. This case study was prepared by Professor Patricia W. Ingraham, Maxwell School of Citizenship and Public Affairs, Syracuse, United States. A more extended version appears in Patricia W. Ingraham, *A Summary of the Experience with Pay for Performance in the United States,* Public Management Occasional Papers, Paris, OECD, 1991.

CITY OF NORFOLK, VIRGINIA, UNITED STATES PERFORMANCE PAY SYSTEM[1]

Norfolk, Virginia, is a seaport with about 300 000 permanent residents. It is home to the world's largest naval base. The economy of the area has been consistently recognised as one of the most stable in the United States. Norfolk is governed by a council/manager form of government; the city manager is responsible for the day to day administration of the city's affairs. The seven person city council is the policy-making body. The current city manager, who has been in Norfolk since 1987, is almost solely responsible for moving the city toward a pay-for-performance system.

The reason for moving to pay-for-performance was to develop a leaner, but better paid organisation. At this point, Norfolk could best be described as having an incipient pay-for-performance system. Only the twelve members of the city manager's cabinet are currently under pay-for-performance. Performance appraisal is being introduced gradually to all other city employees. The city is notable for the extensive time and attention it has devoted to developing and pretesting appraisal instruments, for the level of training provided in performance appraisal, and for its efforts to initiate pay-for-performance across the city administration while reducing staff numbers and cutting back on government expenses generally.

Since late 1987, the city has had a pay-for-performance specialist on its payroll, whose job was initially to examine the feasibility of pay-for-performance, and later to develop performance appraisal forms appropriate for the entire work force. The pay-for-performance office, located in the city's human resources division, currently has a staff of four: the pay-for-performance specialist and three training and development specialists. They are currently training managers for performance appraisal and conducting information meetings for all city employees. In addition, each department has nominated two performance appraisal trainers who have received special instruction from the central performance appraisal staff, and who will conduct more day-to-day training within their departments.

The city has a large number of blue-collar employees on its payroll; it also is struggling with significant illiteracy problems among its employees. The extent to which information sessions have been effective with lower-level employees is not yet clear.

Four different performance appraisal forms have been pilot tested and evaluated in Norfolk. The final versions include a separate form for executives (the city manager's cabinet) and a two-part form for the rest of the work force. The first section is for routine jobs and tasks and contains very specific information and options. The second section, which is designed for the professional staff, relies on a management-by-objectives format, classifying objectives as new project objectives, professional development objectives and routine objectives. Both section one and section two use a five-level rating scale and are designed to produce a numerical final score. The system is being set up so that data from each employee's annual performance appraisal will become part of a central personnel file which will be used to monitor progress of the system.

Performance evaluation for executives is less structured. All executives are rated on four common standards: departmental administration, financial/human resource management, equal employment opportunity/affirmative action, and staff development. Additional standards are added as appropriate and follow a management-by-objectives format. Executive appraisals occur twice a year; 1989 was the first year that pay was affected by the appraisal process.

Executives are eligible for bonuses from zero to 7 per cent of base salary. The performance payments are not currently added to base salary, but the program is viewed as experimental and could be altered. In the first year of the experiment, two of the executives eligible for the bonus received the full 7 per cent. Other executives were in the 5 per cent and below range.

Three years elapsed in Norfolk from the beginning of the analysis process to the first actual performance ratings. City officials estimate that approximately 65 per cent of the city's managers and supervisors are now using the performance appraisal forms and processes. It is very significant, however, that Norfolk is not publicly – or in training and information sessions with employees – linking performance appraisal to pay-for-performance (with the exception of the ''experiment'' in the city manager's cabinet). Although the pay-for-performance staff would like to see the appraisal procedures fully implemented and evaluated before the link to pay is established, there is some unease among other managers and supervisors about the failure clearly to establish the link early on.

Despite the extreme care being taken, the system is already encountering problems. The city manager and most of his immediate staff remain firmly committed to the concept and are convinced that the experiment at their management level has worked. The pay-for-performance staff are also generally pleased with the system's progress. At the next management level, however, there are already some questions, most of which revolve around the ability of managers and supervisors to establish open and frank communication with their employees. Others, including the new Director of Human Resources (who is technically responsible for city-wide implementation of the system), question the system's applicability to many lower-level employees. Still others note that, if the city is not honest about the link between performance appraisal and pay now, trust will be eroded or destroyed when the link is established later. What would initially appear to be a textbook case on how to introduce pay-for-performance correctly is, instead, a continuing search for solutions in Norfolk.

Note

1. This case study was prepared by Professor Patricia W. Ingraham, Maxwell School of Citizenship and Public Affairs, Syracuse, United States. a more extended version appears in Patricia W. Ingraham, *A Summary of the Experience with Pay for Performance in the United States,* Public Management Occasional Papers, Paris, OECD, 1991.

BIBLIOGRAPHY

ADAMS, J. S. (1963), "Toward an Understanding of Inequity", *Journal of Abnormal and Social Psychology, 67,* p. 422-436.

AITKEN, M. J. and R. E. WOOD (1989), "Employee Stock Ownership Plans: Issue and Evidence", *Journal of Industrial Relations,* June 1989, p. 147-168.

BAKER, G. P., M. C. JENSEN and K. J. MURPHY (1988), "Compensation and Incentives: Practice vs Theory", *Journal of Finance, 43,* p. 593-616.

BERNARDIN, H. J. and R. W. BEATTY (1984), *Performance Appraisal: Assessing Human Behavior at Work,* Kent, Boston, Massachussets.

BRETZ, R. and G. MILKOVICH (1989), "Performance Appraisal in Large Organisations: Practice and Research Implictions", *Working Paper 89-17,* Center for Advanced Human Resource Studies, Cornell University, Ithaca, New York.

CARROLL, S. J. and C. E. SCHNEIER (1982), *Performance Appraisal and Review Systems,* Scott/Foresman, Glenview, Illinois.

EHRENBERG, R. G. and G. T. MILKOVICH (1987), "Compensation and Firm Performance", in Kleiner *et al.*, eds., *Human Resources and the Performance of the Firm,* IRRA, Madison, Wisconsin, p. 87-122.

ELLIG, B. (1982), *Executive Compensation – A Total Pay Perspective,* McGraw Hill, New York.

FLYNN, N. (1990), *Public Sector Management,* Harvester Wheatsheaf, London.

FAMA, E. (1980), "Agency Problems and the Theory of the Firm", *Journal of Political Economics,* p. 288-307.

GERHART, B. and G. T. MILKOVICH (1990), "Organizational Differences in Managerial Performance and Financial Performance", *Academy of Management Journal, 33,* p. 663-791.

HEDE, A. and R. COOK (1987), *Victorian Public Service Survey of the Senior Executive Service,* Public Service Board, Melbourne, Victoria.

HORNGREN, C. T. and G. FOSTER (1987), *Cost Accounting: A Managerial Emphasis,* 6th edn., Prentice Hall, Englewood Cliffs, New Jersey.

HUIJER, C. (1990), *Executive Remuneration in the Public Sector: Public Service and Private Reward,* CED, Sydney, New South Wales.

ILGEN, D., J. C. BARNES-FARRELL and D. B. MCKELLIN (1992), "Performance Appraisal Process Research in the 1980s: What has it contributed to appraisals in use?" *Organisational Behaviour and Human Decision Processes.*

INGRAHAM, P. W. (1991), "A Summary of the Experience with Pay for Performance in the United States", *Public Management Occasional Papers* (free document), OECD, Paris.

INGRAHAM, P. W. and P. W. COLBY (1982) "Politics and Government Management: The case of the Senior Executive Service", *Policy Studies Journal,* December 1982, p. 304-317.

JANKELSON, M. B. (1990), "Remuneration Trends and Issues: Looking Forward, Looking Back", *Asia Pacific Human Resource Management,* May 1990, pp. 27-43.

JENSEN, M. C. and K. J. MURPHY, (1990), ''CEO Incentives: It's not how much you pay, but how!'', *Harvard Business Review,* May-June 1990, p. 38-153.

KOCH, R. (1990), ''Development of a Public Personnel Policy for Senior Executives'', *Canberra Bulletin of Public Administration,* July 1990, pp. 53-59.

KOHN, A. (1986), *No Contest: The Case Against Competition,* HoughtonMifflin, Boston, Massachussets.

KONRAD, A. and J. PFEFFER (1990), ''Do You Get What You Deserve? Factors affecting the relationship between pay and productivity'', *Administrative Science Quarterly, 35,* p. 358-85.

KOTTER, J. P. (1982), ''What Effective General Managers Really Do'', *Harvard Business Review, 60,* p. 156-167.

LAWLER, E. E. (1973), *Motivation in Work Organisations,* Brooks/Cole, Monterey, California.

LAWLER, E. E. (1990), *Strategic Pay: Aligning Organizational Strategies and Pay Systems,* Jossey-Bass, San Francisco, California.

LAWLER, E. E. (1981), *Pay and Organizational Development,* Adisson Wesley, Reading, Massachussets.

LOCKE, E. A., D. B. FEREN, V. M. MCCALES, K. N. SHAW and A. T. DENNY (1980), ''The relative effectiveness of four methods of motivating employee performance'', in K.D. Duncan, M.M. Gruneberg and D. Wallis, eds., *Changes in Working Life,* Wiley Ltd., London.

LOCKE, E. A. and G. P. LATHAM (1990), *A Theory of Goal Setting and Task Performance,* Prentice Hall, Englewood Cliffs, New Jersey.

MAHONEY, T. A. (1979), *Compensation and Reward Perspectives,* Irwin, Homewood, Illinois.

MARSDEN, David and Ray RICHARDSON (1991), *Does Performance Pay Motivate? A Study of Inland Revenue Staff,* London School of Economics, London.

MERCHANT, K. A. (1989), *Rewarding Results: Motivating Profit Center Managers,* Harvard Business School Press, Boston, Massachussets.

MILKOVICH, G. and J. NEWMAN (1990), *Compensation,* Richard Irwin, Boston, Massachussets.

MILKOVICH, G. J. and A. K. WIGDOR, eds. (1991), *Pay for Performance: Evaluating Performance Appraisal and Merit Pay,* National Academy Press, Washington, D.C.

MINTZBERG, H. (1975), ''The Manager's Job: Folklore and fact'', *Harvard Business Review,* 53, p. 49-61.

MURPHY, K. and J. CLEVELAND (1991), *Performance Appraisal: An Organizational Perspective,* Allyn and Bacon, Boston, Massachussets.

OECD (1987), *Structural Adjustment and Economic Performance,* Paris.

PAINTER, M. (1988), ''Editorial: Public Management: Fad or fallacy''? *Australian Journal of Public Administration, XLVII, 1,* p. 1-3.

PUBLIC SERVICE BOARD OF VICTORIA (1989), *Review of SES Improvement Planning and Performance Pay System,* Melbourne, Victoria.

REVIEW BODY ON HIGHER REMUNERATION IN THE PUBLIC SECTOR (1987), *Report No. 30,* Stationery Office, Dublin.

STEERS R. M and R. T. MOWDAY (1981), ''Employee Turnover and Post-decision Accommodation Processes'', in L.L. Cummings and B.M. Staw, eds., *Research in Organisational Behaviour,* Vol. 3, JAI Press Inc.

U.S. GENERAL ACCOUNTING OFFICE (1988), *Observations on the Navy's Personnel Management Demonstration Project,* Washington, D.C.

U.S. GENERAL ACCOUNTING OFFICE (1990), *Pay for Performance: State and International Public Sector Pay for Performance Systems,* Washington, D.C.

U.S. GENERAL ACCOUNTING OFFICE (1991), *Review of Evaluation of Personnel Demonstration Project at Commerce,* Washington, D.C.

U.S. MERIT SYSTEMS PROTECTION BOARD (1990), *Working for America: A Federal Employee Survey,* Washington, D.C.

U.S. OFFICE OF PERSONNEL MANAGEMENT (1989), *Implementation Report: NIST Personnel Management Demonstration Project,* Washington, D.C.

U.S. OFFICE OF PERSONNEL MANAGEMENT (1990*a*), *Performance Management and Recognition System 1988 and 1989, A Report to the President and the Congress of the United States,* Washington, D.C.

U.S. OFFICE OF PERSONNEL MANAGEMENT (1990*b*), *The Status of the Senior Executive Service,* Tenth Anniversary Edition, Washington, D.C.

U.S. OFFICE OF PERSONNEL MANAGEMENT (1990*c*), *Second Annual Evaluation Report: NIST Personnel Demonstration Project,* Washington, D.C.

U.S. OFFICE OF PERSONNEL MANAGEMENT (1991), *Results of Title VI Demonstration Projects: Implications for Performance Management and Pay-For-Performance,* Washington, D.C.

VROOM, V. (1964), *Work and Motivation,* Wiley, New York.

WALLACE M. J. and C. H. FAY (1988), *Compensation Theory and Practice,* 2nd edn., Kent, Boston, Massachussets.

WOOD, R. E. (1989), ''Performance Appraisal in the Reform of Public Sector Management Practices'', in Corbett, Selby-Smith and Smith, eds., *Public Sector Personnel Policies for the 1990s,* Public Sector Management Institute, Melbourne, Victoria.

WOOD, R. E. (1991), *Performance Pay and Related Compensation Practices in Australian State Public Sector Organisations,* Public Management Occasional Papers (free document), OECD, Paris.

WOOD, R. E. and T. R. MITCHELL (1990), *Managerial Goal Setting,* unpublished manuscript, Department of Management, University of Western Australia, Perth.

ZUSSMAN, D., and J. JABES (1989), *The Vertical Solitude: Managing in the Public Sector,* Institute for Research on Public Policy, Halifax, Nova Scotia.

MAIN SALES OUTLETS OF OECD PUBLICATIONS
PRINCIPAUX POINTS DE VENTE DES PUBLICATIONS DE L'OCDE

ARGENTINA – ARGENTINE
Carlos Hirsch S.R.L.
Galería Güemes, Florida 165, 4° Piso
1333 Buenos Aires Tel. (1) 331.1787 y 331.2391
Telefax: (1) 331.1787

AUSTRALIA – AUSTRALIE
D.A. Information Services
648 Whitehorse Road, P.O.B 163
Mitcham, Victoria 3132 Tel. (03) 873.4411
Telefax: (03) 873.5679

AUSTRIA – AUTRICHE
Gerold & Co.
Graben 31
Wien I Tel. (0222) 533.50.14

BELGIUM – BELGIQUE
Jean De Lannoy
Avenue du Roi 202
B-1060 Bruxelles Tel. (02) 538.51.69/538.08.41
Telefax: (02) 538.08.41

CANADA
Renouf Publishing Company Ltd.
1294 Algoma Road
Ottawa, ON K1B 3W8 Tel. (613) 741.4333
Telefax: (613) 741.5439

Stores:
61 Sparks Street
Ottawa, ON K1P 5R1 Tel. (613) 238.8985
211 Yonge Street
Toronto, ON M5B 1M4 Tel. (416) 363.3171

Les Éditions La Liberté Inc.
3020 Chemin Sainte-Foy
Sainte-Foy, PQ G1X 3V6 Tel. (418) 658.3763
Telefax: (418) 658.3763

Federal Publications
165 University Avenue
Toronto, ON M5H 3B8 Tel. (416) 581.1552
Telefax: (416) 581.1743

CHINA – CHINE
China National Publications Import
Export Corporation (CNPIEC)
16 Gongti E. Road, Chaoyang District
P.O. Box 88 or 50
Beijing 100704 PR Tel. (01) 506.6688
Telefax: (01) 506.3101

DENMARK – DANEMARK
Munksgaard Export and Subscription Service
35, Nørre Søgade, P.O. Box 2148
DK-1016 København K Tel. (33) 12.85.70
Telefax: (33) 12.93.87

FINLAND – FINLANDE
Akateeminen Kirjakauppa
Keskuskatu 1, P.O. Box 128
00100 Helsinki Tel. (358 0) 12141
Telefax: (358 0) 121.4441

FRANCE
OECD/OCDE
Mail Orders/Commandes par correspondance:
2, rue André-Pascal
75775 Paris Cedex 16 Tel. (33-1) 45.24.82.00
Telefax: (33-1) 45.24.85.00 or (33-1) 45.24.81.76
Telex: 640048 OCDE

OECD Bookshop/Librairie de l'OCDE :
33, rue Octave-Feuillet
75016 Paris Tel. (33-1) 45.24.81.67
(33-1) 45.24.81.81

Documentation Française
29, quai Voltaire
75007 Paris Tel. 40.15.70.00

Gibert Jeune (Droit-Économie)
6, place Saint-Michel
75006 Paris Tel. 43.25.91.19

Librairie du Commerce International
10, avenue d'Iéna
75016 Paris Tel. 40.73.34.60

Librairie Dunod
Université Paris-Dauphine
Place du Maréchal de Lattre de Tassigny
75016 Paris Tel. 47.27.18.56

Librairie Lavoisier
11, rue Lavoisier
75008 Paris Tel. 42.65.39.95

Librairie L.G.D.J. - Montchrestien
20, rue Soufflot
75005 Paris Tel. 46.33.89.85

Librairie des Sciences Politiques
30, rue Saint-Guillaume
75007 Paris Tel. 45.48.36.02

P.U.F.
49, boulevard Saint-Michel
75005 Paris Tel. 43.25.83.40

Librairie de l'Université
12a, rue Nazareth
13100 Aix-en-Provence Tel. (16) 42.26.18.08

Documentation Française
165, rue Garibaldi
69003 Lyon Tel. (16) 78.63.32.23

Librairie Decitre
29, place Bellecour
69002 Lyon Tel. (16) 72.40.54.54

GERMANY – ALLEMAGNE
OECD Publications and Information Centre
Schedestrasse 7
D-W 5300 Bonn 1 Tel. (0228) 21.60.45
Telefax: (0228) 26.11.04

GREECE – GRÈCE
Librairie Kauffmann
Mavrokordatou 9
106 78 Athens Tel. 322.21.60
Telefax: 363.39.67

HONG-KONG
Swindon Book Co. Ltd.
13–15 Lock Road
Kowloon, Hong Kong Tel. 366.80.31
Telefax: 739.49.75

ICELAND – ISLANDE
Mál Mog Menning
Laugavegi 18, Pósthólf 392
121 Reykjavik Tel. 162.35.23

INDIA – INDE
Oxford Book and Stationery Co.
Scindia House
New Delhi 110001 Tel.(11) 331.5896/5308
Telefax: (11) 332.5993

17 Park Street
Calcutta 700016 Tel. 240832

INDONESIA – INDONÉSIE
Pdii-Lipi
P.O. Box 269/JKSMG/88
Jakarta 12790 Tel. 583467
Telex: 62 875

IRELAND – IRLANDE
TDC Publishers – Library Suppliers
12 North Frederick Street
Dublin 1 Tel. 74.48.35/74.96.77
Telefax: 74.84.16

ISRAEL
Electronic Publications only
Publications électroniques seulement
Sophist Systems Ltd.
71 Allenby Street
Tel-Aviv 65134 Tel. 3-29.00.21
Telefax: 3-29.92.39

ITALY – ITALIE
Libreria Commissionaria Sansoni
Via Duca di Calabria 1/1
50125 Firenze Tel. (055) 64.54.15
Telefax: (055) 64.12.57

Via Bartolini 29
20155 Milano Tel. (02) 36.50.83

Editrice e Libreria Herder
Piazza Montecitorio 120
00186 Roma Tel. 679.46.28
Telefax: 678.47.51

Libreria Hoepli
Via Hoepli 5
20121 Milano Tel. (02) 86.54.46
Telefax: (02) 805.28.86

Libreria Scientifica
Dott. Lucio de Biasio 'Aeiou'
Via Coronelli, 6
20146 Milano Tel. (02) 48.95.45.52
Telefax: (02) 48.95.45.48

JAPAN – JAPON
OECD Publications and Information Centre
Landic Akasaka Building
2-3-4 Akasaka, Minato-ku
Tokyo 107 Tel. (81.3) 3586.2016
Telefax: (81.3) 3584.7929

KOREA – CORÉE
Kyobo Book Centre Co. Ltd.
P.O. Box 1658, Kwang Hwa Moon
Seoul Tel. 730.78.91
Telefax: 735.00.30

MALAYSIA – MALAISIE
Co-operative Bookshop Ltd.
University of Malaya
P.O. Box 1127, Jalan Pantai Baru
59700 Kuala Lumpur
Malaysia Tel. 756.5000/756.5425
Telefax: 757.3661

NETHERLANDS – PAYS-BAS
SDU Uitgeverij
Christoffel Plantijnstraat 2
Postbus 20014
2500 EA's-Gravenhage Tel. (070 3) 78.99.11
Voor bestellingen: Tel. (070 3) 78.98.80
Telefax: (070 3) 47.63.51

NEW ZEALAND
NOUVELLE-ZÉLANDE
Legislation Services
P.O. Box 12418
Thorndon, Wellington Tel. (04) 496.5652
Telefax: (04) 496.5698

NORWAY – NORVÈGE
Narvesen Info Center – NIC
Bertrand Narvesens vei 2
P.O. Box 6125 Etterstad
0602 Oslo 6 Tel. (02) 57.33.00
Telefax: (02) 68.19.01

PAKISTAN
Mirza Book Agency
65 Shahrah Quaid-E-Azam
Lahore 3 Tel. 66.839
Telex: 44886 UBL PK. Attn: MIRZA BK

PORTUGAL
Livraria Portugal
Rua do Carmo 70-74
Apart. 2681
1117 Lisboa Codex Tel.: (01) 347.49.82/3/4/5
Telefax: (01) 347.02.64

SINGAPORE – SINGAPOUR
Information Publications Pte. Ltd.
41, Kallang Pudding, No. 04-03
Singapore 1334 Tel. 741.5166
Telefax: 742.9356

SPAIN – ESPAGNE
Mundi-Prensa Libros S.A.
Castelló 37, Apartado 1223
Madrid 28001 Tel. (91) 431.33.99
Telefax: (91) 575.39.98

Libreria Internacional AEDOS
Consejo de Ciento 391
08009 – Barcelona Tel. (93) 488.34.92
Telefax: (93) 487.76.59

Llibreria de la Generalitat
Palau Moja
Rambla dels Estudis, 118
08002 – Barcelona
(Subscripcions) Tel. (93) 318.80.12
(Publicacions) Tel. (93) 302.67.23
Telefax: (93) 412.18.54

SRI LANKA
Centre for Policy Research
c/o Colombo Agencies Ltd.
No. 300-304, Galle Road
Colombo 3 Tel. (1) 574240, 573551-2
Telefax: (1) 575394, 510711

SWEDEN – SUÈDE
Fritzes Fackboksföretaget
Box 16356
Regeringsgatan 12
103 27 Stockholm Tel. (08) 690.90.90
Telefax: (08) 20.50.21

Subscription Agency-Agence d'abonnements
Wennergren-Williams AB
Nordenflychtsvägen 74
Box 30004
104 25 Stockholm Tel. (08) 13.67.00
Telefax: (08) 618.62.36

SWITZERLAND – SUISSE
Maditec S.A. (Books and Periodicals - Livres et périodiques)
Chemin des Palettes 4
1020 Renens/Lausanne Tel. (021) 635.08.65
Telefax: (021) 635.07.80

Librairie Payot S.A.
4, place Pépinet
1003 Lausanne Tel. (021) 341.33.48
Telefax: (021) 341.33.45

Librairie Unilivres
6, rue de Candolle
1205 Genève Tel. (022) 320.26.23
Telefax: (022) 329.73.18

Subscription Agency - Agence d'abonnement
Naville S.A.
38 avenue Vibert
1227 Carouge Tél.: (022) 308.05.56/57
Telefax: (022) 308.05.88

See also – Voir aussi :
OECD Publications and Information Centre
Schedestrasse 7
D-W 5300 Bonn 1 (Germany)
Tel. (49.228) 21.60.45
Telefax: (49.228) 26.11.04

TAIWAN – FORMOSE
Good Faith Worldwide Int'l. Co. Ltd.
9th Floor, No. 118, Sec. 2
Chung Hsiao E. Road
Taipei Tel. (02) 391.7396/391.7397
Telefax: (02) 394.9176

THAILAND – THAÏLANDE
Suksit Siam Co. Ltd.
113, 115 Fuang Nakhon Rd.
Opp. Wat Rajbopith
Bangkok 10200 Tel. (662) 251.1630
Telefax: (662) 236.7783

TURKEY – TURQUIE
Kültur Yayinlari Is-Türk Ltd. Sti.
Atatürk Bulvari No. 191/Kat. 13
Kavaklidere/Ankara Tel. 428.11.40 Ext. 2458
Dolmabahce Cad. No. 29
Besiktas/Istanbul Tel. 160.71.88
Telex: 43482B

UNITED KINGDOM – ROYAUME-UNI
HMSO
Gen. enquiries Tel. (071) 873 0011
Postal orders only:
P.O. Box 276, London SW8 5DT
Personal Callers HMSO Bookshop
49 High Holborn, London WC1V 6HB
Telefax: (071) 873 8200
Branches at: Belfast, Birmingham, Bristol, Edinburgh, Manchester

UNITED STATES – ÉTATS-UNIS
OECD Publications and Information Centre
2001 L Street N.W., Suite 700
Washington, D.C. 20036-4910 Tel. (202) 785.6323
Telefax: (202) 785.0350

VENEZUELA
Libreria del Este
Avda F. Miranda 52, Aptdo. 60337
Edificio Galipán
Caracas 106 Tel. 951.1705/951.2307/951.1297
Telegram: Libreste Caracas

Subscription to OECD periodicals may also be placed through main subscription agencies.

Les abonnements aux publications périodiques de l'OCDE peuvent être souscrits auprès des principales agences d'abonnement.

Orders and inquiries from countries where Distributors have not yet been appointed should be sent to: OECD Publications Service, 2 rue André-Pascal, 75775 Paris Cedex 16, France.

Les commandes provenant de pays où l'OCDE n'a pas encore désigné de distributeur devraient être adressées à : OCDE, Service des Publications, 2, rue André-Pascal, 75775 Paris Cedex 16, France.

12-1992

OECD PUBLICATIONS, 2 rue André-Pascal, 75775 PARIS CEDEX 16
PRINTED IN FRANCE
(42 92 02 1) ISBN 92-64-13823-4 - No. 46319 1993